W9-BIY-823

**RUN
FAST.
EAT
SLOW.**

RISE & RUN.

ALSO BY SHALANE FLANAGAN AND ELYSE KOPECKY,
THE NEW YORK TIMES **BESTSELLERS:**

Run Fast. Eat Slow. Nourishing Recipes for Athletes

Run Fast. Cook Fast. Eat Slow.

Run Fast. Eat Slow. A Runner's Meal Planner

RISE & RUN.

RECIPES, RITUALS, AND RUNS TO FUEL YOUR DAY

SHALANE FLANAGAN & ELYSE KOPECKY

RODALE

NEW YORK

Copyright © 2021 by Shalane Flanagan and Elyse Kopecky
All rights reserved.

Published in the United States by Rodale Books,
an imprint of Random House, a division of
Penguin Random House LLC, New York.
rodalebooks.com

RODALE and the Plant colophon are registered
trademarks of Penguin Random House LLC.

RUN FAST. EAT SLOW. is a registered trademark of Shalane Flanagan
and Elyse Kopecky.

Library of Congress Cataloging-in-Publication Data
is available upon request.

ISBN 978-0-593-23244-6
Ebook ISBN 978-0-593-23245-3

Printed in China

Editor: *Dervla Kelly*
Art Director: *Stephanie Huntwork*
Designer: *Rae Ann Spitzenberger*
Photographers: *Erin Scott (food); lifestyle: Andy Hughes (page 163);
Tiffany Renshaw (pages 2, 4–5, 8, 11, 12–3, 17, 20–21, 23, 24, 40–41,
101, 111, 137, 143, 180, 185, 199, 204, 210, 226, 232, 238 [top], 256, 259,
278, 279, 288 [left]); Cortney White (pages 14, 16, 42, 45, 46, 54, 55,
56–57, 65, 66–67, 68–69, 151, 288 [right]).*
Production Manager: *Jessica Heim*
Production Editor: *Terry Deal*
Composition: *Merri Ann Morrell*
Copy Editor: *Ivy McFadden*
Indexer: *Elizabeth Parson*

10 9 8 7 6 5 4 3 2 1

First Edition

*Dedicated to hardworking
parents everywhere and the
caregivers who support them.
We could not have created this
book without our "crew team":
Andy Hughes, Steven Edwards,
Caren Arlas, Steve Flanagan,
and Monica Flanagan.*

---

*And with love to Lily, Rylan,
Jack Dean, and the next
generation of athletes.
You inspire us each
and every day.*

CONTENTS

INTRODUCTION

There is something special and sacred about mornings–that is, when we slow down long enough to enjoy them. A mountaintop sunrise, a steaming cup of joe, a new beginning. Still, before we started dreaming up this book, we were as guilty of "frantic morning syndrome" as everyone else. The year we wrote this book (2020, RIP) didn't improve matters. But once we began the research and interviews, once we really started listening to our own advice and committed ourselves to early runs and better morning nourishment, writing this book transformed us. We hope reading it has the same effect on you.

It's stating the obvious, but the best part of the morning is–*ding!*–breakfast. For runners, breakfast is the most important meal of the day. Many runners eat two breakfasts–a small and easy-to-digest snack before an early run, and a hearty "second breakfast" for recovery afterward. No wonder it's the most talked about meal among athletes ("I'm dreaming of pancakes after this run," "My breakfast totally fueled my long run," "I just ate breakfast and I'm already hungry again," and on and on).

If you own any of our other cookbooks, you know that breakfast is near and dear to our hearts. We talk about the importance of fueling both before and after a morning run. The idea for *Rise & Run* began with our Superhero Muffins, featured in our previous two books, because we've heard that *you* make them every single week. One fan wrote, "Every Sunday we make a double batch," and another said, "It's the only breakfast we eat before school. Quick, with no fighting from my kids." They're so popular, in fact, that we felt we needed to give readers more. In the pages that follow, you'll find Dark Chocolate Banana Superhero Muffins (page 90), Yam Spice Superhero Muffins (page 103), and all-new savory variations: Pesto-Zucchini (page 75) is Shalane's new favorite, and Everything Bagel (page 77) is Elyse's.

> *The mood of the morning carries through the whole day, so take the time to create meaningful mornings.*
>
> **–SHALANE**

We didn't stop at muffins, though. In addition to twenty-four indulgent and nourishing new Superhero Muffin recipes, more than twenty inspiring weekday power breakfasts, twenty-five memorable brunch recipes, over a dozen snack recipes for when that second breakfast has worn off, twenty hydrating drinks and recovery smoothies, and even ideas on dishes that can double as dinner, this book is *also* a take-back-the-morning manifesto. We want your first hours in the morning to be delicious, active, and inspiring.

To that end, *Rise & Run* gives you the tools to establish a morning routine that can positively impact your whole day, including advice on how to get a great night's sleep; how to clear your head of news, work, and other goblins so you can focus on the here and now; how to avoid injuries; what warm-ups and exercises are best done in the morning; plus–bonus–a training manual filled with running advice from one of America's most decorated distance runner (*pssst*, that's Shalane), with a special section on how to train for a marathon (*pssst*, Elyse is training for her first one and needs all the help she can get). There's even advice and recipes devoted to how to recover from Shalane's training programs!

We tapped everyone we know in the health-wellness-fitness space to ensure this manifesto isn't just our good opinions but is truly built on the backs of experts, people like Shalane's physical therapist and mental-health coach and Elyse's longtime yoga and meditation teacher. You will see their advice–from how running helps anxiety to when to rest with your legs up the wall–peppered throughout these pages.

Writing this book meant committing to slowing down and appreciating the simple things in life–taking the time to heal our bodies or linger over freshly baked bread in order to truly absorb our own lessons. And, of course, going for extra-long adventurous runs with friends. And so, in the end, what we hope to inspire within these pages is a commitment to eliminating "frantic morning syndrome" and a return to prioritizing health and happiness over stress and busyness.

We know hundreds of lives have been transformed by our *Run Fast. Eat Slow.* series–because you tell us in letters and tweets and Instagram posts and reviews. We really can't get enough of those. Your mail tells us we're striking a chord, that we're onto something. Well, *Rise & Run* is the next "something" we're onto. We believe it's the best collection of breakfast foods for athletes ever compiled, with inspiration to start your day with a morning run, whether that's two miles or twenty. And, like everything else in the *Run Fast. Eat Slow.* family–nutrient-dense whole foods, healthy fat, listening to your body, avoiding restrictive diets–it's meant to be a forever habit. We want this to be yet another book that never leaves your counter. Waking right isn't a fad. It's a way of life.

1 | CHASE THE SUN

ROUTINES AND RITUALS TO JUMP-START YOUR DAY

Find passion in your work and you will pop out of bed at sunrise, excited to tackle the day.

—SHALANE

A morning run doesn't have to be far or fast or fierce to positively impact your day. Just about any morning movement done outside will pay dividends. Here are ten reasons we think mornings are an awesome time to get sweaty.

1   Even a short run releases feel-good endorphins to boost mood.

2   A morning run helps flush out toxins via sweat.

3   Direct sunlight first thing in the morning sets your circadian rhythm and will improve the quality of your sleep.

4   Moving in the morning awakens your metabolism.

5   Stressful tasks seem more manageable after a good run. You'll gain confidence and perspective to help you tackle daily challenges.

6   You'll have more energy and increase your focus at work (especially if you follow that run with a brain-boosting breakfast).

7   If you're a parent, starting your day by doing something for yourself enables you to be more patient with your kids later on.

8   Movement naturally releases tension in the body, so you'll feel more relaxed as you move through your day.

9   Being in nature and the rhythmic breathing from running help calm the mind.

10 You'll feel a sense of accomplishment before most people are even awake.

Sounds glorious, right?! But how do you actually find time in your already frantic morning to run? Read on to discover Shalane's "relaxed" a.m. routine, and, for the sane runner (those who don't maintain a 5:20-mile pace in 20-mile workouts!), check out Elyse's working-mom daybreak schedule.

SHALANE'S ELITE-RUNNER MORNING ROUTINE *(before retirement)*

I wake up naturally between five and six thirty a.m. (after going to bed by nine p.m.). This early start allows me to move through my morning at a calm pace, which is important before a hard workout.

I put on cozy sweats and come downstairs for water and coffee (the coffee is ready to go because I set the auto-brew function the night before). I hydrate right when I wake up so that I can flush it through my system before I start running (meaning I'm less likely to have to stop to pee mid-run!). A little caffeine helps me wake up and feel ready to go. If you don't wake up the mind and body properly before a run, you risk injuries like a pulled muscle.

Breakfast before a workout is always simple and essential: either something I made ahead or something that I can prepare in less than 10 minutes in the morning. My pre-run fuel is easy to digest and high in complex carbs, with a little fat and protein to keep me full. My go-to meal is a bowl of oatmeal (pages 136 and 150) or Sunrise Overnight Oats (page 139), and/or a Superhero Muffin (see chapters 5 and 6).

While I sip my coffee and eat, I review the day's plans. I always keep a journal with a written to-do list. I like writing things down instead of using my phone for tracking tasks (this keeps me off my phone first thing). I reflect on everything that needs to get done, add objectives, and then pick a few things to attack that day. It's important to set realistic expectations about how much you can accomplish in one day.

My mind is now awake, but I still like to wake up my body before I head out the door. I love rolling around on the ground on my foam roller, and I do a few light, dynamic stretches. My favorite is rolling out my back. I start at the base of my neck and I gently roll all the way down my spine (I recommend taking a class to learn the proper technique). I can usually hear everything crack and release—it feels glorious! Then I place the roller under my lower back and splay out so I am stretching my back and abdominals. This helps loosen my psoas muscle. Then I lay flat on my back and pull each leg individually up to my chest. This stretches my hamstrings and quad muscles.

Hydration continues throughout my morning. As I move through my routine, I'm sipping water or Lemon Electrolyte Water (page 244), a Matcha Collagen Latte (page 249), and/or coffee with Anti-Inflammatory Cashew Milk (page 250).

Before a workout, I love listening to uplifting music. Sometimes I will dance and play with my cat, Shubie. As adults we often forget to be silly and enjoy the moment. Being playful in the morning helps set the tone for my day. I start my day feeling immense gratitude for my career and health. My whole morning routine takes about two hours. And now I'm ready to run.

SHALANE'S NEW MORNING ROUTINE
(After becoming a coach and a mom!)

Okay, so, not long after I wrote my original morning routine, our son, Jack Dean, came into our lives, and mornings definitely look a little different around here now. Jack dictates my sleep schedule, and there's never enough sleep! Bedtime is between seven and eight p.m. (I try to go to bed at the same time as Jack since we're up in the night), and our built-in baby alarm clock goes off between five and six a.m. I'm the "morning person" in the family, so I'm up with Jack at first light. While he chugs his bottle, this momma is downing her coffee (survival!).

Despite the sleep deprivation, I really treasure these early waking hours with baby Jack. We get in lots of snuggles in comfy pj's while we slowly wake up. Is there anything better than a huggable baby paired with hot coffee?! Best time of the day.

On mornings when we have extra pep in our step or need some good vibes, I turn on music and we dance together. Before heading out for my daily run (now starting from my doorstep to save time), I check my email and send off a few time-sensitive responses. (Jack is at a chill age where he's happy to sit quietly while I do this . . . Elyse says this will soon change!)

Instead of a hearty bowl of oatmeal like I used to have, I'm eating a quick bite like a Chocolate Tart Cherry Seed Ball (page 120), a Superhero Muffin (see chapters 5 and 6), or a Trail Mix Breakfast Cookie (page 115), which is faster and easier to eat than oatmeal while feeding a baby.

Because I have less time to myself now, I do an abbreviation of my foam rolling and stretching routine (sometimes later in the day or only every other day). I also go for shorter runs on weekdays (usually between 30 and 60 minutes) and run much earlier (now that coaching is my main job), so I save my appetite for after my run. And now it's become essential for me to pack my work bag (coaching backpack) the night before to minimize morning stress.

Post-run, when I have the time, I enjoy a hearty and savory breakfast like Chorizo Breakfast Tacos with Guasacaca (page 178) or a Recovery Omelet (page 144). During my run, I'm dreaming up what I'm going to devour when I return home. Especially on chilly or rainy mornings, thoughts of returning to a hot breakfast in my cozy kitchen keep me going. If I'm running behind schedule, my go-to is a smoothie (like Can't Beet Me Smoothie III, page 231, or Raspberry Rival Smoothie, page 228) paired with one of our savory high-protein Superhero Muffins (Pesto-Zucchini, page 75, and Sweet Potato Kale, page 72, are some faves). These are easy to make ahead and grab on my way out the door.

ELYSE'S MORNING ROUTINE

I'm always up between five thirty and six a.m., even on the weekends. I treasure my hour of silence before the kids wake up. I need that time to cook breakfast (prepped the night before), pack lunches, and get dressed (while writing the manuscript for this book, I got up even earlier).

The first thing I do when I wake up is make coffee in our French press. While the coffee is steeping, I'm setting out breakfast for the kids and sipping a tall glass of warm water with lemon and fresh ginger juice (aka Lemon Electrolyte Water, page 244). I always start my day with this concoction (in the summer, I add salt and coconut water for better absorption). It's super soothing to my sensitive digestion. I used to get terrible side stitches during runs until I started this lemon-ginger routine. On days when I'm running, I eat shortly after waking up to give myself time to digest. Or I wait and eat with my kids around seven a.m.

If I had the time, I would eat a rice bowl topped with eggs, veggies, and avocado every single morning (see page 135 for our Breakfast Power Bowl recipe). But time at

the table in the morning is very limited. Therefore, Savory Superhero Muffins (chapter 5), which I bake ahead, have become my morning lifeline. They're super digestible and portable; they keep me full when I'm running midmorning; and they satisfy my salty cravings.

Right now, I don't run every morning; more like every other day–which is about to change when I start Shalane's Marathon Training Program (page 48)! But I do *move* my body every single day. On days when I don't have time to run, I take our dog for a brisk 15-minute walk or I do a 15-minute morning yoga routine (see yoga tips from Rosie Acosta on page 19). Once I had kids, disrupted sleep became the norm for me, but getting outside first thing in the morning definitely helps improve my sleep quality, which is really important.

I look forward to having a slower routine once my kids are a little more self-sufficient. But for now, mornings are frantic in my household, and I'm constantly making tweaks to my routine to find ways to start our day with calm.

REVAMP YOUR OWN MORNING ROUTINE TO FIND CALM

As you've read, we cherish starting our days with a run. But your own routine should be customized to suit your personal needs. Do whatever makes sense. It won't become a healthy habit if it doesn't fit comfortably into your lifestyle. To that end, here are a few tips.

▷ Sleep is as important as a morning workout, so try to get to bed earlier and go to bed at the same time every night (see our top 10 sleep tips on page 60).

▷ Wake up earlier to start your day with the right energy. Frantic mornings can impact your whole day. This is especially important if you have kids. You need time to yourself first thing.

▷ Lay out your clothes and prep breakfast the night before. Look for the clock symbol (🕐) in our recipes for tips on how to save time and prep ahead.

▷ Skip social media and perusing the news in the morning, which sucks up valuable time and can negatively impact your mood. If possible, don't look at your phone at all.

▷ Meet a friend for an early run to keep yourself accountable. This is especially important if you are running in the dark (safety first!).

▷ Layer up. Mornings are always cooler, and it's easier to get out the door if you're wearing layers that you can shed. It's important to start with warm muscles to prevent injuries.

▷ Listen to uplifting music while you get dressed, and don't forget that a little caffeine boost can go a long way.

▷ Out the door you go. Don't make excuses for skipping your run. On days when you don't feel like running, tell yourself you will just go 2 miles. See how you feel after a mile (likely much better), but turn around if you're not feeling it. Two miles is still surprisingly beneficial.

▷ Start early-morning runs super slow to allow the body to warm up gradually. Or try a few dynamic stretches before you head out the door (we've included more stretching advice in chapter 4).

If you aren't someone who can run in the morning, we get it. Maybe you need to run in the evening, after work. Maybe you run at lunch and return to your desk sweaty and content. Maybe you run on a treadmill whenever you get 10 free minutes. Good. Make it a habit. The morning will be waiting for you tomorrow, and you can own it in your own style. Whatever you do, prioritize breakfast so that you have the energy to run, walk, hike, bike, swim, study, or work positively no matter the time of day. And that brings us to chapter 2!

ROSIE ACOSTA ON MORNING RITUALS

Rosie Acosta, nationally recognized yoga and meditation teacher and author of *You Are Radically Loved*, uses her practice to help others access their potential and overcome adversity.

What does your morning routine look like?

I wake up and the first thing I say is "thank you." I refuse to get out of bed in a rush or start my day in a bad mood, feeling overwhelmed. I get out of bed being grateful to live another day. I make some hot water with lemon and head straight to my yoga mat. I practice yoga (movement) for 25 to 35 minutes and I meditate for 30 to 45 minutes. Then I step outside and bask in the sunshine for a few minutes. The morning is the most sacred time we have.

How can yoga help runners?

Yoga is designed to strengthen both the body and mind. We need both body and mind for running. On a physiological level, it helps develop core strength, increases mobility, and opens the hip flexors, which are tight in most runners. On an energetic level, it helps quiet the mind, improves mental focus, and cultivates present awareness.

How can meditation help runners?

Meditation has so many incredible benefits. Being still seems like the antithesis of training for a race, but it's important to balance out the motion with stillness. That doesn't mean you can't achieve a meditative state while you're running; in fact, I love getting into that flow when I'm on a run. There is, however, something different that happens when you set time aside to be still, to connect with your body and your breath. You have to model with your physical body what you want your mental body to achieve.

2 | FUEL YOUR DAY

FIND SUCCESS IN THE KITCHEN

Skip breakfast before your morning run, and you'll be running on empty. Skip a substantial meal after your morning workout, and you'll feel "hangry" all day.

—ELYSE

n this chapter, we dig into why breakfast is the most important meal of the day. We share meal prep tips, timesaving tricks to help you organize your morning, and lists of our favorite kitchen tools, essential pantry staples, breakfast recipes, and meal plans for every season. We've even got a list of recipes to help you overcome common runner's ailments (yes, food is medicine!).

BREAK THE FAST

Athletes know breakfast is the most important meal of the day, but hectic morning routines (or kids!) make sitting down to a complete meal nearly impossible. The lack of time for a nourishing breakfast leads to low energy, mood swings, *hangry* habits, and difficulty concentrating. When our bodies are trying to balance our blood sugar levels all day, we feel hungrier, and this can result in more snacking throughout the day.

If you skipped a real breakfast (packaged bars don't count; they lack micronutrients) and raced out the door, you might have a productive morning, but will likely crash later in the day (we've been there!). Take the time to eat a substantial meal, and although this will take more time, we bet you'll accomplish more on your to-do list later in the morning and feel happier doing it.

Breakfast is meant to "break the fast," which means refueling after your longest stretch of not eating. Your first meal of the day should be indulgent, nourishing, and satiating. While you sleep, your body uses up a lot of its energy reserves for growth and repair. You wake up hungry because your cells were hard at work all night. If you're an athlete, your body is working even harder while you sleep, so you need a substantial meal to start your day.

Even if you have a sensitive digestive system, eating a small meal and hydrating before a morning run is important. You'll feel more energized on your run (whether it's 6 miles or 20 miles) and you'll return happier and ready to tackle your day. If you're a sunrise runner and you're racing out the door within thirty minutes of waking–and it's a shorter run (5 miles or less)–we can understand skipping breakfast. In that case, a few sips of coffee and a couple of dates or one of our Small Bites for Sunrise Runners (page 31) can help get things moving for a better run experience (meaning you'll be less likely to dash into the woods mid-run).

Studies show that people who eat a real breakfast maintain a consistent and healthy weight. Eating breakfast prevents weight gain because it awakens your metabolism, balances your hormones, and leaves you less likely to overindulge later. If your first meal is high in protein, fiber, and healthy fats to keep you full longer, you'll be more likely to make smarter choices throughout the day. If you gulp down a bowl of packaged instant oatmeal at your desk after a morning workout, that low-fat, high-sugar oatmeal will likely keep you satisfied for less than 30 minutes, and you're going to feel hungry the second your blood sugar levels plummet (again, speaking from experience). Poor breakfast choices lead to a dependency on coffee and snack foods. Athletes need an incredible amount of nourishment to stay healthy and injury-free.

We've developed recipes and created menus (page 31) for the following groups:

- Those who run at dawn and only need a bite before they go

- Athletes who run late morning and can digest a complete meal before working out

- Student athletes, who run in the afternoon

- Gym buffs, who work out after school or work and need hearty breakfasts that set up the right burn rate for the whole day

MEAL PREP FOR BREAKFAST SUCCESS

The keys to pulling off homemade breakfast every day are advance planning, keeping a well-stocked pantry, and prepping foods the evening (or weekend) before. When you write out your meal plan and grocery list for the week, don't forget to include breakfast and snack ingredients. We are partial to using the *Run Fast. Eat Slow.* meal planner because it keeps everything organized and has room for you to write out how you felt on your run so you can repeat meals that worked for you.

Here's How Meal Prepping Goes Down in Elyse's Kitchen . . .

When I take the time to meal prep, my family eats healthier all week and we rely less on takeout and packaged foods. Meal prepping means cooking components in advance so that you can pull off home-cooked meals in less time. I block out two hours every Sunday afternoon to meal prep (or Monday afternoons, if our weekend is too packed with outdoor adventures). It's amazing how much you can accomplish in just two hours in the kitchen when you have zero distractions (turn off your phone and get the kids outside!). Having a written plan before you start will help you get organized (plus, checking off what you've accomplished is super rewarding). I typically write out our meal plan and shop for groceries the day before meal prepping.

Breakfast is one of the best meals to prep in advance. I always bake a treat like Trail Mix Breakfast Cookies (page 115) or Superhero Muffins (chapters 5 and 6), which can double as a quick breakfast or a midmorning snack. Since writing this book, Savory Superhero Muffins (chapter 5) are on repeat in my meal prep rotation. I also bake up a double batch of granola (pages 127 and 128), enough to last for several weeks, and prep ingredients for smoothies (see Prep-Ahead Smoothie Packets, page 239). Finally, I'll whip up a batch of Sunrise Overnight Oats (page 139) or Chai Chia Seed Parfait (page 140) to get us through the first couple days of the week. I always have Pancake and Waffle Mix (page 158) on hand, and I'm happy when I have a stash of Make-Ahead Breakfast Sausage (page 184) in my freezer.

Throughout this book, keep an eye out for the clock symbol (⏱) at the bottom of the recipes for tips to simplify your morning routine.

TIME-SAVING TOOLS

It's worth the investment in quality kitchen tools, as good cookware will save you time and inspire you to cook more. Here are the essentials.

Large Cutting Board

Go for an extra-large cutting board if you can, about 20 inches long and 14 inches wide, because you can chop all your produce in one fell swoop. Bamboo cutting boards last longer, look gorgeous, and are easy to clean. You'll also want a smaller cutting board to reserve for fruit. There's nothing worse than apple slices that taste like onions.

Chef's Knife

If you're a fan of our previous cookbooks, you already know that you're going to be chopping a lot of produce. A quality chef's knife with a 7- or 8-inch blade is essential. If you're using a dull knife, you are more likely to cut yourself, because it can slip. We highly recommend getting your knives professionally sharpened at least every 6 months. In between sharpenings, use a honing steel to maintain the blade.

Nonstick Muffin Tins (both a 12-cup standard tin and a 24-cup mini-muffin tin)

You're going to be baking a lot of Superhero Muffins, so trust us: you want a good muffin tin that has a truly nonstick surface. Our favorite brand is USA Pan, which has a quick-release coating. We always use paper liners for easy storage and cleanup. Look for If You Care liners; they're nontoxic, nonstick, and environmentally friendly.

Instant Pot

A multicooker like an Instant Pot is a must-have appliance for anyone cooking for a family. Elyse's current model is the Instant Pot Duo Evo Plus 9-in-1 Electric Pressure Cooker in the 6-quart size, which is perfect for a family of four. This multiuse countertop cooker does it all. In this cookbook, you'll use it to make rice, beans, hard-boiled eggs, steel-cut oatmeal, yogurt, broth, and more. It's a time-saver because you can set it and walk away. Elyse used two models of the Instant Pot, the Duo Evo Plus 9-in-1 and the Duo 7-in-1, to test the recipes that call for a pressure cooker. While we've attempted to use universal terms for functions and settings, be sure to consult your pressure cooker or multicooker's user manual before you attempt the dishes to account for the differences in terminology.

High-Speed Blender

If you like making smoothies, nut milk, nut butter, energy bars, sauces, and pesto, it's worth buying a high-speed blender. They cost more than a standard blender, but you'll use it daily and it will last for years. Elyse is partial to her Vitamix, but there are other good-quality brands on the market.

Nonstick Pan

For eggs, you'll need a good nonstick pan. Look for a quality brand that uses a nontoxic coating, although only expect to get a couple of years out of your pan before the surface starts to wear out. To maintain your nonstick pans, never use them over high heat, handwash only, and avoid using metal utensils when cooking in the pans. We like the brands GreenPan and Zwilling.

Oven-Safe Skillet

You'll want a heavy-bottomed skillet that can go from stovetop to oven. We love our 10-inch Lodge cast-iron skillet, which is inexpensive, will last a lifetime (with proper care), and is great for everything from sautéed veggies to frittatas to pancakes.

Heavy-Bottomed Pot with Lid

A high-quality heavy-bottomed large saucepan or pot with a matching lid is a worthwhile investment. Heavy-bottomed stainless-steel pots like those made by All-Clad conduct heat much better for faster and more even cooking. If you cook a lot, get a set with multiple size options.

Sheet Pans (baking sheets)

You'll want at least two rimmed baking sheets, which are multifunctional and essential tools for baking cookies and roasting veggies. The standard size for home use is a half-sheet pan, which is 13 × 18 inches. Also stock up on unbleached parchment paper for easy cleanup (never cook directly on a sheet pan, because the aluminum can leach into your food). Our favorite brand of parchment paper is If You Care.

Loaf Pan

If you want to get into baking homemade bread (yesss!), invest in a ceramic loaf pan, which will retain heat better than glass or metal. We are partial to the high-quality French brands Emile Henry and Le Creuset.

Cook's Tools

You don't want to overload your kitchen drawers with endless gadgets, but there are several that are essential. To make our recipes, you will need a peeler, box grater, whisk, ladle, heatproof spatula, regular spatula (turner), wooden spoons, tongs, instant-read thermometer, timer, citrus press, pepper mill, measuring cups (for both liquids and dry ingredients), and measuring spoons. Look for OXO brand tools for great quality and affordability.

Glass Jars

We use mason jars in every size for storage. Ball brand widemouthed pint jars are especially versatile, as they're freezer-safe and the ideal size for packing smoothies and overnight oats to go. Half-pint jars are also handy, as their smaller size means faster thawing. Look for reusable plastic lids that fit your jars. They won't rust, so they last longer than the metal lids and rings that come with the jars; that said, we don't recommend them for packing liquids to go, as the seal isn't as good.

Storage Containers

You'll also want to stock up on a variety of storage containers for meal prepping and leftovers. We prefer freezer-safe glass, as it's nontoxic and can go in the microwave. Always avoid abrupt temperature changes when using glass storage to prevent shattering. For example, never pour boiling water into glass that was in the fridge or freezer. We like the durability of OXO Smart Seal glass containers–the large 7- or 8-cup size is the most versatile, but you'll want smaller options as well if you pack your breakfast or lunch to go. For storing muffins and cookies, a BPA-free plastic bakery box with a lid is sufficient. For snacks and freezing ingredients for smoothies, reusable silicone bags in multiple sizes are preferable over single-use plastic zipper bags.

Flour Canisters

To keep your whole-grain flours and oats fresh, you'll want to transfer them out of the bags they came in and into airtight storage containers. Again, glass is preferred–look for canisters with a very large opening, which are easy to fill and easier to scoop from. Elyse has six canisters in her pantry for the flours and blends she uses most frequently– Pancake and Waffle Mix (page 158), all-purpose flour, whole-wheat flour, rolled oats, oat flour, almond flour. For whole-grain flours that you buy in smaller bags (and use less frequently), leave them sealed in the bag and store in the fridge or freezer.

Large Mixing Bowls

You'll want two large mixing bowls. More space equals less spilling when you really put some muscle into your whisking. It's convenient to have at least one mixing bowl with a pour spout, which you'll see us recommend in some of the recipes. Mixing bowls usually come as a set, and having a small and a medium option in addition to large is convenient, too.

Salad Spinner, Colander, and Other Things

If you're following the *Rise & Run* lifestyle, you're going to be washing a lot of produce. Invest in a large salad spinner to easily wash leafy greens and also a colander with feet so that it can sit in the sink to drain. You'll also want a fine-mesh sieve for rinsing tiny grains like quinoa and lentils. And if you plan to make nut milk, a nut-milk bag (like Ellie's Best) is a convenient tool for easier straining.

STOCK YOUR PANTRY FOR SUCCESS

Here is a list of the dry goods that we use most frequently in our cookbooks. You won't be disappointed if you buy any of these nourishing ingredients, as you'll be able to use them in more than one recipe. By keeping your pantry well stocked, grocery shopping becomes a lot easier (this also frees you up to shop at the farmers' market on days when you only need fresh ingredients). On a weekly basis, you'll be mostly shopping for fresh produce, dairy, eggs, and meat. This means you can stick to the outer loop of the grocery store and avoid the endless aisles of packaged foods. A well-stocked pantry will inspire you to cook more, and you'll always be able to find a recipe you can pull off with pantry staples, even if your fridge is starting to look sadly bare.

Oats (rolled, steel-cut, and instant) and Oat Flour

We use a lot of rolled oats in this book. Runners love oats, and for good reason. Oats are high in vitamins, minerals, fiber, and antioxidants. They're a good source of easy-to-digest complex carbs and high in soluble fiber, which is great for digestion and balancing blood sugar levels. If you're avoiding gluten, look for certified gluten-free oats. We use rolled oats most frequently, but if you like oatmeal as much as we do, you'll also want to stock instant oats and steel-cut oats. We love baking with oat flour, as we find it easier to digest than whole-wheat flour. To make your own oat flour, simply grind rolled oats in a food processor or high-speed blender until they're broken down to the consistency of flour. A 2-pound bag of rolled oats will yield about 8 cups oat flour.

Flour

We keep whole-wheat flour, whole-wheat pastry flour, all-purpose flour, and bread flour stocked in our pantries. Baking with whole-grain flours can be tricky, as it can result in dense, dry, or gritty treats. Adding a small amount of white flour can make a big difference and help you achieve a fluffier texture. Although white flour isn't as nourishing as whole wheat, we want to love our homemade baked goods, so we aren't afraid to use all-purpose flour in moderation. You'll find it in our Pancake and Waffle Mix (page 158) and Whole-Wheat Bread (page 170). (We tested these recipes with 100% whole-grain flour and the results weren't as good, sadly.) In most of our recipes you can substitute a cup-for-cup gluten-free flour blend for the all-purpose flour, if you have a gluten allergy.

Gluten-Free Flours
(buckwheat, corn, almond)
We aren't big fans of packaged gluten-free flour blends, as they're often made with highly processed "flours" and additives or fillers, which can be difficult to digest. If you're avoiding gluten because you have a sensitive digestive system, gluten-free flour blends might not be that much better for you. In our gluten-free baked goods, we prefer to use almond flour or almond meal (which can be used interchangeably in these recipes), buckwheat flour, or stone-ground corn flour (fine grind). If you're avoiding almonds, hazelnut flour is a great alternative, and you can grind it yourself from whole raw hazelnuts (no need to remove the skins). Buckwheat flour is a great alternative for those on a grain-free diet, since it's technically not a grain and is high in amino acids. These types of flours (or any whole-grain flour that you use less frequently) should be stored in a sealed container in the fridge or freezer.

Legumes

We buy dried beans and lentils in bulk instead of buying canned, since it's more economical and better for the environment (no aluminum and lighter to ship), and since homemade beans possibly cause less gas (this one is up for debate). Canned beans are great to have on hand when you're in a time crunch, but look for cans that are BPA-free. In this book we use dried black beans, red lentils, and white beans. If you frequently cook beans, also buy kombu, a type of dried seaweed, which naturally contains an enzyme that helps break down the gas-producing carbohydrate in beans.

Whole Grains

The whole grains we use most frequently in this cookbook are quinoa and rice. We are partial to cooking organic short-grain brown rice because we love the chewy texture, but also like jasmine and basmati rice. Rice and quinoa should be rinsed prior to using. It's worth noting that there are concerns about high levels of arsenic in rice, especially brown rice. If you are pregnant, you may want to avoid eating it or cut back on how often you eat it; same goes if you're feeding rice to babies. We also stock farro and whole-grain teff, which are great alternatives to expand your repertoire and limit exposure to toxins.

Seeds

Seeds have won us over as an incredibly versatile superfood. They're high in omega-3 fatty acids, protein, and minerals. We use many varieties of seeds throughout this book, including flax, chia, hemp, sesame, pumpkin, and sunflower seeds. For a longer shelf life, seeds should be stored in the fridge or freezer, especially hemp hearts (hulled hemp seeds) and ground flaxseeds.

Nuts and Nut Butter

We use a wide variety of nuts, including cashews, almonds, walnuts, pecans, peanuts, and Brazil nuts. We love to make rich nut milks with cashews and almonds, and we toss nuts into homemade granola, energy bars, nut butters, and trail mix. Walnuts and pecans are more expensive than other nuts, but they take baked treats like muffins, cookies, and crumbles to a whole new level of awesomeness. We also keep almond butter and peanut butter on hand (especially delicious added to smoothies), and we love making our own nut butters (see pages 269 and 275).

Dried Fruit

Dates are our go-to whole-food sweetener for smoothies and energy bars. We buy dates in bulk since they have a long shelf life. We also recommend stocking unsweetened coconut flakes and shredded coconut, tart cherries or cranberries, dried apricots, and freeze-dried strawberries. Dried fruit is great for tossing into granola, instant oatmeal mix, and homemade bars. Before buying, check the ingredient list and try to avoid dried fruit with added sugar.

Miscellaneous Baking Ingredients

You're about to embark on a lot of baking–baked treats are a mainstay for breakfast in our households. The baking ingredients that you will use most frequently include baking soda, baking powder, instant or active dry yeast, tapioca starch, and vanilla extract. Pure vanilla extract is expensive, so if you're on a budget, it can be left out of most recipes.

Fats/Oils

The oils that we use most frequently are virgin coconut oil and extra-virgin olive oil. Avocado oil is also great to keep on hand for high-heat cooking. For baked treats, we are partial to using butter (yum!), but coconut oil is a great alternative for those avoiding dairy. Although it's not a pantry item, plain whole-milk yogurt or Greek yogurt appears in many of our recipes (to make your own, see page 147). A small amount of yogurt helps muffins and pancakes rise–the acidity of the yogurt reacts with baking soda to create bubbles. We also love adding yogurt to smoothies for a healthy dose of probiotics, calcium, protein, and fat. Many people who are sensitive to dairy find yogurt much easier to digest than other dairy products.

Coffee and Tea

This is a breakfast cookbook, so of course you'll want to stock coffee and tea in your pantry. Our go-to teas are matcha, oolong, green, black, chai, and herbal (for sleep). Nothing pairs better with a breakfast treat than a steaming mug of coffee. Look for organic and Fair Trade coffee. For best results, buy your beans whole and grind them fresh at the store or at home with a coffee grinder. You don't need a fancy coffee maker to make a great mug. Elyse is partial to using a French press, but a good drip coffee maker with auto-on functionality will save you precious morning minutes.

Sweeteners

Our go-to natural sweeteners are honey, blackstrap molasses, and maple syrup. Blackstrap molasses is high in iron, calcium, and other important micronutrients for athletes. Look for pure maple syrup and store it in the fridge. We also love baking with coconut sugar, which has a lower glycemic index than white sugar. Be sure to stock dark chocolate bars (70% or higher), unsweetened cocoa powder, and chocolate chips. Chocolate just makes everything better.

Spices and Salt

The spices we use most frequently include cinnamon, ginger, cardamom, garlic powder, oregano, smoked paprika, cumin, chili powder, and curry powder. It's worth whipping up your own Chai Spice Mix (page 274), which we use in many recipes. Also buy whole black peppercorns and invest in a pepper mill to be able to grind them fresh. Freshly ground black pepper has significantly better taste and nutrition. For salt, we mostly use fine sea salt or fine Himalayan salt. We like Redmond Real Salt, Jacobsen Salt Co., Celtic Sea Salt, and iodized sea salt. It's also nice to keep a flaky salt on hand for a finishing touch on chocolate treats like our Crispy Rice Peanut Butter Bars (page 123).

PRE-RUN FUEL:
ELECTROLYTE DRINKS AND EASY-TO-DIGEST MEALS

Small Bites for Sunrise Runners

These recipes are easy to digest and provide glucose for quick fuel and healthy fats for lasting energy. Everyone's digestion and metabolism vary greatly, so it's important to experiment to learn what works best for you.

Light Meals for Late-Morning Runners

These recipes are balanced, easy to digest, and nutrient-dense and will keep you full longer.

Hearty Breakfasts for Afternoon or Evening Runners

If you work out later in the day, go for a big, nourishing breakfast that will keep you sustained until lunch. A breakfast high in protein, fat, complex carbs, fiber, vitamins, and minerals will help you feel energized all day.

POST-RUN FUEL:
JUMP-START YOUR RECOVERY

If you run in the morning, it's important to make time for "second breakfast" instead of holding off until lunch. Or merge breakfast and lunch and celebrate your hard effort with a hearty brunch. Try to eat within an hour of finishing your workout to help your body recover faster.

On long runs, our minds wander to thinking about what we'll make for brunch upon our return home. Here are a few of our favorites.

HYDRATE

A smoothie is more hydrating than plain water because smoothies contain natural electrolytes, and the fiber helps you retain fluids.

FUEL

These dishes are protein-packed and offer complex carbs and healthy fats to boost your recovery. Fruit and veggies often take center stage to help replenish vitamins and minerals lost on your run. These easy meals can be prepped in advance and finished upon your return.

CELEBRATE

For mornings when you have more time, celebrate with a festive brunch. Check out all the drool-worthy meals in our Brunch chapter (starting on page 178). Here are just a few favorites to share with friends and family.

HEALING RECIPES

Food has an incredible ability to heal our bodies and minds. Without proper nutrition, distance running can take its toll over time. No distance runner is immune to occasional ailments. We hope these recipes will help you come back stronger and healthier than you started. If you have *Run Fast. Eat Slow.*, check out the Runners' Remedies chapter for more information on how to heal common injuries with proper nutrition.

I'd rather eat my way to health.
–SHALANE

RISE & RUN SEASONAL BREAKFAST MEAL PLANS

We lead with Saturday and Sunday since you likely do most of your cooking and longer runs (heartier brunch) on the weekends. Many breakfast leftovers can pair with lunch or dinner. The snack might be eaten before a run if you run early, post-run to hold you over until lunch, or saved for the afternoon. If you are cooking for one or two people instead of a family, you can

FALL

	BREAKFAST	SNACK	DRINK
Saturday	Sheet Pan Brunch with Make-Ahead Breakfast Sausage (*pages 187 and 184*)	Pumpkin Streusel Superhero Muffin (*page 96*)	Digestion Tonic (*page 246*)
Sunday	Recovery Omelet, Sweet Potato Sage Biscuits (*pages 144 and 198*)	Pumpkin Streusel Superhero Muffin (*page 96*)	Iron Almond Milk (*page 252*)
Monday	Apple-Quinoa Parfait with Chai-Spiced Pecans and yogurt (*pages 157 and 126*)	Chocolate Tart Cherry Seed Balls (*page 120*)	Digestion Tonic (*page 246*)
Tuesday	Apple-Quinoa Parfait with Chai-Spiced Pecans and yogurt (*pages 157 and 126*)	Chocolate Tart Cherry Seed Balls (*page 120*)	Iron Almond Milk (*page 252*)
Wednesday	Teff Porridge with Pear and Pecans (*page 169*)	Cinnamon Raisin Seed Bread (*page 175*), hard-boiled egg (*page 142*)	Pumpkin Pie Smoothie (*page 232*)
Thursday	Breakfast Power Bowl (*page 135*)	Molasses Tahini Granola with yogurt (*page 128*)	Matcha Collagen Latte (*page 249*)
Friday	Teff Porridge with Pears and Chai Pecans (*page 169*)	Cinnamon Raisin Seed Bread (*page 175*), hard-boiled egg (*page 142*)	Turmeric Tea (*page 257*)

freeze the leftovers (especially the baked treats and muffins). We give a lot of variety below to inspire you to try new things, but you can repeat these meals and snacks to make the weekly plan stretch longer. The choices shown here are geared toward runners with hearty appetites.

WINTER

	BREAKFAST	SNACK	DRINK
Saturday	Chorizo Breakfast Tacos with Guasacaca (*page 178*)	Yam Spice Superhero Muffin (*page 103*)	Sunrise Juice (*page 243*)
Sunday	Black Bean Quinoa Pilaf (*page 188*) with Guasacaca (*page 178*)	Yam Spice Superhero Muffin (*page 103*)	Sip Me Hot Cocoa (*page 256*)
Monday	Apple Maple Butter Oatmeal Bake (*page 132*)	Sweet Potato Kale Superhero Muffin (*page 72*)	Turmeric Tea (*page 257*)
Tuesday	Breakfast Power Bowl (*page 135*)	Yam Spice Superhero Muffin (*page 103*)	Matcha Collagen Latte (*page 249*)
Wednesday	Apple Maple Butter Oatmeal Bake (*page 132*)	Sweet Potato Kale Superhero Muffin (*page 72*)	Turmeric Tea (*page 257*)
Thursday	Breakfast Power Bowl (*page 135*)	Sprouted Almond Butter on banana or apples (*page 269*)	Matcha Collagen Latte (*page 249*)
Friday	Savory Red Lentil Oatmeal (*page 164*)	Sprouted Almond Butter on banana or apples (*page 269*)	Sunrise Juice (*page 243*)

	BREAKFAST	**SNACK**	**DRINK**
Saturday	Waffles (Pancake-Waffle Mix; **page 158**), Cacao-Hazelnut Spread **(page 271)**	Green Eggs and Hammer On Superhero Muffin **(page 78)**	Raspberry Rival Smoothie **(page 228)**
Sunday	Asparagus and Potato Skillet Frittata **(page 205)**, Make-Ahead Sausage **(page 184)**	Whole-Wheat Bread with Cacao-Hazelnut Spread **(pages 170 and 271)**	Anti-Inflammatory Cashew Milk **(page 250)**
Monday	Leftover Waffle with fried egg (Savory Waffles, **page 163**)	Lily's Chocolate Superhero Muffins **(page 104)**	Chai Tea with Anti-Inflammatory Cashew Milk **(page 250)**
Tuesday	Avocado Toast **(page 167)** with Everything Bagel Seasoning **(page 265)**	Lily's Chocolate Superhero Muffins **(page 104)**	Recovery Cashew Milkshake **(page 251)**
Wednesday	Green Eggs and Hammer On Superhero Muffin **(page 78)**	Trail Mix Breakfast Cookie **(page 115)**	Raspberry Rival Smoothie **(page 228)**
Thursday	Creamy Chai Cauliflower Smoothie Bowl **(page 240)**, Lily's Chocolate Superhero Muffins **(page 104)**	Salted Caramel Sprouted Almond Butter on banana **(page 269)**	Turmeric Tea **(page 257)**
Friday	Waffles, Breakfast Sausage (from freezer)	Trail Mix Breakfast Cookie **(page 115)**	Matcha Collagen Latte **(page 249)**

SUMMER

	BREAKFAST	SNACK	DRINK
Saturday	Tempeh Breakfast Sausage *(page 183)*, Basic Flaky Biscuits *(page 197)*, sautéed greens, burst cherry tomatoes	Strawberry-Rhubarb Superhero Muffin *(page 95)*	Green Vitality Smoothie *(page 234)*
Sunday	Brunch Power Salad *(page 194)*, Soft-Boiled Eggs *(page 142)*, Toast with Blueberry Chia Seed Jam *(page 267)*	Strawberry-Rhubarb Superhero Muffin *(page 95)*	Green Vitality Smoothie *(page 234)*
Monday	Blueberry Bliss Smoothie Bowl *(page 237)* with Goddess Grain-Free Granola *(page 127)*	Crispy Rice Peanut Butter Bar *(page 123)*	Lemon Electrolyte Water *(page 244)*
Tuesday	Sunrise Overnight Oats *(page 139)*	Crispy Rice Peanut Butter Bar *(page 123)*	Lemon Electrolyte Water *(page 244)*
Wednesday	Pesto-Zucchini Superhero Muffin *(page 75)*	Tropical Fruit Salad with Farro *(page 206)*	Can't Beet Me Smoothie III *(page 231)*
Thursday	Pesto-Zucchini Superhero Muffin *(page 75)*, Goddess Grain-Free Granola *(page 127)* with yogurt and fruit	Tropical Fruit Salad with Farro *(page 206)*	Lemon Electrolyte Water *(page 244)*
Friday	Savory Red Lentil Oatmeal *(page 164)*	Popcorn Trail Mix *(page 124)*	Marathon Mocha *(page 255)*

3 | NEXT-LEVEL TRAINING

COACH FLANAGAN'S MARATHON PROGRAM

*Everyone has a little fire
in them that even in tough
times can't be extinguished.*

—SHALANE

I love the fact that not many people can say, "Oh, I went out and ran 20 miles today." I love how much dedication it takes and how much you learn about yourself and your physical and mental limits.

—SHALANE

Ready to take your running to the next level? Let's soak in training and race-day wisdom from Coach Flanagan. The following pages will set you up for success in the marathon, whether it's your first 26.2 or your twentieth. This chapter is geared toward marathoners, but those who are training for shorter distances will be inspired by the workouts and key guidelines to becoming a stronger (and lifelong) runner. If you're ready to elevate your marathon training, check out Shalane's 14-week program on page 47.

Take It Away, Coach!

The marathon is the most exciting running event. From the camaraderie to the memorable courses to the fans, there really is no other sporting event like it. I love that the marathon attracts every type of runner. Beginners get to toe the line in the same race as the best distance runners in the world. No matter your level, you'll experience pure pain and euphoria all on the same day. At around eighteen miles, you'll swear to yourself that you'll never do another marathon, but by the time you return home, you'll be plotting your next race.

The keystone of this chapter is my 14-week training program on page 47. But before you dive into the program, I want to set the stage with my best advice for marathon training. (Hopefully this doesn't make you withdraw your race entry!)

1 **YOU GOTTA GET FIT TO GET FIT!** Translation: You need a base fitness level before you begin training for a marathon. A base means that you're already running consistent mileage. This is essential to prevent injuries. Before you start my program, work your way up to running four or five days per week and also commit to a strength-training program (see chapter 3 for advice). First-time marathoners should be logging at least 20 miles per week as a base before they start their training program, and veteran marathoners should have a base of around 40 miles per week. The general rule of thumb is to increase your mileage by no more than 10 percent per week. The marathon is about conditioning your legs to withstand a lot of pounding and getting used to being on your feet for a long time.

2 **CONSISTENCY.** No one particular workout makes or breaks a marathon buildup; it's truly about putting in the work for many weeks and months. It's not at all sexy, but it works. At the elite level, the goal is to find out how many miles you can log on your legs without breaking down. Getting to the starting line healthy is no easy feat, but if you can run lots of miles, your mind and body will carry you farther than you thought possible!

3 That brings us to **MENTAL STRENGTH**, which is as important as physical strength. Your internal dialogue during a race will be all over the place, swinging from positive to negative to positive in a few minutes. To overcome race-day

hurdles, it's crucial to have a clear plan, written goals, and a *WHY*. Why are you doing this? This answer will get you to the finish line. Write it in a running journal, post it over your bathroom mirror, tattoo it on your arm. Whatever it takes, don't forget your *WHY*.

4   **TUNE INTO YOUR BODY.** A veteran runner will know when to push and when to back off. Is that "twinge" the start of an injury or something you can run through? Do you need to take an extra day off to rest this week? Remember that a training plan is not written in stone. Make adjustments as you go.

5   **FUEL RIGHT.** The more you run, the more nutrient-dense whole foods (see previous chapter) you need to incorporate into your daily diet. Distance runners need an incredible amount of nutrition to stay healthy. As you increase your mileage, you will find yourself hungry ALL THE TIME. You need to dedicate time in the kitchen to keep yourself healthy and satiated.

6   **GET OTHER KINDS OF EXERCISE.** Variety keeps the training interesting and stresses your body in new ways, which enables you to build fitness faster. If you are injury-prone, you'll want to incorporate more cross-training. My favorite cross-training activities include swimming, Spin class, weight training, yoga, and Pilates. You can train for a successful marathon with just four solid runs per week if you are also cross-training two or three times per week.

Also, commit to running some of your mileage on trails to reduce the pounding. Personally, I like to run 50 percent of my mileage on roads and 50 percent on soft surfaces (track, grass field, trails). I also recommend incorporating strides (running short distances while focusing on great form) and drills like bounding and high knees.

7   No matter your goal or level, I highly recommend finding a **COMPATIBLE TRAINING PARTNER AND A COACH.** They will hold you accountable on days when your motivation is low. A coach will help you work through challenges and make adjustments to your training program.

8   **REST IS ESSENTIAL FOR RECOVERY.** That's why we've dedicated a whole section to tips to help you sleep better (see page 60). If you are pushing yourself too hard, injuries will creep in. Signs that you need to back off your training include an elevated heart rate, trouble sleeping, low motivation, and injuries. These are also signs that you might not be fueling right (see #5 above). And remember, your rest days should truly be rest days, which means a Recovery Run (see page 47) or a walk and yoga. I recommend scheduling your rest day for the day after your Long Run (see page 45).

9   **"GET COMFORTABLE BEING UNCOMFORTABLE"** is a great mantra for marathoners. It's going to hurt at times. Just when you're in a groove, something will change. Your buildup to race day will have obstacles. The

weather changes. Your body changes (sometimes meal to meal). Your head changes depending on your sleep, your fuel, your last run. And then there's the blisters and chafing! It's important to stay focused and know that discomfort is part of running, and it's also part of the transformation. You will want to give in or give up, but just keep putting one foot in front of the other. Just like in life. You plan for it. You train for it. You put your best foot forward. And then everything changes. Again and again.

10 This entire list is a long way of saying: **YOU CAN'T JUST RUN THE MILES—YOU NEED TO LIVE THE LIFESTYLE.** If you just focus on the workouts, you are headed for a wall. Proper nutrition, rest, recovery, and mental strength—these are essential intertwined pillars of marathon training. None is more or less important than the others.

Here are the types of weekly workouts I recommend for intermediate to advanced marathoners.

BEST WORKOUTS FOR RUNNERS

Tempo Run

This run—usually 6 to 9 miles—should be done at your goal marathon pace or slightly faster. You'll be able to talk, but it gets harder the farther you go. As you get more fit, this pace will become easier to hold and for longer amounts of time. This run will increase your lactate threshold. Increasing your threshold is important for racing all distances because it allows the body to run

at faster speeds and for a longer amount of time before fatigue hits.

Mile Repeats

This is your most challenging workout, and it will help you gain the most fitness. It will really get your heart rate up. It should be difficult to talk when you're running repeats. Aim to run at your half marathon pace. The recovery is short, 90-second rests between each mile, working up to 6 x 1 mile. This is ideally run at a track, but it can also be done on the road with a watch to track your progress. Before every track workout, I do drills and strides to work on mechanics and good form.

Long Run

This is the cornerstone of marathon training and should be incorporated every week. It builds mental and physical strength and endurance. I find that the Long Run is the best indicator of marathon fitness. You'll start at around 10 miles and build up to 18 to 20 miles. In marathon training, you typically do not run over 20 miles until race day. During my weekly Long Run, I like to visualize the race I'm training for and transport my mind to the course.

Use your Long Run to figure out what fuel works best for you. Keep a running and food journal (We wrote one! It's called *Run Fast. Eat Slow. A Runner's Meal Planner*) and log what you eat before, during (fluids/gels), and after the run. This will allow you to make adjustments as the weeks pass. Every run is an opportunity to learn something about yourself, especially how much fuel, stretching (see pages 68–69), and rest (lots!) you require.

Speed Training and Hills

These are typically 200-, 400-, or 800-meter repeats done at a track, with a continuous jog between the sprints. The goal is to run as fast as you can to improve your leg turnover. You will usually repeat the distance six to eight times to really fatigue your legs. It's important to maintain good running form (knee drive, arms swinging front to back, chin up, relaxed shoulders, relaxed jaw). If you don't have access to a track, you can do this more as a fartlek-style workout

(*fartlek* means "speed play" in Swedish): You speed up for a set amount of time and then slow down for a set amount of time. In the training program on page 48, we give this as an option instead of the track workout.

Another form of speed work are hills. Running hills is a great way to build up leg and glute strength, as well as cardio fitness and mental toughness. Find a hill that is long, but not too steep, so that you can maintain good form. The hill should be long enough for 45 seconds to 2 minutes of hard running. You will build up to 8 repetitions. If you are signing up for a hilly marathon or a trail race, this is a must-do workout.

Strength Training

Two to three times per week I'm in the gym to lift after my run. My focus is core strength, overcoming imbalances, and building muscle for resiliency. Check out my injury-prevention routine on page 66, which can be accomplished from your home with very little equipment.

Recovery Run

Honor the value in the slower run. Listen to your body and have the confidence to run easy so you can bring your best to hard workouts. The Recovery Run is about building easy mileage. It should be done at a conversational pace, which means you can talk during the entire run. This is your chance to really celebrate running, soak up the beauty of your surroundings, catch up with running friends, and appreciate your health.

COACH FLANAGAN'S 14-WEEK TRAINING PROGRAM

This 14-week training program is geared toward seasoned runners who are training for their first marathon and have a time goal, or returning marathoners who want to set a PR. Shalane wrote this training program specifically for Elyse, who is training for her first marathon to celebrate her fortieth birthday. Elyse has been a distance runner since she was twelve years old and always thought she would run a marathon someday, but pregnancy, young kids, and career have meant she's put it off for years. Now with her friend Shalane to guide her, Elyse really has no excuse. She asked Coach Flanagan to write a challenging but realistic training program for busy professionals.

If you're new to the sport or training for your first marathon, consider subbing one of the workout days for just consistent mileage. Customize this to suit your personal goals and lifestyle. For example, Elyse subs one of the run days for swimming since she knows her body can only tolerate so much pounding. For those working toward a finish-time goal, we've also included a pace chart so you have target splits for the workouts.

And remember: At the beginning of a buildup, it's easy to be overwhelmed by the distance and the paces, so focus on the individual weeks instead. The progression toward the goal is subtle and gradual. Patience is truly a virtue in marathon training!

Flanagan's 14-week Marathon Training Program

This is an advanced training program for seasoned runners who want to take their training to the next level. We recommend working with a coach to scale to fit your needs and goals.

*All Tuesday and Thursday workouts should have a 2-mile warmup and 2-mile cooldown.

*The second "OR" workout listed after the track workout is an alternative option for those who don't have access to run at a track or prefer to incorporate the speed work into their regular run.

Week	Sunday	Monday	Tuesday
	Long Run	**Rest Day**	**Speed Training or Hills**
14	8-mile long run	Rest (walk, yoga)	6–8 x 200 w/ a 200 m recovery jog **OR** 6–8 x 1-min. hard, 1-min. easy
13	8–10 mile long run	Rest (walk, yoga)	6–8 x 400 w/ 60–90-sec. rest **OR** 6–8 x 2-min. hard, 90-sec. easy
12	10-mile long run (continuous 4-mile warmup, 2-mile tempo at marathon pace, 4-mile cooldown)	Rest (walk, yoga)	8 x 200 m w/ a 200 m jog (continous) **OR** 8 x 45–60-sec. hill **OR** 8 x 1-min. hard, 1-min. easy
11	10–12-mile long run	Rest (walk, yoga)	8 x 300 w/ 60-sec. rest **OR** 8 x 1:30-hard, 1- min. easy
10	12 mile long run (continuous 4-mile warmup, 3-mile tempo @ marathon pace, 5-mile cooldown)	Rest (walk, yoga)	12 x strides **OR** 12 x 45-sec. hills **OR** 12 x 1-min. hard, 1-min. easy

	5:00–5:15	4:30–4:45	4:00–4:15	3:30–3:45	3:00–3:15
Marathon Pace	11:30–12:00	10:20–10:50	9:10–9:40	8:00–8:30	6:50–7:30
Easy Run/ Long Run	12:00 per mile	11:00 per mile	10:00 per mile	9:00 per mile	8:00 per mile
Mile Repeats	11:15–11:45	10:00–10:30	8:50–9:20	7:45–8:15	6:30–7:10
800/Speed Training	5:00 per 800	4:30 per 800	4:00 per 800	3:30 per 800	3:00 per 800

Wednesday	Thursday	Friday	Saturday	Weekly Mileage Goal
Recovery Run or Cross-Train	**Mile Repeats or Fartlek**	**Recovery Run**	**Recovery Run or Cross-Train**	
5 miles	3 x 1-mile, 90- sec. rest **OR** 3 x 8-min. hard, 90-sec. easy	5 miles	cross-train or 5 miles	30–40s
6 miles	5–6 x (3 min hard, 1-min. easy, 1- min. hard, 1-min. easy)	6 miles	cross-train or 6 miles	40s
7 miles	4 x 1-mile, 90-sec. rest **OR** 4 x 8-min. hard, 90-sec. easy	7 miles	cross-train or 6 miles	40–50s
7 miles	2 x 2-mile, 5-min. rest **OR** 2 x 20-min. hard, 5-min. easy	8 miles	cross-train or 7 miles	50s
7 miles	5 x 1-mile, 90 second rest **OR** 5 x 8-min. hard, 90-sec. easy	8 miles	cross-train or 8 miles	50–60s

Week	Sunday	Monday	Tuesday
	Long Run	**Rest Day**	**Speed Training or Hills**
9	12–14-mile long run	Rest (walk, yoga)	6–8 x strides **OR** 6–8 x 1-min. hard, 1-min. easy
8	12–14-mile long run (continuous 4-mile warmup, 4-mile tempo at marathon pace, 4–6-mile cooldown)	Rest (walk, yoga)	10 x 1-min. hill, jog back down
7	14-mile long run	Rest (walk, yoga)	4 x 400, 4 x 200, 1-min. rest, 3-min. rest between **OR** 4 x 2-min. hard, 1- min. easy, 4 x 1- min. hard, 1-min. easy, 3-min. jog between
6	16-mile long run (continuous 5-mile warmup, 6-mile tempo at marathon pace, 5-mile cooldown)	Rest (walk, yoga)	6–8 x strides **OR** 6–8 x 1-min. hard, 1-min. easy
5	18-mile long run	Rest (walk, yoga)	8–10 strides **OR** 8–10 x 45-sec. hills **OR** 8–10 x 1-min. hard, 1-min. easy
4	20-mile long run	Rest (walk, yoga)	2 x (5 x 200) w/ 200 m continous jog. 3–5-min. rest between sets **OR** 2 x (5 x 1-min hard, 1-min. easy) 3–5-min. jog between sets

Wednesday	Thursday	Friday	Saturday	Weekly Mileage Goal
Recovery Run or Cross-Train	**Mile Repeats or Fartlek**	**Recovery Run**	**Recovery Run or Cross-Train**	
8 miles	6 x 5-min. hard, 1- min. easy	8 miles	cross-train or 8 miles	50–60s
8 miles	6 x 1-mile, 90-sec. rest **OR** 6 x 8-min. hard, 90-sec. easy	8 miles	cross-train or 8 miles	50–60s
8 miles	2 miles, 1-mile, 2 miles, 3–5-min. rest between **OR** 15-min., 8-min., 15-min. hard, 3–5- min. jog between	8 miles	cross-train or 8 miles	50–60s
8 miles	2 x (8 x 400), 200 m jog between, 5- min. rest between sets **OR** 2 x (8 x 2-min. hard, 2-min. easy) 5-min. jog between sets	8 miles	cross-train or 8 miles	50–60s
8 miles	2 x (1-mile, 800, 1-mile, 800) 2-min. rest, 5-min. rest between sets **OR** 2 x (8-min. hard, 4-min. hard, 8-min. hard, 4-min. hard) 2-min. jog between intervals, 5-min. jog between sets	8 miles	cross-train or 8 miles	60s
9 miles	8–10 x 800, 2-min. rest **OR** 8–10 x 4-min. hard, 2-min. jog	9 miles	cross-train or 9 miles	60s

Week	Sunday	Monday	Tuesday
	Long Run	**Rest Day**	**Speed Training or Hills**
3	14–16-mile long run	Rest (walk, yoga)	10 x 1-min. hill **OR** 10 x 1-min. hard, 1-min. easy
2	10–12-mile long run	Rest (walk, yoga)	3 x 2 miles, 5-min. rest between **OR** 3 x (15-min. hard, 5-min. jog)
1	8-mile long run	cross-train or 6 miles	1 mile @ marathon pace, 4 x 400. Fully rest between each **OR** 8 min. at marathon pace, 3–5-min. jog, 4 x 2-min. hard, 3-min. rest

RACE DAY

Wednesday	Thursday	Friday	Saturday	Weekly Mileage Goal
Recovery Run or Cross-Train	**Mile Repeats or Fartlek**	**Recovery Run**	**Recovery Run or Cross-Train**	
8 miles	3 mile, 2 mile, 1 mile w/ 5-min. rest between **OR** 25-min. hard, 15- min. hard, 8-min. hard w/ 5-min. jog between	8 miles	cross-train or 8 miles	50s
6 miles	2 x (1 mile, 4 x 400) 2-min. rest after mile, 90-sec. rest after each 400, 3 min. between sets **OR** 2 x (8-min. hard, 2-min. jog, 4 x 2- min. hard, 90-sec. jog) 3-min. jog between sets	6 miles	cross-train or 6 miles	40s
5 miles	5 miles and 8 strides	Rest Day	3-mile shake-out run	30s

RACE-READY

The work is done and your race is just two weeks away. Now it's time to taper, hydrate, fuel, and relax. In the days leading up to the race, it's important to maintain a normal routine. The excitement will build in the final days, especially if you're traveling to your race. Avoid the temptation to walk miles exploring a new city or spend hours at the race expo. Relax more and stay off your feet as much as possible. The day before the race, do a 3-mile shakeout run and some light stretching.

Eat the foods that you know your body digests best (you'll know this by reviewing the notes you took in your journal after your Long Runs). What you eat in the days leading up to the race is just as important as what you eat the night before. Avoid the endless samples at the race expo. Don't save carbo-loading for the night before, or you'll show up on the starting line feeling bloated. In the week leading up to the race, I incorporate one additional high-carbohydrate snack into my daily routine, but otherwise I stick to my balanced eating habits. My favorite easy-to-digest complex carbs are sweet potatoes and oats. You'll find these two all-star ingredients in several recipes throughout this book.

If you're experiencing race-day jitters, accept it as normal. It's a positive sign that you are ready to race. Do activities that you love to pass the time, and try a few of my calming tips (opposite).

HOW DO YOU FACE RACE-DAY NERVES?

Embrace race-day jitters with a hug! Feeling nervous is a sign that you care. I remind myself that racing is the reward for my hard work and training. This is the *fun* part! Here are a few more calming tips.

1 Look over your running journal to remind yourself of the work you've put in. Looking at the consistency in my own training gives me confidence that I am ready for a race.

2 Outline a race-day plan with a running partner or coach. Having a plan that I know I'm capable of executing calms my mind.

3 Go over what you can control, and accept that there will be things you cannot control on race day. I always tell myself I will go with the flow.

4 Organize your schedule and write out exactly what time you'll be eating, sleeping, getting on the bus, warming up, etc. This organization allows me to enter autopilot mode on the morning of the race, so I'm not wasting energy overthinking the process or rushing to get to the starting line.

5 The night before the race, I lay out my clothes and pack my bag with everything I will need on race day. I have a ritual of taking an ice bath, drinking hot herbal tea, and reading a fluffy novel to help me sleep.

FINAL WORDS OF WISDOM

The hardest part is getting to the starting line. Once you're there, soak in your surroundings and celebrate the day.

Accept that what you are about to do is HARD. But we can do HARD things! And you know what? Overcoming challenges makes us feel ALIVE, proud, and confident.

Lean into the discomfort. You get to decide how hard you are going to work for your goal. If you had a tough day and didn't reach your goal, focus on the next one. Just keep moving forward.

If nothing else keeps you upright, think about what you'll eat post-race–a juicy burger, fries, and a cold beer, please. Post-race meals are the best part of training for a marathon!

4 | PLAY ON

MIND AND BODY RESILIENCY

It's great to be fast, but it's better to be a great person.

—SHALANE

This informative training chapter is half "how to prevent injuries and recover faster" and half "how to set better goals and establish a positive mind-set for a successful race day" (or any big life moment!). Behind every great athlete, there is a team helping them get to the starting line in working order, so we consulted with our favorite experts in the fields of physical therapy, yoga, Pilates, wellness, and mental health to help us put this chapter together. The experts below have been involved in Shalane's career for years and work closely with the elite Bowerman Track Club (BTC).

Recover Faster

In any given year, at least 50 percent of runners will be sidelined with an injury. As any runner knows, not being able to run is heartbreaking, especially if running is your main outlet to manage stress and/or you are training for an important race. Most of us struggle to set aside time to dedicate to cross-training, strength training, and stretching—because we'd rather be running than holding a plank position with a knee in our armpit. But . . .

Running, like an old friend, will always be there for you. Even if you take a break from the sport, running will welcome you back with open arms. I didn't run through pregnancy or nursing. It didn't feel natural to me, and I didn't have the energy. A total of three years off from running in my thirties (I had been running since age twelve) made me return to the sport with more enthusiasm and a newfound love and appreciation. Don't fear time off–embrace it.

—ELYSE

Improving in this sport takes an incredible amount of patience and dedication, and the majority of injuries are due to overtraining and taking on too much, too soon. We spoke with Colleen Little, Shalane's physical therapist, to gather her vital advice for busy runners.

INTERVIEW WITH COLLEEN LITTLE
PT, DPT, OCS, NIKE BOWERMAN TRACK CLUB PHYSICAL THERAPIST

Q *What is the most important injury-prevention advice for runners?*

True recovery days and strength training are essential to preventing injury. Schedule a day off each week where you do yoga or rehab exercises, walk, or bike. Also, run your easy runs truly easy. Far too often, we run our easy runs too hard, which delays recovery.

Schedule time to strength train at least twice per week. A properly designed weight program won't take away from your running. It should complement your training and help build resiliency within the body, in order to adapt to the load and volume you are asking it to do.

Q *Does stretching really do that much? What should we do if we have very little extra time before and after a run?*

Stretching is important, but I like to think of it more as mobility. As runners we need a good balance between stiffness and mobility. I typically suggest dynamic stretching (movement-based stretching with shorter holds) pre-run to help prep the tissue for the run and then longer stretches and joint mobility work post-run (later in the day is totally acceptable) to work on gaining some length in the tissue that tends to be shorter than we'd like. Common areas to focus extra love are hip flexors, calves, hamstrings, and the mid-back. Most of us don't hold stretches long enough to make lasting change, so really work on spending time in each position.

Q *What are the most common causes of injuries and imbalances in runners?*

Taking on too much volume too quickly, without adding targeted strength. Many people run to get in shape or to get fit instead of getting fit first to be able to run without injury. We underestimate the demands that running places on our bodies. Every time our foot hits the ground, our body is absorbing 2.5 to 3 times our body weight. All our soft tissue (muscles, tendons, and ligaments) need time to build up strength and resiliency. It takes a lot of patience.

Q *What can help runners recover faster?*

In addition to easy run days and nutrition/ fuel, sleep is probably the most important factor overall in true recovery, especially following hard efforts.

Check out Colleen's top 5 injury-prevention exercises for runners on page 66 (Shalane's Strength Training Routine).

Prevent Injuries

We wouldn't have to recover from injuries if we managed to successfully prevent them. For that, we spoke to Tracey Katona, the expert Pilates instructor for the BTC team. Tracey has worked with an impressive list of elite female runners, including Shalane, Colleen Quigley, Kate Grace, and Emily Infeld. She knows bodies, and how to build them to last.

INTERVIEW WITH TRACEY KATONA
CERTIFIED ROMANAS PILATES INSTRUCTOR, OWNER, KATONA PILATES

Q *Why is Pilates good for runners?*

Pilates offers a wealth of support for runners to keep them in the sport longer. It focuses on core strength, symmetry and body awareness for function and injury prevention, joint mobility and stability, increased flexibility, better circulation, improved lung capacity, less muscular tension, and decompression of the spine

(continues on page 62)

Sleep Better

We agree with Colleen that sleep is so important for recovery. Many of us live such busy lives that it can be difficult to unwind at the end of the day. Your body might feel exhausted, but the second your head hits the pillow, your mind starts racing and sleep doesn't come as easily as it should.

If you aren't able to get to bed early enough to wake up naturally at six a.m., then maybe sunrise workouts aren't for you. Waking up early to exercise but cutting your sleep short can impact your metabolism. Early-morning gym sessions can backfire if you aren't getting the recommended seven to nine hours of sleep. A lack of quality sleep can lead to more snacking throughout the day as our body strives to counteract the energy gap.

SHALANE AND ELYSE'S TOP 10 TIPS FOR BETTER SLEEP

1 Get outside first thing in the morning to set your circadian rhythm. Your mind and body need direct sunlight in the morning. This means at least fifteen minutes of walking, running, meditation, or yoga outside (summer or winter, rain or shine). Leave the sunglasses at home (you need to absorb those morning rays!). On days when Elyse doesn't have time to run, she takes her dog for a brisk 15-minute walk instead.

2 Limit your caffeine intake. We *love* coffee, but it can stay in your system for longer than eight hours. We limit our caffeine habit to mornings only. On afternoons when we really need a small boost, we switch to green tea, but only in the early afternoon. Caffeine is a really powerful stimulant, and some people metabolize it slower than others. Elyse is so sensitive to caffeine that she cannot even eat chocolate in the evenings (sigh).

3 Stay off electronic devices at night, especially one hour before bed. It's tempting to want to use this time after the kids are asleep to work or scan social media, but the blue light that emanates from our screens is really detrimental to sleep. Apps are designed to keep our minds stimulated. Your body won't start making hormones essential for sleep, like melatonin, until you begin to unwind from your day. Even a quick scroll on Instagram activates way too many thought processes and FOMO anxiety.

4 Most nutrition experts recommend not eating before bed. A 12-hour fast can be beneficial for digestion, detoxification, and sleep. But personally, we feel a light snack before bed can help you sleep deeper. Runners are always hungry, and if you eat dinner early (five thirty p.m. for us) by nine p.m., you're craving a snack. Instead of reaching for a bag of pretzels or sugary cereal, which won't sustain you, eat a snack that is high in protein, fat, and minerals (minerals like magnesium and calcium are essential for sleep). Elyse's go-to bedtime snack is whole-milk yogurt topped with homemade granola (high in minerals from the nuts, seeds, and molasses; see our recipes on pages 147 and 127). During intense training, you may want to try a supplement to help your muscles relax, like NOW Foods magnesium glycinate.

5 Turn down the lights in the evenings and invest in blackout drapes. Even the smallest light coming from an electronic device can disrupt your sleep. If you wake up in the night to go to the bathroom, keep the lights as dim as possible.

6 Shalane enjoys drinking herbal tea instead of alcohol in the evenings to unwind. If you are going to enjoy a glass of wine or a beer, have it before or during dinner, so your body has time to metabolize the alcohol and you have time to rehydrate before going to bed. Our favorite dried herbs to steep into tea for better sleep are chamomile, calendula, peppermint, hops, and lavender (see our Dreamer's Tea recipe on page 258).

7 Deep breathing, meditation, light stretching, foam rolling, or simply lying on your back with your legs up the wall are great exercises to do before bed. Elyse learned the legs-up-the-wall trick from Shalane: Lie on your back with your butt snug against the wall and place your legs straight up so you are in an L shape. This releases the lower back, stimulates blood flow for recovery, and stretches your hammies. Hang out there for 5 to 10 minutes while practicing deep breathing.

8 Reading a good book in bed does wonders to shift your mind away from focusing on your busy day. Never read a thriller, mystery, or self-help book right before bed (too stimulating!). We prefer reading over watching TV, as Netflix always leads to unintended binge watching.

9 On nights when you're lying in bed and can't seem to turn off your mind, try deep breathing and counting backward. Start at 10 and slowly count down to 0 while taking one deep breath on every count. This will hopefully put you into a slumber before you complete the countdown.

10 The worst thing you can do is stress so much about sleep that you end up *not* sleeping. Remember, everyone experiences a disruptive night of sleep every once in a while. Simply remind yourself that a bad night tonight means tomorrow night you'll sleep like a baby.

We'll give the last word on sleep to Brad Stulberg, who writes the "Do It Better" column for *Outside* magazine and understands the athlete's mind like no other:

> *Don't freak out about not sleeping. The first rule of sleep is that you should prioritize it because it is one of the most important things for health. The second rule of sleep is not to stress out if you don't get it. So much of what keeps people awake is freaking out about not getting sleep. Sleep like your life depends on it. And if you are up in the middle of the night or not sleeping well, release from the fact that your life depends on it—because it doesn't!*

Check out more vital advice from Brad on page 63.

and joints (much needed after a long run). Pilates is therapy for the entire body. Every exercise strengthens you, stretches you, and gives you better muscle control.

Q What can help runners recover faster?

A commitment to regular Pilates (mat exercises at home and/or at a studio on Pilates apparatuses) will noticeably reduce your recovery time. Ideally, a runner should strive for at least two lessons per week, but it can also be done daily at home for optimal achievement.

Busy runners should prioritize the exercises that target their weaknesses. Some find it great as a warm-up and a way to connect to their core before heading out the door, and some find it great to decompress and lengthen the body after a run.

Pilates helps you run more efficiently. You will find yourself less tired, sore, and stiff after long runs and workouts.

Q If you have just 10 minutes before heading out for a run, what warm-up exercises are best?

I recommend activating your core with an exercise like the Pilates 100 and doing a rotational exercise (stand with legs bent, activate your abs, arms raised, and slowly twist back and forth, only moving above your waist). This connects you to your core (we call it your "powerhouse"), gets the blood circulating, and loosens up your mid-back. You could also do wall sits—sit into a squat with your legs at a right angle and your back and neck long against a wall. It will remind you of the importance of good posture and will activate your abs and glutes before you take off.

Q How can runners who sit at a desk all day improve their posture?

I tell my clients to pay attention to how they are sitting. It's easy to get lost in your computer, and the next thing you know, the day has flown by and your back hurts. This happens because we collapse into the lower back and slouch (rounding the upper body with neck extended forward). This puts great strain on your spine—your back will let you know it.

By supporting your low back with your stomach in and sitting aligned tall, you take pressure off your spine and decompress your lungs so you can breathe properly, and this lifts your waistline so your organs aren't crowded. You will feel better and look more confident!

Also, don't cross your legs! Over time, this will lead to one hip being physically higher than the other hip. You will eventually feel this strain in your knees and back. Keep your feet even so your hips are even. Ideally you want to sit with your weight toward the front of your sitz bones, with your low stomach muscles pulled in to support your lumbar spine. Your shoulders should be above your hips (not behind them) with your ears right above your shoulders. Alignment is beautiful and beneficial!

INTERVIEW WITH BRAD STULBERG

AUTHOR, *THE PRACTICE OF GROUNDEDNESS*,
PEAK PERFORMANCE, AND *THE PASSION PARADOX*

IMPROVE MENTAL HEALTH AND CHASE DREAMS

We gained a wealth of knowledge by speaking to author and mental-health expert Brad Stulberg about the importance of mind-set. "Where the mind goes, the body follows" is so true in this sport. Running has the power to heal the mind and body. If harnessed correctly, it can help people overcome stress, anxiety, and trauma.

Brad was instrumental in helping Shalane realize her potential after she retired from competitive racing. He helped her overcome the anxiety she felt about transitioning out of professional running and into a new role as an elite coach. We are grateful to be able to share Brad's wisdom with you.

Q *A lot of people get into running to alleviate stress or anxiety—how does running help?*

Running changes your biology by helping to promote an ideal balance of neurochemicals in your brain. Running changes your psychology by giving you a) confidence; b) something you have full control over; and c) something from which your results are tangible and directly proportionate to the work you put in (which is rare in today's world, especially for knowledge-economy workers). It gives you the chance to pursue a clear goal on your own terms.

Running also helps you connect and bond with others. There is a huge community element. For these reasons, running is so effective at dealing with depression,* anxiety, and stress—it works on both underlying biology and underlying psychology. And not just running—the same could be said for most forms of physical activity, including fast-paced walking.

Q *What attributes and habits do you see in successful athletes?*

Successful athletes (and executives, entrepreneurs, etc.) have a growth-oriented mind-set, which enables them to stick to a schedule and healthy habits.

The other important attributes that I see include: Strong core values. Good nutrition. A solid community of support (they seek mentorship and coaching). Patience!

Successful elite runners play the long game. They take recovery seriously, but keep it simple (eat well, sleep well, don't stress about much else). They have other hobbies or passions outside their sport–doesn't need to be many, but at least one.

Successful athletes care deeply about what they do, which makes them vulnerable. They aren't afraid of vulnerability. If you want to have highs, you need to accept the lows, and hold it all with a big heart of love, kindness, compassion, and community.

*It is important to note that running is not a replacement for therapy or medication, but it is another tool in the toolbox.

Q *What's your stance on to-do lists?*

To-do lists can help you stay on track, but I am much more in favor of NOT-to-do lists . . . on these lists goes all the stuff that sucks the life out of us, all the crap that we'd be wise to cut, like social media and endless text messages. It's amazing how much you can come up with and how much time, attention, and energy you can get back in your life by cutting this stuff.

Q *What's your advice for busy achievers who feel like there's never enough time in the day to accomplish everything?*

There isn't enough time in the day to accomplish everything! True fact. And that's okay! Life is a constant prioritization of what is important to you. This can, and probably will, change over the course of your lifetime. Release yourself from trying to find balance. It's an illusion.

If you are a driven pusher who likes to go all in on things, that's great. But you can't go all in on everything at once. There are seasons for certain things in life. Trying to be great at everything all the time will lead to frustration, fatigue, and burnout. Figure out what you want to prioritize now and go hard. Just constantly evaluate what you're giving up, the trade-offs, and adjust and adjust and adjust as life evolves.

Q *How can runners set more effective goals (work, life, or running related)?*

Once you set a big goal, it's important to release from it and focus on the process instead. Set micro-milestones, which have more to do with time, energy, and effort than measurable results. And nail those milestones. The big goal then will take care of itself.

Also, whatever goals you are setting, try to have them work in service of ultimate life goals. For instance, set a goal to become a stronger, kinder, and wiser person. We are all running to the same finish line. The big race is our life. All our goals should be about living the life we want to live, becoming the person we want to become, contributing what we want to contribute to society.

Q *Any tips to help someone find the motivation to run before work?*

Stop trying to find motivation! Just show up and get started. Mood follows action, not the other way around. You don't need to feel good and motivated to get going. You need to get going and then you'll feel good and motivated. Just get through the first 10 minutes of your workout. After that, you can quit. But I bet you won't.

The desire to have motivation is a false premise. If I waited to be motivated, I would never write essays, let alone books! Mood follows action. Mood follows action. Mood follows action. I've had a coaching client almost tattoo this on her wrist!

Forced time off due to an injury is frustrating, but it's often a hidden blessing. Time away from running allows you the chance to invest in other areas of your life. During one of my longest breaks due to injury, I became a foster parent to two teenage girls, took a much-needed vacation, had more time for friends and family, and had downtime to recover physically and mentally.

After this injury setback, I had one of my greatest athletic achievements: winning the 2017 NYC marathon. I truly believe the injury was a blessing that led to fulfilling a lifelong goal. I now look at injuries in a new light. It's your body's way of saying, "Slow down, rest, and take the time to become a better athlete and version of you!!"

—SHALANE

Shalane's Strength Training Routine

In the following pages, Shalane shares top exercises you can do at home—first, a 15-minute strength routine from Colleen, her team's physical therapist, and then a 15-minute stretching routine. To go along with these lessons, you'll need resistance bands, a kettlebell or hand weight, a chair, and a mat. Any time you are starting a new exercise regimen, we recommend working with an expert to ensure proper form.

TOP 5 INJURY-PREVENTION EXERCISES FOR RUNNERS

Lateral Band Walks

Place an exercise band around your thighs just above your knees. Hold an athletic stance. Sidestep back and forth, keeping the bands tight.

For a second exercise, place a band just above your ankles, hold an athletic stance, and slowly walk forward and backward.

Runner Clam

Place an exercise band just above your knees. Hold one leg out in front with your knee bent and the other leg slightly behind you. The standing leg stays still while the lifted leg rotates out against the band and slowly back. Repeat 10 times on each leg.

Single-Leg RDL

Perform a slow single-leg Romanian deadlift motion (RDL), focusing on balance and control. Drop your hands toward the ground while you lengthen and raise one leg behind you. As you get stronger, add a kettlebell or weight. End in a tall runner's position. Repeat 10 times on each leg.

Side Plank Runner

Hold a side plank position, but drive the top knee up and touch knee to elbow. If you have a partner, add a band for more resistance.

Single-Leg Squat to Wall Knee Drive

Do a slow single-leg squat to a box (or chair), pause, and drive up from the seated position to the wall. Push your hands into the wall and drive your opposite knee up to 90 degrees. Repeat 10 times on one leg and then switch legs.

Shalane's Stretching Routine

Shalane's favorite stretches are yoga-inspired and focus on common areas of tightness for runners including the hips, hamstrings, and low back. She enjoys doing twists, hip openers, forward fold, warrior pose, downward dog, and upward dog. The following photos explain her routine best. For more stretching advice, read our interview with Colleen on page 58.

5 | SAVORY SUPERHERO MUFFINS

SWEET POTATO KALE
SUPERHERO MUFFINS

for a protein-packed super-start to your day

MAKES 12 TO 15 MUFFINS (DEPENDING ON SIZE OF EGGS)

GLUTEN-FREE: Use certified GF oats. // **VEGETARIAN** //

Athletes usually crave salt in the morning because their bodies need the sodium to hydrate properly before a morning sweat session. That's what inspired us to create savory versions of our coveted Superhero Muffins. This portable winner (and those on the following pages) will seriously change your approach to breakfast. They are unlike any muffin out there, loaded with easy-to-digest protein (thanks to eggs, yogurt, cheese, oat flour, almond flour, and sweet potato) in a springy baked package that will even appeal to finicky kids. Don't think "frittata in a muffin cup." Think "muffins minus sugar, plus cheesy addictiveness with hidden veggies." This version is Elyse's go-to weekday breakfast for the whole family. And "12 eggs" is not a misprint. Twelve eggs! You won't regret it.

---

1 cup almond flour or almond meal

1 cup oat flour (see note, page 75)

2 teaspoons dried oregano

1¼ teaspoons fine sea salt

1 teaspoon baking soda

12 eggs

1½ cups grated peeled sweet potato or yam (about 1 large)

1 cup loosely packed chopped kale

1 cup crumbled feta or your favorite grated cheese

⅓ cup plain whole-milk yogurt

Time Saver Tip:
Look for a muffin tin with a quick-release coating, like those made by USA Pan, which are much easier to clean. The best nontoxic paper liners are If You Care baking cups.

1 Position a rack in the center of the oven. Preheat the oven to 350°F. Line a 12-cup nonstick muffin tin with paper liners. Using your fingers, lightly oil the bottom of each paper liner with a drop of olive oil.

2 In a medium bowl, combine the almond flour, oat flour, oregano, salt, and baking soda.

3 In a separate large bowl, whisk the eggs, then stir in the sweet potato, kale, cheese, and yogurt. Add the dry ingredients to the egg mixture and stir until combined.

4 Use a ⅓-cup measuring cup to scoop the batter into the prepared muffin cups, filling each to the brim (do not overfill). Bake until the muffins are light brown on top, 30 to 35 minutes.

5 Place the muffin tin on a cooling rack and allow the muffins to cool for 15 minutes. Use a knife to loosen the muffins, then remove them from the tin and place them on the rack. Serve warm or cool completely prior to storing.

6 Store leftover muffins in an airtight container in the fridge for up to 5 days or in the freezer for up to 3 months. Reheat in the oven at 300°F for 10 minutes or microwave on low power for 30 seconds.

MIX IT UP: Sub ½ cup chopped fresh parsley and ½ cup chopped scallions for the kale for a refreshing herby flavor.

I made the savory recipe you sent me while I was in Park City at altitude training camp. The Bowerman Track Club women loved having them after their morning run and before they hit the weights in the gym. The muffin tides them over before lunch and helps them stay focused in the gym! Finally I've found a snack that is super satisfying without any sweeteners.

—SHALANE

BACON
BLACK BEAN
SUPERHERO MUFFINS
for post-run recovery fuel

MAKES 12 TO 15 MUFFINS
(DEPENDING ON SIZE OF EGGS)

GLUTEN-FREE: Use certified GF oats. //
VEGETARIAN: Skip the bacon and add
an extra ¼ teaspoon salt. //

This Superhero deserves its own special category. The unusual muffin combo of black beans, bacon, sour cream, and chili powder might have you flipping to the next page, but this recipe should not be missed. It's high in protein (over 10 grams per muffin) and complex carbs, and hits all the taste buds to leave you happy and satisfied.

If you have leftover bacon from making a pound of our Easy Oven Bacon (page 201), this is a fun and creative way to use it. Serve to friends on game day for a memorable snack.

¾ cup almond flour
or almond meal

½ cup oat flour
(see note, page 75)

1 tablespoon plus
1½ teaspoons chili powder

¼ to ½ teaspoon cayenne
pepper, to taste

1¼ teaspoons fine sea salt

1 teaspoon baking soda

10 eggs

⅓ cup sour cream

1 cup grated peeled
sweet potato or yam
(about 1 medium)

1 cup black beans
(canned or Basic Black
Beans, page 166),
drained and rinsed

¾ cup finely chopped
cooked bacon
(about 10 slices)

1 Preheat the oven to 350°F. Line a 12-cup nonstick muffin tin with paper liners.* Drizzle a couple drops of olive oil in the bottom of each paper liner and spread with your fingers to coat.

2 In a medium bowl, combine the almond flour, oat flour, chili powder, cayenne, salt, and baking soda.

3 In a separate large bowl, whisk the eggs and sour cream thoroughly. Stir in the sweet potato, black beans, and bacon. Add the dry ingredients to the egg mixture and stir until combined. The batter will be runny.

4 Use a ⅓-cup measuring cup to scoop the batter into each muffin cup, filling just to the brim (do not overfill). Bake until the muffins are light brown on top and a knife inserted into the center comes out clean, 30 to 35 minutes.

5 Use a knife to loosen the muffins from the tin and place them on a cooling rack. Serve warm, or cool completely prior to storing. Store leftover muffins in an airtight container in the fridge for up to 5 days or in the freezer for up to 3 months. Reheat in the oven at 300°F for 10 minutes or microwave on low power for 30 seconds.

Use high-quality paper liners like the If You Care brand. These parchment-style liners are easy to peel off the muffins once they cool; inexpensive liners will stick. Also, if your muffin tin does not have a quick-release coating (see our pan recommendation on page 25), you may want to lightly oil the bottoms and sides of the tin before you put in the liners.

PESTO-ZUCCHINI
SUPERHERO MUFFINS
for supercharging your day

MAKES 12 TO 15 MUFFINS
(DEPENDING ON SIZE OF EGGS)

GLUTEN-FREE: Use certified GF oats. //
VEGETARIAN //

Have you ever woken up craving a slice of pizza? This muffin is your new bestie. Elyse's kids call these "pizza muffins." To whip them up in less time than it takes to make pancakes, stock your freezer with Presto Pesto (page 262). Any time we make pesto, we make a double batch and freeze half (thaw prior to using).

1 cup almond flour
or almond meal

1 cup oat flour
(see note, below)

1¼ teaspoons fine sea salt

1 teaspoon baking soda

½ teaspoon ground
black pepper

12 eggs

1 cup grated zucchini
(about 1 medium)

½ cup grated Parmesan
or aged cheddar cheese

1 cup pesto, homemade
(page 262) or store-bought*

*If using store-bought pesto,
reduce the salt by ¼ teaspoon.*

NOTE: *To make your own oat flour, grind rolled oats in a food processor or high-speed blender until they have the consistency of flour. The resulting flour is so much fresher than store-bought. You'll be using a lot of oat flour throughout this book, so grind 2 pounds of oats at once (yields approximately 8 cups) and store the oat flour in a large airtight canister in the pantry.*

1   Position a rack in the center of the oven. Preheat the oven to 350°F. Line a 12-cup nonstick muffin tin with paper liners. Using your fingers, lightly oil the bottom of each paper liner with a drop of olive oil.

2   In a medium bowl, combine the almond flour, oat flour, salt, baking soda, and pepper.

3   In a separate large bowl (preferably with a pour spout), whisk together the eggs, zucchini, and cheese. Stir in the pesto until fully combined. Add the dry ingredients to the egg mixture and stir until combined. Allow the batter to rest for 15 minutes to absorb moisture.

4   Use a ⅓-cup measuring cup to scoop the batter into each muffin cup, filling to the very brim (or if the bowl has a spout, simply pour into each cup). Bake until the muffins are browned on top and a knife inserted into the center of a muffin comes out clean, 30 to 35 minutes.

5   Immediately transfer the muffins to a cooling rack. Enjoy warm. Store leftover muffins in an airtight container in the fridge for up to 5 days or in the freezer for up to 3 months. Reheat in the oven at 300°F for 10 minutes or microwave on low power for 30 seconds.

One hundred percent, mornings are the time to run. That way, nothing can get in between me and my workout. Plus, it always sets me up for my day with a clear mind and open heart.

–RICH ROLL,
ultra-runner, author, and top wellness podcast host

EVERYTHING BAGEL
SUPERHERO MUFFINS

for a crave-worthy balanced-breakfast at the ready

MAKES 12 MUFFINS

VEGETARIAN //

This savory Superhero variation will seriously remind you of salty, oniony, seed-covered everything bagels. They have a crave-worthy bready texture with a tinge of sweetness from grated sweet potato, which contrasts perfectly with the seasoned muffin tops (the best part!). Slice in half and serve topped with cream cheese or butter, just like you would a bagel. So good!

¼ cup plus 2 tablespoons extra-virgin olive oil

1 yellow onion, finely chopped (about 1½ cups)

Fine sea salt

1½ cups whole-wheat flour

1 cup rolled oats

¾ cup almond flour or almond meal

¼ cup Everything Bagel Seasoning Mix (page 265)

1 teaspoon baking powder

½ teaspoon baking soda

6 eggs

½ cup plain whole-milk yogurt

1½ cups grated peeled sweet potato or yam (about 1 large)

NUT ALLERGY? *You can substitute an additional ½ cup whole-wheat flour for the almond flour and increase the olive oil to ⅓ cup. The muffins will be a little more dense but still delicious.*

1 Position a rack in the center of the oven. Preheat the oven to 350°F. Line a 12-cup nonstick muffin tin with paper liners.

2 Heat 2 tablespoons of the oil in a skillet over medium-high heat. Add the onion and a pinch of salt and sauté, stirring occasionally, until softened, about 5 minutes. Set aside to cool.

3 In a medium bowl, combine the whole-wheat flour, oats, almond flour, 2 tablespoons of the everything bagel seasoning mix, baking powder, baking soda, and a ½ teaspoon salt.

4 In a separate large bowl, thoroughly whisk the eggs, yogurt, and remaining ¼ cup of olive oil. Stir in the sweet potato. Add the dry ingredients to egg mixture and stir until combined. Stir in the cooked onions.

5 Spoon the batter into the muffin cups, filling to just above the brim. Sprinkle the remaining 2 tablespoons of everything bagel seasoning mix on top of the muffins and press it slightly into the batter. Bake until the muffins are light brown on top and a knife inserted into the center of a muffin comes out clean, 30 to 35 minutes.

6 Transfer the muffins to a cooling rack or cool in the muffin tin. Serve warm, or cool completely prior to storing. Store leftover muffins in an airtight container in the fridge for up to 5 days or in the freezer for up to 3 months. Reheat in the oven at 300°F for 10 minutes or microwave on low power for 30 seconds.

GREEN EGGS AND HAMMER ON
SUPERHERO MUFFINS
for easy-to-digest protein

MAKES 12 TO 15 MUFFINS
(DEPENDING ON SIZE OF EGGS)

GLUTEN-FREE: Use almond flour or certified GF oats. // **VEGETARIAN** //

This Savory Superhero Muffin wins the easiest-to-digest award–especially handy for building up energy *before* a morning run. There's no cheese in this one, to keep it lighter, and less fiber, to avoid that leaden feeling some might get. What's it got more of? Iron! It comes in the form of spinach. When we posted a sneak peek of this recipe on Instagram, we loved all your recipe name ideas–from "Hulk Yeah" to "Popeye's Muffin" to "Clean Green Machine." Thank you to Ashley Montgomery for the winning name! We recommend including the walnuts to give these muffins texture.

2 cups grated russet potato (about 2)

10 eggs

4 cups loosely packed baby spinach

¼ cup whole-milk Greek yogurt or sour cream

¼ cup extra-virgin olive oil

1 cup oat flour (see note, page 75), almond flour, or almond meal

1½ teaspoons fine sea salt

½ teaspoon baking soda

1 teaspoon dried oregano

1 teaspoon garlic powder

½ teaspoon ground black pepper

½ cup chopped walnuts (optional)

1 Position a rack in the center of the oven. Preheat the oven to 350°F. Line a 12-cup nonstick muffin tin with paper liners. Lightly oil the bottom of each paper liner with a drop of olive oil.

2 Place the grated potato in a clean, thin kitchen towel and squeeze over the sink to remove as much moisture as possible. Set aside.

3 In a high-speed blender, combine the eggs, spinach, yogurt, and olive oil and blend on medium speed just until liquefied.

4 Add the oat flour, salt, baking soda, oregano, garlic powder, and pepper to the blender. Pulse again until smooth. Use a rubber spatula to stir in the potato and walnuts, if using (do not blend).

5 Use a large spoon to divide the batter between the muffin cups, distributing the potatoes evenly. Fill to the brim. If you have a little extra batter, you can place a muffin cup inside a metal (not plastic or silicone) ½-cup measuring cup and cook the extra batter at the same time. Bake until the muffins are firm on top with some browning, 30 to 35 minutes.

6 Use a knife to loosen the muffins from the tin. Serve warm or place on a cooling rack to cool completely prior to storing. Store leftover muffins in an airtight container in the fridge for up to 5 days or in the freezer for up to 3 months. Reheat in the oven at 300°F for 10 minutes or microwave on low power for 30 seconds.

*I'm strong to the finish
'cause I eats me spinach!*
—POPEYE

APPLE CHEDDAR
SUPERHERO MUFFINS
for a savory jump-start

MAKES 12 MUFFINS

VEGETARIAN //

This Superhero is a hybrid, for those who crave a little natural sweetness (apples and sweet potatoes!) as well as salt (cheese, butter!) in the morning. Really, the veggies and fruits melt into this whole-grain, fluffy muffin, so it just has an essential, healthy deliciousness that's hard to describe and harder to stop eating. Note that the yogurt is necessary, as its acidity reacts with the baking soda to help the muffins rise.

2 cups spelt flour or whole-wheat flour

2 teaspoons baking soda

1½ teaspoons fine sea salt

3 eggs

1½ cups grated cheddar cheese

1 cup grated peeled sweet potato or yam (about 1 medium)

½ cup plain whole-milk yogurt

½ cup (1 stick) unsalted butter, melted

2 large Granny Smith apples, peeled and cored

1 Position a rack in the center of the oven. Preheat the oven to 350°F. Line a 12-cup nonstick muffin tin with paper liners.

2 In a medium bowl, combine the flour, baking soda, and salt.

3 In a large bowl, whisk together the eggs, 1 cup of the cheese, sweet potato, yogurt, and butter. Grate one of the apples and chop the second apple into small pieces. Stir in the apple. Add the dry ingredients to the wet ingredients and stir until combined.

4 Scoop the batter into each muffin cup, filling to the brim. Sprinkle the remaining ½ cup of cheese on top of the muffins. Bake until the muffins are toasty brown on top and a knife inserted into the center of a muffin comes out clean, 30 to 35 minutes.

5 Transfer the muffins to a cooling rack to cool. Store leftover muffins in an airtight container in the fridge for up to 5 days or in the freezer for up to 3 months. Reheat in the oven at 300°F for 10 minutes or microwave on low power for 30 seconds.

Time Saver Tip: The batter can be made the night before and stashed in the fridge. Or better yet, bake your muffins on Sunday and simply reheat in the microwave or oven.

SUBSTITUTIONS: *If you're allergic to oats, you can substitute a gluten-free flour blend for the oat flour. If you have nut allergies, substitute all-purpose flour for the almond flour.*

MINUTE-MUG SWEET POTATO CHEDDAR
SUPERHERO MUFFIN

for a recovery muffin in a pinch

MAKES 1 EXTRA-LARGE MUFFIN

GLUTEN-FREE: Use certified GF oats. //
VEGETARIAN //

If you experience a sudden craving for a Superhero Muffin but don't have time to bake an entire batch, this recipe is for you: a single-serving muffin made in the microwave. Wholesome and fluffy in 2 minutes flat!

This is the perfect recipe for student-athletes living in a dorm without access to an oven (if you're really dedicated, you could even pull this off in a hotel room). Our favorite part about it is the minimal number of dishes: just one! The batter is mixed and cooked directly in a large mug.

Whether you are craving sweet or savory, we've got you covered– see page 107 for a lime-raspberry sweet variation.

1 tablespoon
unsalted butter

¼ cup almond flour
or almond meal

¼ cup oat flour
(see note, page 75)

¼ teaspoon baking powder

⅛ teaspoon fine sea salt

1 egg

¼ cup finely grated peeled
sweet potato or yam

¼ cup grated
cheddar cheese

1 Microwave the butter in a large microwave-safe mug* until just melted, about 30 seconds. Add the almond flour, oat flour, baking powder, and salt and stir to combine.

2 Add the egg, sweet potato, and cheese. Stir thoroughly with a fork to combine (it's important to make sure the egg is fully incorporated). Use a spoon to ensure no unincorporated flour is stuck to the bottom of the mug.

3 Microwave on high for 1 minute 30 seconds to 2 minutes (cooking time will vary based on microwave power). Let sit for 5 minutes. Devour with a spoon right out of the mug, or use a knife to loosen the edges and invert the muffin onto a plate.

*If you don't have a large enough mug, you can cook this in a microwave-safe cereal bowl. The "muffin" won't have the shape of a muffin, but it will still taste delicious.

 Nutrition Tip: You can make this recipe without the oats. Simply increase the almond flour to ½ cup.

ZUCCHINI-CHEDDAR CORNBREAD
SUPERHERO MUFFINS

for a makeover to a classic

**MAKES 12 MUFFINS
(OR 24 MINI MUFFINS)**

GLUTEN-FREE // **VEGETARIAN** //

Our Raspberry-Zucchini Cornbread Superhero Muffins (page 109) turned out so well that we were inspired to craft a savory variation with cheese and jalapeños. For a brunch-inspired menu serve these with baked beans (page 200), Brunch Power Salad (page 194), or a frittata (pages 191 and 205). For dinner, they pair well with chili. For serving to a crowd, we recommend the mini muffin size.

1½ cups fine stone-ground corn flour

1½ cups almond flour or almond meal*

1½ teaspoons fine sea salt

1 teaspoon baking soda

3 eggs

2 cups grated zucchini (about 2 medium)

1 cup grated cheddar cheese

½ cup extra-virgin olive oil

2 to 3 jalapeños, diced (optional)

1 Position a rack in the center of the oven. Preheat the oven to 350°F. Line a 12-cup standard muffin tin or a 24-cup mini-muffin tin with paper liners.

2 In a large bowl, combine the corn flour, almond flour, salt, and baking soda.

3 In a separate bowl, whisk together the eggs, zucchini, cheese, olive oil, and jalapeños (if using). Add to the dry ingredients and mix until combined. The batter will be thick. Allow it to rest for 15 minutes to absorb moisture from the zucchini.

4 Spoon the batter into the muffin cups, filling each to the brim. Bake until a knife inserted into the center of a muffin comes out clean and the tops are golden, 30 to 35 minutes (25 minutes for mini muffins).

5 Store leftover muffins in an airtight container in the fridge for up to 5 days or in the freezer for up to 3 months. Reheat in the oven at 300°F for 10 minutes or microwave on low power for 30 seconds.

***NUT ALLERGY?** You can sub all-purpose flour for the almond flour.*

QUINOA VEGGIE
SUPERHERO MUFFINS

for the ultimate make-ahead power breakfast

MAKES 12 TO 15 MUFFINS (DEPENDING ON SIZE OF EGGS)

GLUTEN-FREE // VEGETARIAN: Substitute tempeh sausage (page 183). // **DAIRY-FREE:** Skip the feta. //

If you have zero time to cook in the morning but want to start your day with a veggie-loaded power breakfast, this is the recipe to make on a Sunday. While this one takes more time and love than our other muffins, it's worth it, because you're making twelve balanced meals (or six, if you have a hearty appetite) all in one swoop.

A power trio of easy-to-digest proteins–quinoa, eggs, and sausage–makes this especially satisfying, and a little advance planning will help you accomplish this recipe faster (for best results, buy high-quality breakfast sausage from your local butcher or online at ButcherBox.com). The next time you cook quinoa for bowls or salads, cook extra and stash it in the fridge for up to 3 days. The veggies and sausage can be prepped ahead, too (see tip).

---

8 ounces bulk breakfast sausage (see note)

½ yellow onion, diced

3 cups chopped stemmed kale

1½ cups cooked quinoa

1 cup almond flour or almond meal

1¼ teaspoons fine sea salt

1 teaspoon baking soda

6 eggs

1 cup grated zucchini (about 1 medium)

1 cup grated peeled carrots (about 2)

½ cup crumbled feta cheese

NUT ALLERGY?
Substitute oat flour for the almond flour and add 2 tablespoons olive oil to the batter.

*See our muffin tin and paper liner recommendations on page 25.

1   Position a rack in the center of the oven. Preheat the oven to 350°F. Line a 12-cup nonstick muffin tin with paper liners.* Drizzle a couple drops of olive oil in the bottom of each paper liner and spread with your fingers to lightly coat the bottom of the liners.

2   Heat a large skillet over medium heat. Add the sausage and onion and cook, breaking up the sausage into bite-size pieces and stirring occasionally, until the sausage is lightly browned, about 6 minutes (no extra oil is needed—the veggies will cook in the fat from the sausage; don't strain off this fat). Add the kale and sauté until wilted, about 1 minute. Remove from the heat and set aside.

3   In a medium bowl, combine the quinoa, almond flour, salt, and baking soda.

4   In a separate large bowl, whisk together the eggs, zucchini, carrot, and feta. Add the dry ingredients to the egg mixture and stir until combined. Stir in the sausage and kale mixture. The batter will be thick.

5   Use a ⅓-cup measuring cup to scoop a heaping amount of batter into each muffin cup. Bake until the muffins are browned on top and a knife inserted into the center of a muffin comes out clean, 35 to 40 minutes.

Nutrition Tip:

Using raw sausage adds way more flavor than precooked packaged breakfast sausage. And, if you can buy the sausage in bulk instead of in casings, it is easier to cook. If you can't find a high-quality breakfast sausage at the grocery store, you can order it online from ButcherBox, our favorite source for high-quality, humanely raised meat; or make your own (see page 184).

Time Saver Tip:

Cook the quinoa and sauté the sausage, onion, and kale the day before, let cool, then stash, covered, in the fridge. You can also grate the carrot and zucchini in advance. If your sausage is cold when you're adding it to the batter, increase the baking time by 5 minutes.

6 Immediately transfer the muffins to a cooling rack. Enjoy warm, or cool completely prior to storing. Store leftover muffins in an airtight container in the fridge for up to 5 days or in the freezer for up to 3 months. Reheat in the oven at 300°F for 10 minutes or microwave on low power for 30 seconds.

PERFECT QUINOA: Rinse and drain 1 cup quinoa; transfer to a medium saucepan. Add 1½ cups water and bring to a boil over high heat. Reduce the heat to low, cover, and simmer until the quinoa is tender and all the water has been absorbed, 15 minutes. Transfer to a large bowl, fluff with a fork, and set aside to cool. This makes about 4 cups cooked quinoa, so you will have leftovers. Perfect for Breakfast Power Bowls (page 135)!

6 | CLASSIC SUPERHERO MUFFINS

ORIGINAL SUPERHERO MUFFIN 2.0

A makeover of our award-winning muffin

MAKES 12 MUFFINS (OR 24 MINI MUFFINS)

GLUTEN-FREE: Use certified GF oats. //
VEGETARIAN // DAIRY-FREE //

Our original Superhero Muffin recipe from *Run Fast. Eat Slow.* wins the award for most Instagram posts. It started a #superheromuffin movement, and for good reason. Superhero Muffins can now be spotted at running events across the country. They've become a popular go-to breakfast and snack among endurance athletes.

We've taken the original fan-favorite recipe and revamped it. It's now made with fewer ingredients and is less expensive (less almond flour) and easier to make (using just one bowl). This variation is also dairy-free and slightly less sweet than the original. If you prefer a sweeter muffin, include the chocolate chips. This doesn't mean we've abandoned our first Superhero baby or love it any less. Our Superhero 2.0 is just the evolution of the movement.

---

1 cup grated zucchini
(about 1 medium)

1 cup grated peeled
sweet potato or yam
(about 1 medium)

3 eggs

⅓ cup maple syrup or honey

¼ cup virgin coconut
oil, melted

1½ cups rolled oats

1 cup oat flour
(see note, page 75)

1 cup almond flour
or almond meal

⅓ cup chopped walnuts or
chocolate chips (optional)

2 teaspoons ground
cinnamon

1 teaspoon baking soda

¾ teaspoon fine sea salt

½ teaspoon ground nutmeg,
cardamom, or ginger

1   Position a rack in the center of the oven. Preheat the oven to 350°F. Line a 12-cup standard muffin tin or a 24-cup mini-muffin tin with paper liners.

2   In a large bowl, combine the zucchini, sweet potato, eggs, maple syrup, and melted coconut oil and whisk thoroughly to combine.

3   Add the oats, oat flour, almond flour, walnuts (if using), cinnamon, baking soda, salt, and nutmeg. Stir with a rubber spatula until combined; the batter will be thick.

4   Spoon the batter into the prepared muffin cups, filling each to the brim. Bake until the muffins are nicely browned on top and a knife inserted into the center of a muffin comes out clean, 25 to 30 minutes for large muffins or 20 to 25 minutes for mini muffins.

5   Store leftover muffins in an airtight container in the fridge for up to 1 week or in the freezer for up to 3 months. Reheat in the oven at 300°F for 10 minutes or microwave on low power for 30 seconds.

"These muffins save the day when I need to eat something small and easy to digest before an early run. I love how fast this recipe comes together. I'm never too tired to whip up a batch."

—SHALANE

DARK CHOCOLATE BANANA
SUPERHERO MUFFINS
for a sweet beginning

**MAKES 12 LARGE MUFFINS
(OR 28 MINI MUFFINS)**

GLUTEN-FREE: Use certified GF oats. //
VEGETARIAN //

Introducing our most decadent muffin recipe, crafted for serious chocoholics (pretty much all distance runners!). Lucky for you, dark chocolate makes the health food podium, since it's high in essential minerals (iron and magnesium and zinc, oh my!) and inflammation-fighting antioxidants. These gold-medal muffins taste like brownies, even though they're gluten-free and sweetened with just bananas and honey. They're wholesome enough to count as breakfast (you have our permission!) but can also double as dessert.

Shalane's coach, Jerry Schumacher, inspired this recipe. We wanted to prove that our nourishing muffins could satisfy his relentless sweet tooth. Mission accomplished, Coach!

2 cups oat flour
(see note, page 75)

1½ cups hazelnut
flour, almond flour,
or almond meal

¾ cup dark chocolate
chunks (chopped from a
bar) or chocolate chips

½ cup chopped
walnuts (optional)

⅓ cup unsweetened cocoa
powder or cacao powder

1 teaspoon baking soda

½ teaspoon fine sea salt

3 eggs

1 cup mashed very ripe
bananas (2 large or 3 small)

⅓ cup plain
whole-milk yogurt

⅓ cup honey

4 tablespoons (½ stick)
unsalted butter, melted

1 teaspoon vanilla extract

1 Position a rack in the center of the oven. Preheat the oven to 350°F. Line a 12-cup standard muffin tin or a 24-cup mini-muffin tin with paper liners.

2 In a large bowl, combine the oat flour, hazelnut flour, chocolate, walnuts (if using), cocoa powder, baking soda, and salt.

3 In a separate bowl, whisk together the eggs, bananas, yogurt, honey, melted butter, and vanilla. Add the wet ingredients to the dry ingredients and mix until combined.

4 Spoon the batter into the prepared muffin cups, filling each to the brim. Bake until a knife inserted into the center of a muffin comes out clean, 30 to 35 minutes for large muffins or 20 to 25 minutes for mini muffins.

5 Store leftover muffins in an airtight container in the fridge for up to one week or in the freezer for up to 3 months. Reheat in the oven at 300°F for 10 minutes or microwave on low power for 30 seconds.

Nutrition Tip: Birthday bash? Bake these as mini muffins, decorate them with Yogurt Buttercream Frosting (page 277), and you've got Superhero cupcakes!

LEMON CHIA BLUEBERRY
SUPERHERO MUFFINS

for treating yourself right

MAKES 12 MUFFINS

GLUTEN-FREE: Use certified GF oats. //
DAIRY-FREE //

Take the classic lemon poppy seed muffin to a whole new level by using power-packed chia seeds instead of poppy seeds. Stir in summer's peak blueberries, and you have a muffin that will impress all your running buddies.

When Elyse went berry picking in Hood River and came home with over ten pounds of blueberries, she made these muffins on a whim, and they're now vying for a spot on the podium as Best Muffin in our collection. This is by far the favorite muffin of the Bowerman Track Club women–they make them on the regular.

These muffins are best served right out of the oven. For a fancier look, we recommend using almond flour instead of almond meal, which keeps the muffins the color of lemons. Also, if available, use yellow or white carrots instead of orange so they blend in.

2 cups almond flour or almond meal

1½ cups rolled oats

3 tablespoons chia seeds

1 teaspoon baking soda

½ teaspoon fine sea salt

3 eggs

1 cup grated yellow or white carrots (about 2)

½ cup honey

Zest of 1 lemon

¼ cup fresh lemon juice (about 2 lemons)

¼ cup virgin coconut oil, melted

1 cup fresh or frozen blueberries

1. Position a rack in the center of the oven. Preheat the oven to 350°F. Line a 12-cup standard muffin tin with paper liners.

2. In a large bowl, combine the almond flour, oats, chia seeds, baking soda, and salt.

3. In a separate bowl, whisk together the eggs, carrots, honey, lemon zest, lemon juice, and melted coconut oil. Add the wet ingredients to the dry ingredients and mix until just combined (do not overmix). Stir in the blueberries.

4. Spoon the batter into the prepared muffin cups, filling each to the brim. Bake until the tops are golden and a knife inserted into the center of a muffin comes out clean, 25 to 30 minutes.

5. Store leftover muffins in an airtight container in the fridge for up to 1 week or in the freezer for up to 3 months. Reheat in the oven at 300°F for 10 minutes or microwave on low power for 30 seconds.

GRAIN-FREE PINEAPPLE-COCONUT
SUPERHERO MUFFINS

for a digestion-soothing energizing snack

MAKES 24 MINI MUFFINS

GLUTEN-FREE // GRAIN-FREE // VEGETARIAN // DAIRY-FREE //

Craving an escape to the beach? Bake these tropical-inspired muffins. They're tiny but mighty, and they check all the boxes for those following a gluten-free, Paleo, grain-free, dairy-free, or low-glycemic diet. They're high in energizing fats, making them an ideal snack any time of day. Stash them in your gym bag to prevent skipping your workout due to hunger. Since they're easy to digest, you can eat them right before or after training.

A true superhero, these muffins are high in vitamins A and C, as well as iron from the pumpkin and pineapple, and they have immune-boosting superpowers thanks to the coconut.

1½ cups almond flour or almond meal

¾ cup unsweetened shredded coconut

⅓ cup coconut flour

1 teaspoon baking soda

½ teaspoon fine sea salt

3 eggs

¾ cup canned pure pumpkin puree

¼ cup virgin coconut oil, melted

¼ cup honey

1 teaspoon vanilla extract

1 heaping cup frozen pineapple tidbits*

*If your frozen pineapple is in larger chunks, chop the pieces into tidbits. You can substitute fresh pineapple for frozen when in season (March through July).

1 Position a rack in the center of the oven. Preheat the oven to 350°F. Line a 24-cup mini-muffin tin** with paper liners.

2 In a large bowl, combine the almond flour, shredded coconut, coconut flour, baking soda, and salt.

3 In a separate bowl, whisk together the eggs, pumpkin, melted coconut oil, honey, and vanilla. Stir the wet ingredients into the dry ingredients. Stir in the pineapple. The batter will be thick.

4 Spoon the batter into the prepared muffin cups. Try to evenly distribute the pineapple chunks. You can use your hands to shape the tops of the muffins since this batter is thick. Bake until the muffins are well browned on top, about 25 minutes. Cool completely before removing from the tin.

5 Store leftover muffins in an airtight container in the fridge for up to one week or in the freezer for up to 3 months. Reheat in the oven at 300°F for 5 minutes or microwave on low power for 30 seconds.

**GOT MINIS? We like to make these as mini muffins so they're less crumbly (coconut flour is fragile). Mini muffins are the ideal size for snacking. You can use a standard muffin tin instead, but don't fill the cups all the way to the brim, and increase the baking time by 8 minutes.*

Nutrition Tip: Add the leftover pumpkin to smoothies (like our Pumpkin Pie Smoothie, page 232) for a vitamin boost. If you can't find pumpkin puree, substitute applesauce.

My morning ritual is eating breakfast while soaking my feet in a bucket of hot water with Epsom salts. My feet are my biggest asset. I do my best to take care of them.

–BRENDA MARTINEZ,
Olympian and IAAF World Championship medalist

When someone tells you something cannot be done, it is more of a reflection of their limitations, not yours.

—ADRIANNE HASLET,
Boston Strong survivor, para athlete

STRAWBERRY-RHUBARB
SUPERHERO MUFFINS
for lazy summer mornings

MAKES 12 MUFFINS
(OR 24 MINI MUFFINS)

GLUTEN-FREE: Use certified GF oats. //
VEGETARIAN //

Take your Superhero game to the next level with these fancy Oregon-inspired winners. They taste like a cross between a strawberry-rhubarb crisp and a healthy bowl of oatmeal. The hazelnut flour adds a perfect contrast, but you can substitute almond flour if you prefer. Oregon produces 99 percent of our nation's hazelnuts, so we love celebrating this local crop.

Every time we bake these muffins and share them with friends, we feel happier and more hopeful. The mini size is perfect for a brunch party. These are best eaten the day they're baked.

2 cups hazelnut flour*

1½ cups rolled oats

1 teaspoon baking soda

½ teaspoon fine sea salt

⅛ teaspoon ground nutmeg

3 eggs

⅓ cup maple syrup

4 tablespoons (½ stick) unsalted butter or ¼ cup virgin coconut oil, melted

1 teaspoon vanilla extract

1½ cups chopped fresh strawberries (about 8 ounces)

1 cup chopped rhubarb (about 1 large stalk)

*Hazelnut flour is more expensive than almond flour, but we love it for special occasions. You can substitute almond flour or almond meal if you prefer. Or make your own hazelnut flour by grinding whole, raw hazelnuts in a high-speed blender or food processor.

1 Position a rack in the center of the oven. Preheat the oven to 350°F. Line a 12-cup standard muffin tin or a 24-cup mini-muffin tin with paper liners.

2 In a large bowl, combine the hazelnut flour, oats, baking soda, salt, and nutmeg.

3 In a separate bowl, whisk together the eggs, maple syrup, melted butter, and vanilla. Add the wet ingredients to the dry ingredients and mix until just combined. Fold in the strawberries and rhubarb. The batter will be thick.

4 Spoon the batter into the prepared muffin cups, filling each to the brim. Bake until the muffins are nicely browned on top and a knife inserted into the center of a muffin comes out clean, 30 to 35 minutes for large muffins or 25 minutes for mini muffins.

5 Store leftover muffins in an airtight container in the fridge for up to 1 week or in the freezer for up to 3 months. Reheat in the oven at 300°F for 10 minutes or microwave on low power for 30 seconds.

Time Saver Tip: *For mini muffins, chop the strawberries and rhubarb even smaller to better fit the small cups. Lightly press the batter down into the cups and add a rounded spoonful of batter on top of each so you get 24 perfectly sized muffins. Our favorite mini-muffin tin, which has a quick-release coating, is made by USA Pan.*

PUMPKIN STREUSEL
SUPERHERO MUFFINS
for celebrating all things fall

MAKES 12 MUFFINS

GLUTEN-FREE: Use certified GF oats. //
VEGETARIAN //

Who needs a pumpkin latte when you have these Superheroes?! The buttery pecan streusel topping is not to be missed, as it seals the deal on this recipe. These are the muffins you'll want to take to fall-themed festivities or a holiday brunch. Your friends and family will surely ask for the recipe, and you have our permission to share!

1¼ cups oat flour (see note, page 75)

1¼ cups rolled oats

1 cup almond flour or almond meal

½ cup chopped pecans

1 tablespoon Chai Spice Mix (page 274) or pumpkin pie spice

1 teaspoon baking soda

½ teaspoon fine sea salt

3 eggs

1 (15-ounce) can pure pumpkin puree

6 tablespoons (¾ stick) unsalted butter, melted

⅓ cup maple syrup

TOPPING
⅓ cup finely chopped pecans

⅓ cup rolled oats

2 tablespoons unsalted butter, cubed, at room temperature

2 tablespoons coconut sugar

¼ teaspoon fine sea salt

1 Position a rack in the center of the oven. Preheat the oven to 350°F. Line a 12-cup nonstick muffin tin with paper liners.

2 In a large bowl, combine the oat flour, oats, almond flour, pecans, chai spice mix, baking soda, and salt.

3 In a separate large bowl, whisk together the eggs, pumpkin, melted butter, and maple syrup. Add the wet ingredients to the dry ingredients and stir until combined.

4 To make the topping, in a small bowl, combine the pecans, oats, butter, sugar, and salt. Use your fingers to work the butter into the oats and sugar until the mixture begins to clump.

5 Spoon the batter into the prepared muffin cups. Scoop a heaping tablespoon of the topping onto each muffin. Spread the topping evenly over the top and lightly press down so it sinks into the batter. Bake until the muffins are firm on top and a knife inserted into the center of a muffin comes out clean, 30 to 35 minutes. Transfer the muffins to a cooling rack to cool.

6 Store leftover muffins in an airtight container in the fridge for up to 1 week or in the freezer for up to 3 months. Reheat in the oven at 300°F for 10 minutes or microwave on low power for 30 seconds.

I always say, a run in the morning is like eating a fruit a day: it chases the doctor away. It is good for your mind.

—ELIUD KIPCHOGE,
marathon champion, first marathoner to break the 2-hour barrier

PEACH CARDAMOM
SUPERHERO MUFFINS

for a healthy treat to celebrate post-run

MAKES 12 MUFFINS

VEGETARIAN //

Just when we thought we couldn't possibly come up with another muffin recipe, we dreamed up this creative combo. These muffins are naturally sweet from the peaches, carrots, and honey. We love how well the zesty cardamom pairs with the peppery olive oil and nutty whole-wheat flour for a complex flavor profile. If these muffins had real superpowers, they would transport us to a running retreat on the Mediterranean, where we would toast each of you with Turmeric Tea (page 257) and muffins (dreaming!).

1½ cups rolled oats

1 cup almond flour or almond meal

¾ cup whole-wheat flour

1 teaspoon baking soda

1 teaspoon ground cardamom

½ teaspoon ground cinnamon

½ teaspoon fine sea salt

3 eggs

1 cup grated carrots (about 2)

⅓ cup extra-virgin olive oil

⅓ cup honey

1½ cups chopped peeled ripe peaches (about 2)*

When peaches are not in season, sub ripe pears, or use frozen peaches (thaw and chop before using).

1 Position a rack in the center of the oven. Preheat the oven to 350°F. Line a 12-cup standard muffin tin with paper liners.

2 In a large bowl, combine the oats, almond flour, whole-wheat flour, baking soda, cardamom, cinnamon, and salt.

3 In a separate bowl, whisk together the eggs, carrots, oil, and honey. Add the wet ingredients to the dry ingredients and mix until just combined. Fold in the peaches. The batter will be thick.

4 Spoon the batter into the prepared muffin cups, filling each to the brim. Bake until the tops are golden with browned edges and a knife inserted into the center of a muffin comes out clean, 25 to 30 minutes.

5 Store leftover muffins in an airtight container in the fridge for up to 1 week or in the freezer for up to 3 months. Reheat in the oven at 300°F for 10 minutes or microwave on low power for 30 seconds.

SUPERHERO SMASH MUFFINS

for a low-glycemic baked treat

**MAKES 12 MUFFINS
(OR 24 MINI MUFFINS)**

GLUTEN-FREE: Use certified GF oats. //
VEGETARIAN // **DAIRY-FREE:** See tip. //

These moist muffins with zero added sweeteners are ideal for anyone looking for low-glycemic baked goods. They are sweetened with only fruit and veggies. We call them "smash muffins" because Elyse baked them for her son Rylan's first birthday, instead of a "smash cake" topped with a mound of blue icing. Carrying on the tradition, Shalane's baby, Jack, is now a big fan. For older kids who might want them sweeter, add ½ cup chocolate chips. Also, remember that the riper the banana, the sweeter the muffin, so plan ahead and stash a few bananas in your pantry for a week (or check out our fast banana-ripening trick on page 223).

---

2 cups oat flour
(see note, page 75)

1¼ cups almond flour
or almond meal

¼ cup ground flax (optional)

2 teaspoons ground
cinnamon

1 teaspoon baking soda

½ teaspoon fine sea salt

3 eggs

1 cup mashed ripe bananas
(2 large or 3 small bananas)

1 cup grated carrots
(about 2)

½ cup smooth unsweetened
applesauce (see tip)

6 tablespoons (¾ stick)
unsalted butter, melted

1 Position a rack in the center of the oven. Preheat the oven to 350°F. Line a 12-cup standard muffin tin or a 24-cup mini-muffin tin with paper liners.

2 In a large bowl, combine the oat flour, almond flour, ground flax (if using), cinnamon, baking soda, and salt.

3 In a separate bowl, whisk together the eggs, bananas, carrots, applesauce, and melted butter. Add the wet ingredients to the dry ingredients and mix until combined.

4 Spoon the batter into the prepared muffin cups, filling each to the brim. Bake until the muffins are browned on top and a knife inserted into the center of a muffin comes out clean, 30 to 35 minutes for large muffins or 25 minutes for mini muffins.

5 Store leftover muffins in an airtight container in the fridge for up to 1 week or in the freezer for up to 3 months. Reheat in the oven at 300°F for 10 minutes or microwave on low power for 30 seconds.

 Nutrition Tip: If your applesauce is store-bought, check the label to find a brand with no added sugar or preservatives.

DAIRY-FREE? Sub in ⅓ cup virgin coconut oil for the butter, or look for cultured butter, which is easy to digest.

SPELT BLUEBERRY YOGURT
SUPERHERO MUFFINS

for a classic muffin, revamped

MAKES 12 MUFFINS

VEGETARIAN //

Blueberry muffin recipes, even the healthy-sounding whole-grain ones, are often made with an entire cup of sugar and cheap vegetable oil. Our fluffy blueberry muffins are sweetened naturally with just honey and grated apple. When you bake with real butter, you can use a lot less sweetener because the butter adds a delicious richness. Also, if you've read our first two cookbooks, you know why we love butter (see the Nutrition Tip for a recap).

Make these muffins with any whole-grain flour, but don't skip the almond flour. By incorporating a small amount of almond flour, you'll get a much fluffier result (trust us, we've tested hundreds of flour combinations).

1½ cups spelt flour or whole-wheat flour

1 cup rolled oats

½ cup almond flour or almond meal

2 teaspoons ground cinnamon

1 teaspoon baking powder

½ teaspoon baking soda

½ teaspoon fine sea salt

3 eggs

½ cup (1 stick) unsalted butter, melted

½ cup plain whole-milk yogurt

1 cup grated peeled apple

⅓ cup honey

1½ cups frozen blueberries

1 Position a rack in the center of the oven. Preheat the oven to 350°F. Line a 12-cup standard muffin tin with paper liners.

2 In a large bowl, combine the spelt flour, oats, almond flour, cinnamon, baking powder, baking soda, and salt.

3 In a separate bowl, whisk the eggs, melted butter, yogurt, apple, and honey. Add the wet ingredients to the dry ingredients and mix until just combined (do not overmix). Gently fold in the blueberries. The batter will be thick.

4 Spoon the batter into the prepared muffin cups, filling them to slightly above the brim. Bake until the muffins are golden brown on top and a knife inserted into the center of a muffin comes out clean, 30 to 35 minutes.

5 Store leftover muffins in an airtight container in the fridge for up to 1 week or in the freezer for up to 3 months. Reheat in the oven at 300°F for 10 minutes or microwave on low power for 30 seconds.

Nutrition Tip: Yes, butter is good for you! High-quality (grass-fed or organic) butter provides vitamins A, D, and E. Butter is also rich in antioxidants and conjugated linoleic acid, an essential fatty acid for recovery.

YAM SPICE
SUPERHERO MUFFINS
*for easy-to-digest
long-run fuel*

MAKES 12 MUFFINS

GLUTEN-FREE // **VEGETARIAN** //
DAIRY-FREE: Sub 3 tablespoons virgin
coconut oil for the butter. //

Picking a favorite Superhero Muffin is like trying to pick a favorite book. We find comfort in so many different styles and combos of ingredients depending on our mood, cravings, and training schedule. This Yam Spice Superhero Muffin has become our go-to fuel before long runs and intense workouts. We've always honored sweet potatoes and oats as the best easy-to-digest complex carbs for endurance. The fresh ginger is a bonus to soothe digestion before cranking out the miles. Grating fresh ginger is worth the effort, but if you're in a time crunch, replace it with 1 teaspoon ground ginger.

2 cups almond flour
or almond meal

1½ cups rolled oats

1 teaspoon baking soda

1 teaspoon ground
cinnamon

½ teaspoon fine sea salt

½ cup chopped walnuts
or pecans (optional)

3 eggs

2 cups grated peeled sweet
potato or yam (about 2)

⅓ cup maple syrup or honey

4 tablespoons (½ stick)
unsalted butter, melted

2 tablespoons grated
fresh ginger

1 Position a rack in the center of the oven. Preheat the oven to 350°F. Line a 12-cup standard muffin tin with paper liners.

2 In a large bowl, combine the almond flour, oats, baking soda, cinnamon, salt, and walnuts (if using).

3 In a separate bowl, whisk together the eggs, sweet potato, maple syrup, melted butter, and ginger. Add the wet ingredients to the dry ingredients and mix until just combined. The batter will be thick.

4 Spoon the batter into the prepared muffin cups, filling each to the brim. Bake until the muffins are nicely browned on top and a knife inserted into the center of a muffin comes out clean, 30 to 35 minutes.

5 Store leftover muffins in an airtight container in the fridge for up to 1 week or in the freezer for up to 3 months. Reheat in the oven at 300°F for 10 minutes or microwave on low power for 30 seconds.

LILY'S CHOCOLATE SUPERHERO MUFFINS

for kids who love to bake

MAKES 24 MINI MUFFINS

GLUTEN-FREE: Use certified GF oats. //
VEGETARIAN // DAIRY-FREE //

When Elyse's daughter, Lily, was five years old, she wrote this recipe all on her own and surprised Elyse with it as a gift on Mother's Day. Like mother, like daughter. We were so impressed with it, and in love with her spelling, that we had to work her recipe into *Rise & Run*.

The only ingredients we added to improve things were maple syrup for sweetness and applesauce for moisture. At first we thought lemon wouldn't go with chocolate, but actually, adding a small amount of lemon juice to baked goods is brilliant. The acid in the lemon juice reacts with the baking soda for a fluffier result.

This is our simplest muffin recipe, great for picky eaters who love to bake. The muffins are allergy-friendly and nut-free, which makes them ideal for school lunches.

2 cups oat flour
(see note, page 75)

¼ cup unsweetened
cocoa powder

1 teaspoon baking soda

½ teaspoon fine sea salt

2 eggs

1 cup unsweetened
applesauce

⅓ cup maple syrup

¼ cup virgin coconut
oil, melted

1 tablespoon fresh
lemon juice

½ cup chocolate chips

Nutrition Tip:
Sub plain whole-milk yogurt for half the applesauce and skip the lemon juice.

1 Position a rack in the center of the oven. Preheat the oven to 350°F. Line a 24-cup mini-muffin tin with paper liners.

2 In a large bowl, combine the oat flour, cocoa powder, baking soda, and salt.

3 In a separate bowl, whisk together the eggs, applesauce, maple syrup, melted coconut oil, and lemon juice. Add the wet ingredients to the dry ingredients and mix until combined. Stir in half the chocolate chips.

4 Spoon the batter into the prepared muffin cups, filling each to the brim. Top the muffins with the remaining chocolate chips, pressing them lightly into the batter. Bake until the tops are firm, 20 to 25 minutes.

5 Store leftover muffins in an airtight container in the fridge for up to 1 week or in the freezer for up to 3 months. Reheat in the oven at 300°F for 5 minutes or microwave on low power for 30 seconds.

 "Definitely our easiest muffin recipe. I love that you can whip them up in less than 15 minutes."

–SHALANE

choclite mufin
By Lily Kopecky

lemense
cokunut oyol
ot flewr
egs
coco pawdr
choclit chips

These muffins taste like chocolate cake, which kids will love, but they're a lot healthier than cake, so my mom is happy. We eat a lot of muffins.

—LILY

VEGAN RED VELVET
SUPERHERO MUFFINS

for an energizing antioxidant-rich snack

MAKES 12 MUFFINS
(OR 24 MINI MUFFINS)

GLUTEN-FREE: Use certified GF oats. //
VEGAN //

Eggs and butter will not be missed in this antioxidant-rich dark chocolate muffin, definitely our best-ever vegan Superhero variation. The beets and cocoa powder add rich flavor and help replace minerals lost after a sweat session.

We named these red velvet muffins because the batter has a deep red hue thanks to the grated beets. If you were to top these muffins with homemade frosting (see page 277), you could easily pass them off as healthier cupcakes.

1½ cups grated peeled raw beet (about 1 medium)

1 cup canned unsweetened full-fat coconut milk (see tip)

⅓ cup coconut sugar

1 tablespoon fresh lemon juice

2 cups oat flour (see note, page 75)

1½ cups almond flour or almond meal

½ cup dark chocolate chunks (chopped from a bar) or chocolate chips

½ cup chopped walnuts (optional)

⅓ cup unsweetened cocoa powder

1 teaspoon baking soda

½ teaspoon fine sea salt

1 Position a rack in the center of the oven. Preheat the oven to 350°F. Line a 12-cup standard muffin tin or a 24-cup mini-muffin tin with paper liners.

2 In a large bowl, combine the beet, coconut milk, sugar, and lemon juice.

3 In a medium bowl, combine the oat flour, almond flour, chocolate, walnuts (if using), cocoa powder, baking soda, and salt. Add the dry ingredients to the wet ingredients and stir to combine.

4 Spoon the batter into the prepared muffin cups, filling each to the brim. Bake until firm on top and a knife inserted into the center of a muffin comes out clean, 30 to 35 minutes for large muffins or 25 minutes for mini muffins.

5 Store leftover muffins in an airtight container in the fridge for up to 1 week or in the freezer for up to 3 months. Reheat in the oven at 300°F for 10 minutes or microwave on low power for 30 seconds.

Nutrition Tip: If your coconut milk is solidified on top or separated, empty the contents of the can into a microwave-safe bowl and microwave for 30 seconds, or heat in a small saucepan on the stovetop just until warm. Stir together before measuring.

Time Saver Tip: This batter can be made the night before; cover the bowl and store in the fridge, then bake the muffins fresh in the morning. If the batter is refrigerated, add 5 minutes to the baking time.

MINUTE-MUG LIME-RASPBERRY
SUPERHERO MUFFIN

for a recovery muffin in a minute

MAKES 1 EXTRA-LARGE MUFFIN

GLUTEN-FREE: Use certified GF oats. //
DAIRY-FREE // VEGETARIAN //

This recipe saves those mornings when you have a sudden sweet Superhero Muffin craving, but no time to bake an entire batch. It's also a fun one to make for an after-school snack that you can feel good about. If you're craving something savory instead, check out our sweet potato–cheddar variation on page 82.

1 teaspoon virgin coconut oil

¼ cup almond flour or almond meal

¼ cup instant oats

¼ teaspoon baking powder

Pinch of fine sea salt

1 egg

1 tablespoon honey

1 tablespoon fresh lime juice

¼ cup fresh or frozen raspberries, thawed if frozen

1 Microwave the coconut oil in a large microwave-safe mug* until just melted, about 30 seconds. Add the almond flour, oats, baking powder, and salt and stir to combine.

2 Add the egg, honey, and lime juice. Stir thoroughly with a fork to combine (it's important to make sure the egg is fully incorporated). Stir in the raspberries.

3 Microwave on high for 1 minute 30 seconds. Let sit for 5 minutes. Devour with a spoon right out of the mug, or use a knife to loosen the edges and invert the muffin onto a plate.

If you don't have a large enough mug, you can cook this in a microwave-safe cereal bowl. The "muffin" won't have the shape of a muffin, but it will still taste delicious.

 Nutrition Tip: *To make this recipe without the oats, simply increase the almond flour to ½ cup.*

RASPBERRY-ZUCCHINI CORNBREAD
SUPERHERO MUFFINS
for a gluten-free makeover

MAKES 12 MUFFINS

GLUTEN-FREE // VEGETARIAN //

We love the simplicity of 100% stone-ground corn flour. It's a delicious gluten-free flour option for those with sensitivities to oats and wheat. And it doesn't contain additives like a lot of gluten-free flour blends. Yes, the main ingredients–raspberries, zucchini, and olive oil–sound like an unusual mix, but the sweet-and-savory combination won us over on the very first taste test.

1½ cups fine stone-ground corn flour

1½ cups almond flour or almond meal*

1 teaspoon baking soda

¾ teaspoon fine sea salt

3 eggs

2 cups grated zucchini (about 2 medium)

⅓ cup extra-virgin olive oil

⅓ cup honey

¼ cup plain whole-milk yogurt

1 heaping cup fresh or frozen raspberries

*NUT ALLERGY?
You can sub all-purpose flour or whole-wheat pastry flour for the almond flour. If you do, increase the olive oil to ½ cup.

1 Position a rack in the center of the oven. Preheat the oven to 350°F. Line a 12-cup standard muffin tin with paper liners.

2 In a large bowl, combine the corn flour, almond flour, baking soda, and salt.

3 In a separate bowl, whisk together the eggs, zucchini, oil, honey, and yogurt. Add the wet ingredients to the dry ingredients and mix until just combined. Gently fold in the raspberries. The batter will be thick. Allow the batter to rest for 15 minutes to absorb moisture from the zucchini.

4 Spoon the batter into the prepared muffin cups, filling each to just above the brim. Bake until the tops are golden and a knife inserted into the center of a muffin comes out clean, 25 to 30 minutes.

5 Store leftover muffins in an airtight container in the fridge for up to 1 week or in the freezer for up to 3 months. Reheat in the oven at 300°F for 10 minutes or microwave on low power for 30 seconds.

RACE-DAY
SUPERHERO MUFFINS
for easy-to-digest stamina

**MAKES 12 MUFFINS
(OR 24 MINI MUFFINS)**

GLUTEN-FREE: Use certified GF oats. //
VEGETARIAN //
DAIRY-FREE //

Bananas with peanut butter. Oatmeal with nuts and honey. Baked sweet potato. Scrambled eggs with toast.

What if we combined those four tried-and-true race-day meals into one magical dish? You'd get a muffin like this one. The banana, oats, and sweet potato provide complex carbs, and the honey provides simple sugars for quick fuel. And there's just enough fat and protein in the eggs and peanut butter to ensure you won't feel hungry when you toe the starting line.

These Superhero Muffins were born out of a need for a packable, balanced, and easy-to-digest breakfast for marathon morning. We've made these dairy-free, gluten-free, and even almond flour–free for those with the most sensitive stomachs. You may be an athlete who can eat two large muffins just an hour before running, while others may only tolerate a mini muffin two hours before the race. Try these before Long Runs, to dial in what works best for you. Never try anything new on race day. (And we highly recommend eating at least 2 hours before a race.) Pack to-go muffins in a hard-sided container, not a bag.

---

2 cups oat flour
(see note, page 75)

½ cup rolled oats

1 teaspoon baking powder

1 teaspoon baking soda

¾ teaspoon fine sea salt

½ teaspoon ground
cinnamon

3 eggs

1 cup grated peeled sweet
potato or yam (about
1 large; see tip, opposite)

1 cup mashed ripe
bananas (2 to 3 medium)

⅓ cup unsalted creamy
peanut butter*

⅓ cup honey

1 Position a rack in the center of the oven. Preheat the oven to 350°F. Line a 12-cup standard muffin tin or a 24-cup mini-muffin tin with paper liners.

2 In a large bowl, combine the oat flour, oats, baking powder, baking soda, salt, and cinnamon.

3 In a separate bowl, whisk together the eggs, sweet potato, bananas, peanut butter, and honey. Add the wet ingredients to the dry ingredients and mix until combined.

4 Spoon the batter into the prepared muffin cups, filling each to the brim. Bake until a knife inserted into the center of a muffin comes out clean, 30 to 35 minutes for large muffins or 20 to 25 minutes for mini muffins.

5 Store leftover muffins in an airtight container in the fridge for up to 1 week or in the freezer for up to 3 months. Reheat in the oven at 300°F for 10 minutes or microwave on low power for 30 seconds.

If your peanut butter is salted, reduce the salt to ½ teaspoon.

Time Saver Tip: *Instead of grating the sweet potato, peel and quarter it, then pulse it in a high-speed blender or food processor until finely chopped. The batter can be made the night before and stored, covered, in the fridge, then baked in the morning. Add an extra 5 minutes to the baking time if the batter is chilled.*

7 | ANYTIME SNACKS AND PACKABLE TREATS

The hardest part about running is getting out the door. Once you're out there, the fresh air, sunshine, nature, rhythmic breathing, quiet, and calm will keep you going.

—ELYSE

TRAIL MIX BREAKFAST COOKIES

for running up mountains

MAKES 20 COOKIES

GLUTEN-FREE: Use certified GF oats. //
VEGETARIAN // DAIRY-FREE: Sub
6 tablespoons virgin coconut oil. //

This recipe was a late addition to the lineup and is now our go-to power snack for early-morning adventures. When Shalane and Elyse woke up at four a.m. for a sunrise photo shoot for this book and ran a rugged 13 miles for the camera, these cookies saved the day. They have similar ingredients to a loaded bowl of oatmeal but are much easier to eat when you're racing out the door.

If you didn't wake up hungry but know you have a big day ahead, pack these cookies to go. They're easy to eat on your drive to the trailhead and easy to digest if you prefer to fuel up midway through a run or hike. Also, they're high in complex carbs, real-food protein, and healthy fats to replenish depleted reserves.

1½ cups rolled oats

1 cup oat flour
(see note, page 75)

½ cup almond flour
or almond meal

½ cup coarsely chopped
walnuts, pecans, or peanuts

⅓ cup chocolate chips

⅓ cup unsweetened
dried tart cherries,
cranberries, or raisins

⅓ cup unsweetened
shredded coconut

¼ cup ground flax

1 teaspoon ground
cinnamon

1 teaspoon fine sea salt

½ teaspoon baking soda

½ cup (1 stick) unsalted
butter,* slightly melted

⅓ cup coconut sugar
(or cane sugar)

1 egg, whisked

¼ cup honey

1 teaspoon vanilla extract

*If your butter is salted,
reduce the salt in the
recipe to ¾ teaspoon.*

1   In a large bowl, combine the oats, oat flour, almond flour, walnuts, chocolate chips, dried fruit, coconut, flax, cinnamon, salt, and baking soda.

2   In a separate bowl, whisk the melted butter and sugar until combined. Add the egg, honey, and vanilla and whisk until well blended. Add the wet ingredients to the dry ingredients and mix until combined. Cover and chill the dough in the fridge for 1 hour (or in the freezer for 30 minutes).

3   Position a rack in the center of the oven. Preheat the oven to 350°F. Line a baking sheet with parchment paper.

4   Use your hands to roll the dough into golf ball–size balls (applying pressure to ensure all the mix-ins hold together) and set them on the prepared baking sheet, spacing them 1 inch apart. Use your palm to flatten them slightly.

5   Bake for 14 to 16 minutes, until golden brown on the edges. Use a spatula to transfer the cookies to a cooling rack to cool.

Time Saver Tip: Keep a container of these cookies stashed in your freezer so you're always prepared for a last-minute invite to hit the trails.

FLOURLESS PB CHOCOLATE CHIP COOKIES

for a grain-free sweet treat

MAKES 24 SMALL COOKIES

GLUTEN-FREE //
VEGETARIAN //

Chocolate and peanut butter are essential ingredients in a runner's diet. These minimalist grain-free cookies satisfy that crunchy-meets-sweet craving that comes on fast and must be satisfied immediately (you know the one). High in protein and healthy fats, these two-bite cookies are multitasking champs. They're easy to digest for instant fuel before a sunrise run, and they're happy to be packed for an on-the-go afternoon snack. The ingredients are simple enough to keep stocked so that you can whip up a batch any time you're heading out on a weekend adventure.

1 cup creamy peanut butter*

⅓ cup coconut sugar

¼ cup raw sesame seeds

2 tablespoons raw sunflower seeds

1 egg

1 teaspoon vanilla extract

½ teaspoon baking soda

½ teaspoon fine sea salt

¼ cup chocolate chips

Check the label on your peanut butter: peanuts (and sometimes salt) should be the only ingredient listed. Many brands add unnecessary sugar and hydrogenated oils. Our favorite brands are Santa Cruz Organic and Adams. Oil separation is natural—stir thoroughly before using. If your peanut butter is salted, reduce the salt in the recipe to ¼ teaspoon.

1 Position a rack in the center of the oven. Preheat the oven to 350°F. Line a baking sheet with parchment paper.

2 In a large bowl, combine the peanut butter and sugar. Stir in the sesame seeds, sunflower seeds, egg, vanilla, baking soda, and salt. The batter will be thick. Stir in the chocolate chips.

3 Use a tablespoon to scoop the dough, roll into balls, and place on the prepared baking sheet. Use your hands to flatten the cookies slightly. If they break apart because of the chocolate chips, just mold them back together.

4 Bake for 12 to 14 minutes, until the bottoms and edges are browned. Cool for 10 minutes on the baking sheet, then use a spatula to transfer to a cooling rack. Store in an airtight container in the pantry for up to 1 week or in the fridge for up to 1 month.

NUTTY CHAI ENERGY BITES

for an anti-inflammatory energy boost

MAKES 18 BITE-SIZE BALLS

GLUTEN-FREE //
VEGAN //

When Shalane and Elyse met up for a week of recipe testing in Bend, Oregon, this is the recipe that fueled their early-morning trail runs. This was one of those rare recipes that required no tweaking from conception to kitchen testing. The sweet-salty-spiced flavor turned out perfectly balanced the first time Shalane whirled them together.

These energy balls provide ideal easy-to-digest energy for a quick bite before an early run. We like to keep them stashed in the fridge at all times.

1 cup raw almonds

1 cup raw walnuts

¼ cup raw hemp hearts (hulled hemp seeds)

¼ cup raw sesame seeds or sunflower seeds

1 tablespoon Chai Spice Mix (page 274)

¼ teaspoon fine sea salt

6 Medjool dates, pitted and halved*

1 tablespoon virgin coconut oil

Medjool dates are large and dried but not dehydrated. They have a higher moisture content than Deglet Noor dates, so they're stickier and better for bars. Find them in the produce aisle at most grocery stores. If you can't find Medjools, substitute 1 cup of Deglet Noor dates.

1 Position a rack in the center of the oven. Preheat the oven to 300°F.

2 Place the almonds and walnuts on a rimmed baking sheet and lightly toast in the oven for 10 to 15 minutes, stirring every 5 minutes, until fragrant but not browned. Set aside to cool completely.

3 In a food processor or high-speed blender, pulse the toasted nuts, hemp hearts, sesame seeds, chai spice mix, and salt until the nuts are coarsely ground. Add the dates and coconut oil. Pulse or blend (if blending, begin on low speed, slowly increasing the speed to high, and use the tamper tool) until the mixture is rollable and doughlike, with no visible chunks of dates. Stop as needed to scrape underneath the blade. Be careful not to overprocess, or it will become oily.

4 Use your hands to roll the mixture into bite-size balls. Place in a storage container with a lid. Chill in the fridge for 1 hour prior to eating. Store leftovers in the fridge for up to 1 month. These bites are best eaten cold, as they melt easily.

NEXT LEVEL: *Add 1 tablespoon gelatinized maca powder for an extra boost. Consume with water or a sports drink.*

BUCKWHEAT CHOCOLATE MOLASSES COOKIES

for a sweet break from a fast pace

MAKES 24 COOKIES

GLUTEN-FREE: Substitute a gluten-free flour blend for the all-purpose flour. // **VEGETARIAN** //

So this isn't exactly breakfast food, but we had to include this recipe because these memorable cookies pair dreamily with coffee for a midmorning break. Also, we could argue that this sweet treat is more nutritious than your average breakfast cereal, since the cookies are made with magnesium-rich buckwheat flour. Buckwheat contains essential amino acids and is high in fiber.

When baking with buckwheat, it's important to combine it with regular flour, or your treats will turn out grainy and dense. We chose all-purpose flour for accessibility, but you could use a gluten-free cup-for-cup flour blend instead.

Plan ahead. This batter needs to chill for 2 hours (or up to overnight) in the fridge. Baking times vary based on ovens and size of cookie. These cook fast and can go from perfect to burnt in a couple of minutes, so keep a careful watch.

½ cup (1 stick) unsalted butter

½ cup coconut sugar or cane sugar

2 eggs

¼ cup blackstrap molasses

¾ cup buckwheat flour

¾ cup all-purpose flour

½ cup chocolate chips

½ teaspoon baking powder

½ teaspoon baking soda

½ teaspoon fine sea salt

Time Saver Tip: *Shalane and her husband, Steven, love to eat these cookies chilled, and they keep them stashed in the fridge for a late-afternoon pick-me-up. Steven was skeptical of the ingredients, but these are now his favorite cookies!*

1   Melt the butter in a small saucepan over very low heat (or quarter the butter and melt in the microwave, using low power and 30-second increments to avoid splattering). Pour into a large bowl and use a rubber spatula to get every last bit (never waste butter!).

2   Add the sugar, eggs, and molasses to the butter and whisk well to combine.

3   In a medium bowl, combine the buckwheat flour, all-purpose flour, chocolate chips, baking powder, baking soda, and salt. Add the dry ingredients to the wet ingredients and stir to combine. Cover the bowl and refrigerate for at least 2 hours or up to overnight.

4   Position a rack in the center of the oven. Preheat the oven to 375°F. Line two baking sheets with parchment paper.

5   Dampen your hands to prevent sticking. Scoop heaping tablespoons of the batter into your hands, then roll each portion into a ball, placing them 2 inches apart on the prepared baking sheet. Bake for 9 to 12 minutes, until slightly firm on top but still soft. Use a spatula to transfer the cookies to a cooling rack.

CHOCOLATE TART CHERRY SEED BALLS

for energy on the run

MAKES 16 BALLS

GLUTEN-FREE //
VEGAN //

Introducing nut-free energy bites that are sweet, salty, and tart to please all your discerning taste buds. They're low-glycemic and packed with a heart-healthy trifecta of energizing seeds, including pumpkin, sunflower, and our favorite powerhouse, hemp seeds.

Seeds are high in protein, healthy fats, and essential minerals, and are shown to help balance hormones and boost your mood. These brave balls are packable and ready to join you on your next endurance adventure—whether that's a day at the office or a mountain trail run.

¾ cup raw pumpkin seeds

¼ cup raw sunflower seeds

¼ cup raw hemp hearts (hulled hemp seeds)

½ cup Deglet Noor dates, pitted

¼ cup unsweetened dried tart cherries*

¼ cup chocolate chips

2 tablespoons virgin coconut oil

1 tablespoon unsweetened cocoa powder

¼ teaspoon fine sea salt

We like the tartness of sour cherries as a contrasting flavor to the sweet dates, but if you can't find tart cherries, substitute dried cranberries.

1. In a food processor or high-speed blender, combine the pumpkin seeds, sunflower seeds, and hemp hearts. Pulse a couple of times to break up the seeds. Add the dates, cherries, chocolate chips, coconut oil, cocoa powder, and salt. Pulse or blend on high, stopping as needed to scrape underneath the blade, until the mixture is rollable and doughlike (it will be slightly oily, but will firm up once chilled).

2. Use your hands to roll the mixture into bite-size balls. Place in a glass storage container. Chill in the fridge for 30 minutes prior to eating. Store leftovers in the fridge for up to 1 month.

SPROUTED ALMONDS

for gold-medal snacking

MAKES 3 CUPS

GLUTEN-FREE //
VEGAN //

Almonds are probably the number one snack food for athletes. They're high in protein, healthy fats, antioxidants, and minerals. But in large quantities, raw or roasted nuts can be difficult to digest. Nuts are high in antinutrients like phytic acid and lectins, which can block nutrient absorption. Soaking the nuts ahead of time helps remove the phytic acid and awakens the germ, which makes the nutrients in the nuts easier to absorb. To maximize your intake of key nutrients, including calcium, magnesium, potassium, vitamin E, and other essential trace minerals, sprouting is worth the effort.

Dehydrating at a low temperature helps keep the nuts' healthy fats intact. It's incredible how delicious sprouted almonds taste. They're sweet, salty, and perfectly crunchy without the any added oils or seasonings. If you don't have time to dehydrate, you can eat the soaked almonds straight up. (They taste like snap peas!) Once you get into a rhythm of sprouting your almonds, we bet you'll never go back.

---

3 cups raw almonds
3 cups water
1 tablespoon fine sea salt

Time Saver Tip:
This recipe can easily be doubled. Here's an ideal schedule: Soak your nuts before dinner the first night. The next night, place them in the oven 12 hours before the time you wake up (i.e., if you normally wake up at seven a.m., put them in the oven at seven p.m.). Check them as soon as you wake up; if they need more time, keep them in the oven for another hour or two (best to save this project for a non-work day). Set a reminder on your phone so you don't accidentally leave them in there all day.

1 In a large bowl or ½-gallon jar, combine the almonds, water, and salt. Stir to dissolve the salt. Cover with a lid or light towel. Soak at room temperature for 24 hours (if you need to soak them for longer than 24 hours, store them in the fridge).

2 Set the oven to its lowest heat setting, 150° to 170°F max.

3 Rinse the nuts thoroughly, then drain. Dry the almonds really well with a towel, then spread them over a baking sheet (no parchment paper). Dehydrate in the oven for 12 hours (overnight). After 12 hours, taste an almond: it should be crunchy. If not, return the almonds to the oven for another 1 to 2 hours, then check again. Set a reminder on your phone so you don't forget they're in there!

4 Sprouted almonds are activated (like fresh produce) and should be stored in an airtight container in the fridge. They'll stay fresh for up to 2 weeks.

CRISPY RICE PEANUT BUTTER BARS

for a better bar

MAKES 16 SMALL SQUARES

GLUTEN-FREE // **VEGAN:** Substitute maple syrup for the honey. //

These peppy bars will wake you up better than coffee will. They taste like a peanut butter cup and Rice Krispies Treat combo. They're loaded with healthy fats and simple ingredients to keep you sustained between meals. Try a square with green tea when you're craving a sweet midmorning break. They're not exactly a breakfast food, but some days you just need to treat yourself.

Our crispy rice bars are best served chilled. Their lower sugar content means they're more crumbly than packaged bars.

2 cups crispy rice cereal

½ cup chopped roasted almonds or peanuts

⅓ cup NOW Real Food Organic Triple Omega Seed Mix*

¾ cup unsalted creamy peanut butter**

3 tablespoons virgin coconut oil, melted

3 tablespoons honey

1 teaspoon vanilla extract

¼ teaspoon fine sea salt

4 ounces dark chocolate bar (70% cacao)

½ teaspoon flaky sea salt, for topping (optional)

*You can use any combination of chia seeds, flaxseeds, hemp seeds, and/or sesame seeds. We like NOW Real Food's Organic Triple Omega Seed Mix because it has all our favorite powerhouse seeds combined for convenience.

**Freshly ground peanut butter or runny peanut butter won't work as well in this recipe. Look for a mainstream brand made from 100% peanuts; our favorites are Santa Cruz Organic and Adams.

1 Line an 8-inch square baking dish with parchment paper leaving a 2-inch overhang on two sides..

2 In a large bowl, combine the cereal, almonds, and seed mix.

3 In a medium bowl, stir together the peanut butter, melted coconut oil, honey, vanilla, and salt. Pour over the cereal mixture and stir to combine.

4 Scoop the cereal–peanut butter mixture into the prepared baking dish. Spread out and press down evenly and firmly with the back of a spatula.

5 In a small saucepan, melt the chocolate over the lowest heat setting, stirring occasionally, until fully melted. Drizzle the chocolate evenly over the bars and use a rubber spatula to spread it to coat the top completely. Sprinkle with the flaky sea salt, if desired. Chill the bars in the fridge or freezer for 1 hour, or until the chocolate solidifies.

6 Use the parchment paper to lift the bars out of the baking dish and onto a cutting board. Cut into 16 squares. Serve chilled. Store in an airtight container in the fridge for up to 1 month or the freezer for up to 3 months.

Nutrition Tip: Look for chocolate with a cacao content of 70%. Dark chocolate is high in iron and antioxidants. In the baking aisle at natural foods stores, you can often find dark chocolate bars designed for baking/melting. They're the same as the high-quality chocolate that you find in the snack aisle, but at a lower price. They're also marked with ounce measurements.

POPCORN TRAIL MIX

for a snack attack

MAKES ABOUT 7 CUPS

GLUTEN-FREE // VEGAN //

Warning: This perfectly spiced snack is highly addictive. We suggest sharing it with a friend.

We subbed popcorn for oats in this sweet-and-savory gluten-free snack mix that's a cross between trail mix and granola. Any time you pop your own kernels, it's worth making enough popcorn for this recipe–plus, if you follow the recipe, you'll have leftovers for movie night. Simply drizzle the extra popcorn with butter or coconut oil and add salt to taste.

½ cup raw almonds

½ cup raw cashews

½ cup raw sunflower and/or pumpkin seeds

3 tablespoons olive oil

2 tablespoons maple syrup

7 cups plain unsalted popcorn (see below)

1 teaspoon chili powder

½ teaspoon ground cinnamon

½ teaspoon ground turmeric

½ teaspoon fine sea salt

¼ teaspoon cayenne pepper (optional)

1 Preheat the oven to 300°F. Line a rimmed baking sheet with parchment paper.

2 In a large bowl, toss the almonds, cashews, and sunflower seeds with 1 tablespoon of the oil and 1 tablespoon of the maple syrup. Add the popcorn and drizzle the remaining 2 tablespoons oil and 1 tablespoon maple syrup over the top. Use your hands to toss well.

3 In a small bowl, combine the chili powder, cinnamon, turmeric, salt, and cayenne (if you like spice). Sprinkle the seasoning over the popcorn mixture and toss well to evenly combine. Be sure that some of the seasoning coats the nuts.

4 Spread the popcorn mixture over the prepared baking sheet. Bake for 10 minutes, then stir and bake for 10 to 15 minutes more, until the nuts are golden. While still warm (but not too hot), taste the popcorn and add another sprinkle of salt if needed. Cool completely before serving or storing.

5 Store in a glass jar with a lid at room temperature for up to 1 week.

POP YOUR OWN KERNELS

3 tablespoons virgin coconut oil   ½ cup popcorn kernels

1 Heat the oil in a large heavy-bottomed pan with a lid over high heat. Add the kernels, cover with the lid, and give the pan a little shake. When the popping starts, turn the heat down to medium-low.

2 When the popping slows, remove the pan from the heat but keep it covered for another minute, until the popping stops. Remove the lid. Transfer the popcorn to a large bowl to cool.

Homemade kettle corn meets trail mix. I would have never thought to bake popcorn, but now I'll probably do it every time I watch a movie. It transforms the texture. Spice mixture was spot on. Sweet, salty, savory, crunchy.

—Recipe tester **MICHAEL WEISBERG**

CHAI-SPICED PECANS

for a decadent start

MAKES 3 CUPS

GLUTEN-FREE // **VEGAN:** Substitute maple syrup for the honey and coconut oil for the butter. //

These festive nuts can transform a simple bowl of morning oatmeal, and they beg to be snacked on straight out of the jar. If you love them and want to make them faster the second time around, keep our Chai Spice Mix (page 274) on hand, as you'll use it in several recipes throughout this book. These pecans pair perfectly with coffee and tea. Save some to sprinkle on Teff Porridge (page 169) and our Apple-Quinoa Parfait (page 157).

3 cups (12 ounces) raw pecans

2 tablespoons honey

2 tablespoons unsalted butter, melted

1½ teaspoons Chai Spice Mix (page 274)

¼ teaspoon plus ⅛ teaspoon fine sea salt

1 Position a rack in the center of the oven. Preheat the oven to 300°F. Line a rimmed baking sheet with parchment paper.

2 In a large bowl, combine the pecans, honey, and butter. Sprinkle the chai spice mix and salt evenly over the top and stir to combine.

3 Spread the nuts over the prepared baking sheet. Roast for 6 minutes, then stir and roast for 6 to 8 minutes more, until the pecans are fragrant and slightly darker in color. Cool completely and then transfer to a 1-quart jar and cover with a lid.

4 Store in the pantry for up to 1 week or in the fridge for up to 1 month.

"I lay out my clothes the night before practice, and my backpack is mostly packed. Inside my bag are my running shoes, post-workout snacks, and gear that I will need for the workout. I always pack a change of clothes because nothing is worse than hanging out in a wet sports bra after practice. This helps me recover quicker because it keeps me from getting cold and tight."

—SHALANE

GODDESS GRAIN-FREE GRANOLA

for summiting mountains

MAKES 4¼ CUPS

GLUTEN-FREE // **VEGAN:** Skip the egg white and use 3 tablespoons virgin coconut oil instead of the butter. //

This is the granola you make when you want to climb mountains—or beat your friends to the top. It's our most energizing granola to date thanks to the power combo of nuts, seeds, and real butter—don't skimp on the buttah!

This granola is only lightly sweetened, which means you can feel good about snacking on it here, there, and everywhere. You might think it has too many ingredients, but trust us, it's totally worth it! Every ingredient has a purpose, from the mineral-rich seeds to the selenium-rich Brazil nuts to the soothing spices.

Allow to cool completely prior to storing so you don't disturb those oh-so-perfect crunchy clusters. The egg white helps the granola clump, but you can leave it out if you don't eat eggs.

½ cup chopped raw Brazil nuts

½ cup chopped raw pecans or walnuts

½ cup unsweetened coconut flakes

½ cup chopped dates

½ cup raw sunflower seeds

½ cup raw pumpkin seeds

¼ cup raw sesame seeds

3 tablespoons coconut sugar

1 teaspoon ground cinnamon

½ teaspoon ground ginger

½ teaspoon fine sea salt

2 tablespoons unsalted butter

1 egg white

1 teaspoon vanilla extract

1 Position a rack in the center of the oven. Preheat the oven to 275°F. Line a rimmed baking sheet with parchment paper.

2 In a large bowl, stir together the nuts, coconut flakes, dates, seeds, coconut sugar, cinnamon, ginger, and salt.

3 In a microwave-safe bowl, melt the butter. Add the egg white and vanilla and whisk to combine. Pour the wet ingredients over the dry ingredients and stir thoroughly to combine.

4 Spread the mixture in an even, but clumped-together, layer on the prepared baking sheet. Bake for 20 minutes. Remove from the oven and stir. Bake for 15 minutes more, or until the nuts and coconut flakes are lightly browned. Cool completely before storing. (The granola will still be moist at the end of baking, but will morph into crunchy goodness once it cools.)

5 Store in a lidded glass jar at room temperature for up to 1 week, or stash in the fridge for up to 1 month.

Nutrition Tip: Did you know Brazil nuts are high in selenium? Selenium is an essential mineral and a powerful antioxidant—good for hormone balance and cardiovascular health. A little goes a long way, and too much selenium can be toxic, so eat Brazil nuts in moderation. If you can't find Brazil nuts, substitute raw almonds.

MOLASSES TAHINI GRANOLA

for a mineral-rich snack

MAKES ABOUT 9 CUPS

GLUTEN-FREE: Use certified GF oats //
VEGETARIAN // **VEGAN:** Substitute
maple syrup for the honey. //

Elyse is so obsessed with the Ginger Molasses Granola recipe from our first cookbook that she has made a batch of it every few weeks since its conception years ago. It's become her go-to bedtime snack with whole-milk yogurt because of its high mineral content (good for deep sleep) and soul-satisfying flavor.

Over the years, she's made tweaks to the recipe, and this is now her favorite version (it even comes along on family vacations). This recipe checks all the winning boxes—it's sweet, savory, and buttery, and has huge clusters. Elyse's three-year-old, Rylan, asks to help make a batch any time the jar in the pantry runs low.

This recipe is flexible, so feel free to sub in any assortment of your favorite nuts and seeds. If you're allergic to nuts, substitute a combination of pumpkin seeds and coconut flakes.

3½ cups rolled oats

1 cup raw mixed nuts (almonds, cashews, Brazil nuts, walnuts, pecans), chopped

½ cup raw sunflower seeds or pumpkin seeds

¼ cup raw sesame seeds

2 teaspoons ground cinnamon

1 teaspoon ground ginger or cardamom

1 teaspoon fine sea salt

¼ cup tahini

¼ cup extra-virgin olive oil

¼ cup blackstrap molasses

¼ cup honey

SPICE IT UP: *If you want to punch up the sweet spices, replace the cinnamon and ginger or cardamom with 1 tablespoon Chai Spice Mix (page 274).*

1 Preheat the oven to 275°F. Line a rimmed baking sheet with parchment paper.

2 In a large bowl, stir together the oats, nuts, seeds, cinnamon, ginger, and salt.

3 In a small bowl, combine the tahini, olive oil, molasses, and honey. Stir thoroughly until smooth. Add the wet ingredients to the dry ingredients and use your muscles to mix well. The oats will seem dry at first, but keep mixing.

4 Spread the mixture over the prepared baking sheet. Bake for 20 minutes, stir, and bake for 20 minutes more. The granola will still be moist at the end of baking. This granola has a dark color, but don't worry—you didn't burn it. Cool completely before breaking up the clusters and storing.

5 Store in a lidded glass jar at room temperature. The granola will stay fresh for several weeks but will likely be devoured long before expiring.

NEXT LEVEL: *Brighten your granola by mixing in 1 cup freeze-dried strawberries or freeze-dried raspberries.*

Nutrition Tip: Check the label of your blackstrap molasses. A top-quality brand will have a higher mineral content. Iron per serving should be 20% of the recommended daily value. For tahini, we like Once Again, Artisana, and 365 brands. Some brands of tahini are thicker and may be more difficult to mix in.

8 | WEEKDAY POWER BREAKFASTS

APPLE MAPLE BUTTER
OATMEAL BAKE
for thriving on Monday mornings

SERVES 6

GLUTEN-FREE: Use certified GF oats. //
VEGETARIAN //

Tired of eating the same bland, gloppy oatmeal day in and day out? You will fall back in love with oatmeal after making this recipe. Baked oatmeal is our supreme make-ahead weekday breakfast solution that brings even picky kids to the table. It reminds us of apple cake, but it's packed with the same wholesome ingredients that runners love in their bowl of heart-healthy oatmeal.

If mornings are for meditation in your household, not cooking, follow the Time-Saver Tip below. Also, the leftovers (if there are any!) are delicious reheated the next day.

---

2 cups rolled oats

¼ cup ground flax

1½ teaspoons ground cinnamon

½ teaspoon ground cardamom (optional)

¼ teaspoon fine sea salt

1 teaspoon baking powder

4 tablespoons (½ stick) unsalted butter, plus more for the baking dish

2 eggs

1½ cups whole milk, nut milk, or water*

¼ cup maple syrup, plus more for serving

2 cups cored and chopped apples (about 2)

⅓ cup chopped nuts or raisins (optional)

Whole-milk yogurt, for serving (optional)

Elyse typically uses half water and half whole milk.

1 Position a rack in the center of the oven. Preheat the oven to 400°F. Grease an 8-inch square baking dish with butter.

2 In a large bowl, combine the oats, flax, cinnamon, cardamom (if using), salt, and baking powder.

3 In a small microwave-safe bowl, melt 2 tablespoons of the butter.

4 Make a well in the center of the dry ingredients and crack the eggs into the well. Whisk the eggs, then add the milk, maple syrup, and melted butter. Whisk thoroughly, then stir to combine with the remaining dry ingredients. Stir in the apples and nuts (if using).

5 Pour the oatmeal into the prepared baking dish and spread it into an even layer. Cut the remaining 2 tablespoons butter into small cubes and sprinkle them over the oatmeal. Bake for 40 to 45 minutes, until set in the middle and golden and crispy on top.

6 Allow to cool slightly, then slice into squares. Serve warm, topped with yogurt and an extra drizzle of maple syrup, if desired.

Time Saver Tip: Make the batter the night before. Pour it into the greased baking dish and dot with the remaining butter. Cover and refrigerate. The next day, bake as directed, but increase the baking time by 5 minutes.

Nutrition Tip: Add 1 cup grated peeled sweet potato to the batter.

I wake up at seven, and I like to have enough time to eat breakfast, drink coffee, and get in all my activation drills before my run.

—EVAN JAGER,
steeplechase Olympic Silver medalist and American record holder

BREAKFAST POWER BOWLS

for powering your day

SERVES 2

GLUTEN-FREE // VEGETARIAN // VEGAN: Sub tempeh sausage for the scrambled eggs. //

If you've read *Run Fast. Cook Fast. Eat Slow.*, you know Power Bowls are our favorite weeknight meal. But Power Bowls can also double as a breakfast of champions. This is the breakfast to eat if you want to stay focused and motivated until lunch (there's nothing more disruptive than stomach grumbles).

Savory breakfast bowls are a great way to incorporate veggies into your morning meal. The below recipe is our go-to combo, but get creative and substitute any seasonal veg. Up the power by adding any of the following: Tempeh Breakfast Sausage (page 183), Make-Ahead Breakfast Sausage (page 184), Parsnip Fries (page 193), Classic Baked Beans (page 200), Vegan Spinach-Walnut Pesto (page 264), or Everything Bagel Seasoning Mix (page 265).

---

4 eggs

¼ cup crumbled feta or your favorite grated cheese

1 tablespoon whole milk or water

Fine sea salt and ground black pepper

2 tablespoons extra-virgin olive oil

2 cups cooked rice

3 cups chopped stemmed kale or other dark leafy green

2 garlic cloves, minced

1 avocado, sliced (optional)

Pico de Gallo (page 266), Guasacaca Sauce (see page 178), or a spicy condiment (optional)

1 Place the eggs in a medium bowl and whisk until the whites and yolks are fully combined. Add the cheese, milk, and a couple pinches each of salt and pepper. Set aside.

2 Heat 1½ teaspoons of the oil in a nonstick skillet over medium heat. Add the rice (if using day-old rice, add a splash of water as well). Cook just until heated through, about 1 minute. Divide between two bowls. Cover the bowls with pot lids or a clean kitchen towel to keep warm.

3 Return the skillet to the heat and add another 1½ teaspoons of the oil. Add the kale, garlic, and a pinch of salt. Cook, stirring occasionally, just until wilted, 1 to 2 minutes. Divide the kale between the two bowls and cover.

4 Heat the remaining 1 tablespoon oil in the same skillet over low heat. Pour in the egg mixture. As curds begin to form, slowly stir with a rubber spatula (use a folding motion, scraping the egg from the bottom of the pan and folding it over the top). Don't overcook the eggs—they'll continue to cook from residual heat when removed from the skillet.

5 Divide the eggs between the two bowls. Serve topped with avocado and Pico de Gallo, Guasacaca, or a spicy condiment, if desired.

Nutrition Tip: For a grain-free option, substitute quinoa, lentils, Basic Black Beans (page 166), or Simply Roasted Potatoes (page 211) for the rice.

INSTANT OATMEAL MIX

for convenience without the sugar overload

MAKES 5½ CUPS

GLUTEN-FREE: Use certified GF oats. //
VEGAN //

Instant oatmeal packets and packaged cups are convenient for travel, but when you're home, save the environment and your budget by creating your own instant mix. Plus, most store-bought oatmeal mixes are high in sugar and lacking in ingredients to sustain you.

By making your own instant oatmeal mix in one big batch, you can customize with your favorite nuts, seeds, and dried fruit or any ingredients you have left over after making Goddess Grain-Free Granola (page 127). We recommend keeping a canister of this mix stashed in your pantry so you can simply scoop, add boiling water, and plow on. A bowl of oatmeal with nuts and seeds is Shalane's go-to meal before every Long Run (page 45) and marathon.

4 cups quick-cooking oats*

1 cup unsalted nuts
(pecans, walnuts, or
almonds), chopped

½ cup chopped unsweetened
dried fruit (apricots,
date pieces, cranberries,
tart cherries, or freeze-
dried strawberries)

⅓ cup unsweetened
shredded coconut

⅓ cup chia seeds

⅓ cup ground flax or hemp
hearts (hulled hemp seeds)

2 teaspoons ground cinnamon

1 teaspoon fine sea salt

½ teaspoon ground
cardamom or ginger (optional)

FOR SERVING

Whole milk or nut milk
(such as Vanilla Almond
Milk, page 253), warmed

Honey or molasses (optional)

Chopped fresh fruit (berries,
pear, peach, banana; optional)

1 In a large canister or bowl with a lid, combine the oats, nuts, dried fruit, coconut, chia seeds, flax, cinnamon, salt, and cardamom (if using). The mix can be stored in the pantry for up to 3 months (however, if you're including ground flax, we recommend storing it in the fridge).

2 To make one serving, shake the canister or stir to recombine the ingredients, then scoop ½ cup of the oatmeal mix into a cereal bowl. Add ½ cup boiling water (or ¾ cup, if you will not be adding milk), stir, and cover. (Covering the bowl is important to retain the heat—you can simply use the lid from a pot.) Let stand for 3 minutes.

3 Stir in warm milk to your desired thickness. Top with a drizzle of honey or molasses and chopped fresh fruit, if desired, then enjoy.

Instant oats, which may also be labeled "quick-cooking" or "1-minute" oats, are simply rolled oats that have been rolled even flatter and cut smaller for a faster cooking time. You can find bags of plain instant oats at most natural foods stores, and some stores offer instant oats in their bulk bins. Recipe tester Melissa says she lightly pulses regular rolled oats in her blender to break them down into smaller pieces to avoid having to buy and store multiple types of oats.

OVERNIGHT OATS
for racing out the door

SERVES 1

⅓ cup Instant Oatmeal Mix (page 136)

⅓ cup plain whole-milk yogurt

⅓ cup nut milk (such as Vanilla Almond Milk, page 253), plus more for serving

Chopped fresh fruit (berries, apple, pear, or peach)

Chopped nuts (optional)

Honey, maple syrup, or blackstrap molasses

Use our Instant Oatmeal Mix to quickly make overnight oats before you hit the sack. For a treat, drizzle with Cacao-Hazelnut Spread (page 271). We love packing our overnight oats into individual-serving-size mason jars for grab 'n' go convenience.

1 In a 1-pint glass jar or cereal bowl, combine the oatmeal mix, yogurt, and nut milk. Cover and store in the fridge overnight.

2 In the morning, stir in another splash of milk to desired thickness. Add your favorite fresh fruit and nuts (if desired), and drizzle with your preferred sweetener to taste.

SUNRISE OVERNIGHT OATS

for rushed mornings

SERVES 3

GLUTEN-FREE: Use certified GF oats. //
VEGETARIAN //

This stamina-building recipe will have you chasing dreams. During the craziness of the past year, this creative combo became another dependable breakfast for Shalane and Elyse.

For a healthy digestive system, it's important to regularly incorporate raw fruit and vegetables, so we've sneaked in carrots and apples, which add digestion-enhancing enzymes as well as vitamins, minerals, and crunch. This bowl is best served cold (in summer) or at room temp (in fall and spring). If it's snowing outside as you're reading this, turn to page 150 for our warming steel-cut oatmeal recipe.

---

1 Honeycrisp, Granny Smith, or other crisp apple, halved and cored

½ cup grated carrot (about 1 small)

1 cup Vanilla Almond Milk (page 253) or Anti-Inflammatory Cashew Milk (page 250),* plus more if needed

½ cup plain whole-milk yogurt (see page 147)

½ cup rolled oats

½ cup walnuts, pecans, or almonds (or Sprouted Almonds, page 121), toasted and chopped

¼ cup chia seeds

½ teaspoon ground cinnamon

Honey

Our homemade nut milks add significant nutrition and flavor to this recipe, so it's worth the extra effort to make them. If you're using store-bought nut milk, whisk in 1 to 2 tablespoons almond butter or peanut butter for extra fat and flavor and add ¼ teaspoon ground cinnamon and a pinch of salt.

1 Grate one half of the apple on the large holes of a box grater (see tips) and chop the other half.

2 In a medium bowl with a lid,** combine the apple, carrot, milk, yogurt, oats, nuts, chia seeds, and cinnamon. Cover and refrigerate overnight or for up to 3 days.

3 In the morning, stir the mixture; if needed, add another splash of milk to desired texture (the consistency should still be thick). Drizzle with honey to taste, and enjoy.

**Elyse preps this dish directly in a 7- or 8-cup glass storage container, which provides plenty of room to stir and can go straight into the fridge.

Time Saver Tips: Instead of grating the apple half and carrot, Shalane uses her blender to pulse the apple and then the carrot until finely chopped. // Add this recipe to your weekend meal prep routine. Pack it into widemouthed 1-pint glass jars for grab 'n' go convenience.

"Children love to be included, but cooking is messy. I like to make breakfast the night before with my little one when the kitchen is still a disaster from cooking dinner. This way, when I wake up, breakfast is done and I only have one mess to clean."

—GWEN JORGENSEN, *Olympic gold medalist*

CHAI CHIA SEED PARFAIT

for a calming start to the day

MAKES 1 PARFAIT

GLUTEN-FREE //
VEGETARIAN //

You're exhausted at the end of a long day and the last thing you feel like doing is prepping breakfast for the next day. Sweat no more. This creamy, dreamy parfait comes together in minutes and makes the perfect to-go breakfast. Stash it in the fridge overnight and then toss the jar into your purse, backpack, or gym bag in the morning.

Chia seeds are tiny, but mighty. They're high in omega-3s, soluble fiber, and minerals. They're soothing to our overworked digestive systems and will keep you feeling full longer. We always keep a jar of chia seeds in our pantry for parfaits, Instant Oatmeal Mix (page 136), Sunrise Overnight Oats (page 139), Marathon Peanut Butter (page 272), and jam (page 267).

½ cup unsweetened nut milk or Anti-Inflammatory Cashew Milk (page 250), plus more if needed

½ cup plain whole-milk yogurt or nondairy yogurt

3 tablespoons chia seeds

1 tablespoon maple syrup or honey

¼ teaspoon Chai Spice Mix (page 274) or ground cinnamon

TOPPINGS
(pick 1 from each category)

FRUIT: raspberries, strawberries, or blueberries; sliced banana; diced peach or mango; chopped apple or pear

CRUNCH: toasted pumpkin seeds, toasted pecans toasted coconut flakes, hemp hearts (hulled hemp seeds), Granola (see pages 127 and 128)

DRIZZLES: honey, maple syrup, blackstrap molasses, almond butter, peanut butter

1 In a widemouthed 1-pint jar (or cereal bowl), combine the milk and yogurt. Sprinkle in the chia seeds while stirring to avoid clumping. Stir in the maple syrup and chai spice mix. Cover and refrigerate overnight or for at least 2 hours. (The chia mixture, without toppings, can be stored in the fridge for up to 4 days.)

2 When you're ready to eat, stir the mixture; if it's too thick, add more milk as needed. Add your favorite toppings and enjoy the parfait straight from the jar (or bowl).

Time Saver Tip: This recipe should be made the night before (or at least 2 hours before) you plan to enjoy it, as chia seeds need time to absorb moisture. Chia seeds should never be consumed dry.

NOTE: This recipe is easy to double (or quadruple!) to ensure you have breakfast at the ready for busy weekdays.

PERFECT EGGS, 5 WAYS *for mastering the art of eggs*

GLUTEN-FREE // VEGETARIAN //

SCRAMBLED EGGS

SERVES 2

4 or 5 eggs

1 tablespoon whole milk or water

¼ cup favorite grated cheese (aged cheddar and Gruyère are our go-tos)

Pinch of fine sea salt

Pinch of ground black pepper

1 tablespoon butter or olive oil

The key to creamy scrambled eggs is to slowly cook them over medium heat. If your eggs cook too quickly, they will end up rubbery. It's also important to whisk the eggs with any other ingredients before pouring them into the hot pan instead of cracking them directly into the pan. And we highly recommend cooking them in buttah! Serve with toast and pesto (page 262) for bonus points.

1 Crack the eggs into a medium bowl and whisk until the whites and yolks are fully combined. Whisk in the milk, cheese, salt, and pepper.

2 Melt the butter in a 10 to 12-inch nonstick skillet over medium heat. Pour in the egg mixture and cook, stirring slowly with a wooden spoon or rubber spatula (never use metal utensils on nonstick pans). As soon as curds begin to form, reduce the heat to low and switch to folding the eggs onto themselves until cooked through.

3 Divide the eggs between two warmed plates.

(recipe continues)

SOFT-BOILED EGGS

Elyse discovered her love of jammy eggs while living abroad in Switzerland. Nothing beats dipping a hunk of fresh baguette into a runny yolk for a quick and easy breakfast. The key to achieving the lustrous yolk is to set a timer for exactly 7 minutes.

4 large eggs
Fine sea salt and ground black pepper

Bring a large pot of water to a rolling boil. Use a spoon to slowly lower the eggs into the boiling water. Reduce the heat to keep the water simmering, not boiling furiously (you don't want your eggs to crack). Set a timer for 7 minutes. Keep a watch on the water to make sure it holds a gentle simmer. When the timer goes off, immediately use a spoon to transfer the eggs to a bowl. Let cool for a few minutes before peeling.

FRENCH SERVING STYLE: Place each egg in an individual egg cup (find these online). Tap the top of the shell with a spoon and peel it off. Slice off the top of the egg white to reveal the yolk. Sprinkle the yolk with salt and pepper. Dip bread into the yolk and savor. Use a spoon to eat the remaining egg white.

HARD-BOILED EGGS

We have an endless debate in our family about the best method for hard-boiling eggs so they're easy to peel. We tested several methods to determine the winning way.

Place 4 to 6 eggs in a large pot and add water to cover them by at least 1 inch. Bring to a boil over high heat. Cover the pot, turn off the heat, and set a timer for 10 minutes. Remove the eggs from the water and submerge them in a bowl of ice water; let cool, then drain. Stash in the fridge for up to 5 days. Peel just before serving.

Tips for buying eggs: We use a lot of eggs in this book. The labeling on egg cartons at grocery stores is confusing and misleading. In general, look for "organic" and "free-range" labels. "Cage-free" and "all-natural" don't mean much. Find a brand of eggs that tastes amazing and has deep orange yolks. When you can, buy your eggs directly from local farmers for the highest quality and nutrient density. It's worth the extra cost.

INSTANT POT HARD-BOILED EGGS

If peeling hard-boiled eggs is your least fave kitchen task, try pressure cooking them, the fastest method for the easiest-to-peel eggs. See page 25 for information about the Instant Pot.

Place a steamer rack or egg steamer trivet in your Instant Pot. Add 2 cups water. Arrange 4 to 7 eggs on the rack or trivet. Secure the lid on the pot and close the pressure-release valve. Cook on high pressure for 4 minutes. Once the cook time is complete, allow the pressure to release naturally for 10 minutes (the eggs will continue to cook during this time), then quick-release any remaining pressure. Open the lid, remove the eggs, and submerge them in a bowl of ice water. When cool, drain and store in an airtight container in the fridge for up to 5 days.

FRIED EGGS (OVER EASY)

A flawless fried egg makes us ridiculously happy. The goal is to achieve crispy edges with the whites fully cooked and the yolks still runny. You want that yolk to ooze across your toast, biscuit (see page 197), or bowl (see page 135) when your fork first dives into the center.

Olive oil, coconut oil, or butter
2 eggs
Fine sea salt and ground black pepper

Heat a nonstick skillet over medium-high heat. Add enough oil or butter to coat the bottom of the pan. Crack an egg into each side of the pan. Sprinkle with salt and pepper. Cook just until the whites set, about 1 minute 30 seconds. Carefully flip the eggs and cook on the second side for 30 seconds, then remove from the pan and enjoy on top of toast, rice, quinoa, savory oatmeal, or a waffle.

RECOVERY OMELET

for refueling and repairing

SERVES 2

GLUTEN-FREE // VEGETARIAN // DAIRY-FREE: Use nut milk, skip the cheese, and use olive oil, not butter. //

Mix up your scrambled-egg routine by introducing omelets into your life. Omelets are fun to make and can be filled with a variety of veggies, cheese, and extra protein, from beans to sausage.

We call this a recovery recipe because it's high in protein and micronutrients to repair your body after pounding the pavement. For best results, eat within an hour of finishing your workout.

Serve with toasted Olive Garlic Whole-Wheat Bread (page 171) or Simply Roasted Potatoes (page 211). Follow our technique once, and you'll be able to create your own fancy omelets without a recipe.

---

3 tablespoons unsalted butter

4 ounces cremini mushrooms, stems trimmed, thinly sliced (about 1¼ cups)

¼ teaspoon fine sea salt

3 cups loosely packed baby spinach

5 eggs

2 tablespoons whole milk or plain whole-milk yogurt

⅛ teaspoon ground black pepper

½ cup grated cheddar or Gruyère cheese

½ cup black beans (canned or Basic Black Beans, page 166), drained and rinsed (optional)

Chopped fresh chives, basil, or parsley, for garnish (optional)

Spicy condiment or Pico de Gallo (page 266), for serving (optional)

1 Melt 2 tablespoons of the butter in a 10- or 11-inch nonstick pan over medium-high heat. Add the mushrooms and ⅛ teaspoon of the salt and cook for 5 minutes, stirring once, until browned. Add the spinach and cook, stirring continuously, for 1 minute, or until wilted. Transfer to a bowl and cover with a lid to keep warm; set the pan aside.

2 In a medium bowl, whisk together the eggs, milk, remaining ⅛ teaspoon salt, and the pepper.

3 Melt ½ tablespoon of the butter in the same pan over medium heat. Pour half the egg mixture into the pan. Use a rubber spatula to pull the egg from the edges toward the center of the pan and then tilt the pan in a circle to fill the bottom (this will help evenly cook and distribute the egg).

4 Sprinkle the eggs with half the cheese and half the beans (if using). Drain off any liquid from the mushrooms and spinach and then spread half the mixture over the beans. Use a spatula to fold one side of the omelet over the fillings. Cook for 1 minute, or until the eggs are set and the cheese has melted, then carefully flip the omelet. (If the omelet is too large to flip, you can use the spatula to divide it in half.) Cook on the second side for 1 minute, or until golden. Transfer to a plate. Wipe out the pan and return it to the heat. Melt the remaining ½ tablespoon butter and repeat the steps above with the remaining eggs and fillings to cook a second omelet.

5 Sprinkle the omelets with fresh herbs, top with a spicy condiment or Pico de Gallo, if desired, and enjoy.

🕐 **Time Saver Tip:** Omelets are best made fresh, but the fillings can be prepped before your run. Grate the cheese and sauté the veggies, then stash in the fridge until ready to use. If your beans are in the freezer, remember to thaw them. If you're cooking for one, you can save the extra fillings for the next day and just combine them in one container.

INSTANT POT WHOLE-MILK YOGURT

for boosting your digestion

MAKES 7½ CUPS YOGURT

GLUTEN-FREE //
VEGETARIAN //

We've heard from our recipe-testing team that it can be hard to find plain whole-milk yogurt in mainstream grocery stores. We love a true European-style yogurt that is slowly cultured to make it rich in probiotics and easier to digest. Homemade yogurt is lower in lactose from the culturing process, so for runners who are sensitive to dairy (the vast majority of us!), making your own yogurt is a great way to get the calcium boost without the bloat. This style of yogurt is thinner than store-bought and a perfect texture to eat with granola (pages 127 and 128). If you prefer a thicker Greek-style yogurt, you can strain it.

See page 25 for information about the Instant Pot, the special equipment needed for this recipe. Elyse adapted the recipe from the Instant Pot manual and includes a lot of additional information and tips to make the process as simple as possible.

The best way to culture your first batch of yogurt is to use store-bought yogurt as the starter. This works better than buying a yogurt-making kit or active cultures. You can buy a small container of high-quality yogurt with active cultures to use for your first batch; for subsequent batches, use 2 tablespoons of yogurt from the previous batch.

---

2 quarts (64 ounces) organic whole milk

2 tablespoons plain yogurt with active cultures

1 **Sterilize your Instant Pot.** When making yogurt, it's important that the pot is completely clean. See page 148 for instructions.

2 **Heat the milk.** Pour the milk into the Instant Pot, cover, and set the valve to Seal. Press the Yogurt button and use the dial or Adjust button until the display reads Boil (older models) or Pasteurize (newer models). Press Start. When it's done, after about 15 minutes, you'll hear a beep and the display will say Yogt (older model) or End (newer model). Uncover the pot, being careful not to let condensation from the lid drip back in.

(recipe continues)

3 **Add your starter culture.** Remove the inner pot and place it on a hot pad on your counter. Let the milk cool to at least 115°F (use an instant-read thermometer). For faster cooling, you can make an ice bath in your sink and submerge just the bottom of the pot.

4 Pour about ½ cup of the cooled milk into a medium bowl. Whisk in the yogurt. Pour the milk-yogurt mixture back into the pot with the rest of the milk and stir with a clean rubber spatula.

5 **Culture while you sleep.** Set the inner pot back inside the Instant Pot. Seal the lid and set the valve to Vent. Select the Yogurt function and use the dial or + button to select Ferment (newer models); set to ferment for 8 to 12 hours on Normal. You can leave it to culture for the entire day while you're at work or overnight while you sleep. For a more tart yogurt that is nearly lactose-free, culture the yogurt for up to 24 hours (Elyse typically does hers for 12 hours).

6 **Storage.** When fermentation is complete, the Instant Pot will beep (set an additional reminder on your phone so you don't forget to transfer the finished yogurt to the fridge). Use a large spoon or ladle to transfer the yogurt to glass storage containers. Use a fork to whisk the yogurt until smooth. Cover and refrigerate for at least 8 hours before serving. Homemade yogurt will stay fresh in the fridge for up to 1 month. (Remember to set aside 2 tablespoons to make your next batch!) If you prefer it thicker, you can pour the yogurt into a fine-mesh sieve lined with cheesecloth and set over a bowl, and strain it in the fridge overnight.

STERILIZE YOUR INSTANT POT: *Keep your multicooker clean. Odors can remain from cooking savory dishes, and you probably don't want your oatmeal to taste like chicken. To sterilize your Instant Pot, pour about a cup of water into the pot, seal the lid, close the valve, and set to cook on high pressure for 5 minutes. When the timer goes off, quick-release the pressure and rinse the pot.*

MANGO WHOLE-MILK YOGURT

for a fruit yogurt without the sugar overload

MAKES 3 CUPS

GLUTEN-FREE //
VEGETARIAN //

Elyse's kiddos go nuts for this flavored yogurt, which they eat for breakfast or "bedtime snack." Since most store-bought flavored yogurts are high in sugar and low in healthy fat, Elyse started making her own variations. Mango with a pinch of cardamom is always the winner. You can double the recipe below to have enough for the week. This recipe is delicious topped with Molasses Tahini Granola (page 128).

2 cups frozen mango chunks (one 10-ounce bag)

1 tablespoon virgin coconut oil

¼ teaspoon ground cardamom

2 cups plain whole-milk yogurt (homemade, page 147, or store-bought)

1 tablespoon honey (optional)

1 In a medium saucepan with a lid, combine the mango, coconut oil, and cardamom and heat over medium heat. Once the oil has melted and the mango begins to thaw, reduce the heat to low, cover, and simmer, stirring occasionally, until the mango softens, about 10 minutes. Transfer to a blender and let cool completely.

2 Add the yogurt to the blender. Pulse on low speed just until the mango blends into the yogurt (some texture from the mango is good; overblending will liquefy the yogurt). Taste and, if needed, add the honey. Blend briefly to incorporate.

3 Transfer to a container with a lid and store in the fridge for up to 2 weeks.

INSTANT POT STEEL-CUT OATMEAL

for a hot breakfast at the ready

SERVES 3

GLUTEN-FREE: Use gluten-free certified oats. //
VEGAN: Use nut milk and nut butter. //

A hearty bowl of creamy steel-cut oatmeal is light-years more satisfying than instant oats, but steel-cut oats take about 45 minutes to cook. At that point, we know you would melt into a hangry blob, so we came up with these two shortcut methods for runners on a mission.

Toss the ingredients into your Instant Pot before you head out for a run, and this soul-warming breakfast will be ready and waiting upon your return. The best part about cooking oatmeal in a multicooker is that you can use the warming function to keep it hot while you're out training. This is also ideal for family members who like to eat breakfast at different times of day.

See page 25 for information about the Instant Pot, the special equipment needed for this recipe. No Instant Pot? No problem. Use our overnight soaking method below to make creamy steel-cut oatmeal in just 10 minutes. This recipe is delicious with our Chai Honey Nut Butter (page 275); if you do use the nut butter, you can skip the cinnamon, butter, and honey called for here.

---

1 cup steel-cut oats

1 teaspoon ground cinnamon

¼ teaspoon fine sea salt

2½ cups water (if adding milk at the end, use ¼ cup less water)

2 tablespoons unsalted butter or nut butter

2 tablespoons maple syrup or honey

TOPPINGS

Whole milk or nut milk

Toasted walnuts or Chai-Spiced Pecans (page 126)

Fresh blueberries, chopped strawberries or peaches, or Pumpkin-Pear Butter (page 268)

1 Combine the oats, cinnamon, salt, and water in your Instant Pot* (or other pressure cooker or multicooker).

2 Secure the lid on the pot and close the pressure-release valve. Cook on high pressure for 10 minutes. Once the cook time is complete, allow the pressure to release naturally for 10 minutes.

3 Use the warming function to keep the oatmeal hot until ready to serve. Remove the lid and stir in the butter or nut butter and syrup or honey. If the oatmeal is too thick, add a splash of milk. Spoon into bowls and top with nuts and/or fruit.

SPEEDY STOVETOP STEEL-CUT OATMEAL: The night before, bring 2 cups water to a boil in a large saucepan over high heat. Stir in the oats, turn off the heat, cover, and let stand on the stovetop overnight. In the morning, add ½ cup milk (or enough to reach your desired thickness), raisins (if using), cinnamon, and salt and simmer over low heat for 10 minutes, or until the oats are soft. Stir in the butter, if desired, and syrup or honey, add your toppings, and enjoy.

Sterilize your Instant Pot (see page 148).

Sunrise is the most sacred time of day. Create a meaningful morning, because it will impact your whole day.
–SHALANE

A.M. BONE BROTH

for a healing start

MAKES ABOUT 12 CUPS

GLUTEN-FREE //
DAIRY-FREE //

This recipe makes a rich, healing, and nutrient-dense broth. Bone broth is surprisingly delicious for breakfast any time you're feeling under the weather or in need of extra comfort. It's especially soothing for a stressed mind and digestive system, and it should be sipped and savored.

Once you get your flow down, you'll be able to pull off a fresh batch every month. The hardest part about making broth is the storage and cleanup. Reserve this project for a rainy weekend.

2 to 3 pounds chicken bones (left over from 2 roasted whole chickens)

12 cups cold filtered water

2 tablespoons apple cider vinegar

3 carrots, unpeeled, cut into thirds

3 celery sticks, cut into thirds

1 large yellow onion, unpeeled, quartered

½ bunch parsley (with stems; optional)

3 bay leaves

1 teaspoon whole black peppercorns

1 If your chicken bones are frozen, thaw them overnight in the fridge. Place the bones in a 6-quart or larger slow cooker or Instant Pot. Add the water and vinegar (use enough water to cover the bones but do not fill past the max line).

2 Rinse all the vegetables well. Add the carrots, celery, onion, parsley (if using), bay leaves, and peppercorns to the pot. If using an Instant Pot, secure the lid, close the pressure-release valve, and cook on high pressure for 2 hours. Once the cook time is complete, allow the pressure to release naturally. If using a slow cooker, cover and cook on Low for 12 to 24 hours, occasionally checking on the pot and adding more water if the bones are no longer submerged. (You may want to set up the slow cooker near a window that can be left open to prevent your whole house from smelling like broth.)

3 Strain the broth through a large fine-mesh sieve placed over a large heatproof bowl with a pour spout. Discard the vegetables and bones. Pour the broth into freezer-safe widemouthed 1-pint jars and seal with lids. Chill in the fridge. Once cool, skim the fat off the top and discard.

4 Store in the fridge for up to 5 days or in the freezer for up to 3 months. (If freezing, thaw overnight in the fridge.) Reheat in a pan overlow heat until hot, but not boiling.

Miso paste and/or sea salt

Spicy condiment

Soft-boiled egg
(page 142; peeled
and halved), greens,
or cooked noodles

Pour hot broth into a mug or bowl and stir in sea salt and/or miso paste to taste. Add a spicy condiment, if desired. Sip it straight up or add noodles, greens, and/or a soft-boiled egg to make it a meal.

Bone Broth Tips

▶ Freeze leftover bones right after finishing a roasted chicken (see *Run Fast. Eat Slow.* for our Whole Roasted Chicken recipe). Remove any remaining meat from the bones. Place the bones and any skin (adds flavor) in a 1-gallon zipper bag. Keep this bag stashed in your freezer and add to it whenever you cook a chicken.

▶ Read the recipe entirely before you begin. Plan your hours so that you start the broth first thing in the morning to finish before bed, or start in the evening so the broth cooks overnight (if slow cooking).

▶ Make sure you have the right equipment before you begin. You will need a large fine-mesh sieve (strainer), a large bowl with a pour spout, and freezer-safe jars.

▶ Store the broth in the freezer. Thaw overnight in the fridge. For a quick thaw, partially submerge the jar in a few inches of warm (not boiling) water, then, as soon as the broth thaws enough to release from the jar, turn it out into a saucepan and thaw it the rest of the way (and heat until hot).

▶ This makes a rich broth; if the flavor is too strong, you can dilute it with water.

MORNING MISO SOUP

for healing your mind and body

SERVES 4

GLUTEN-FREE //
VEGAN //

Years ago Elyse had the opportunity to take a cooking class in Tokyo. One of her top memories from Japan is the bowl of soup she slurped for breakfast when she got there. It was soul-satisfying and revitalizing after a long day of traveling.

Since that adventure abroad, she's discovered that many cultures serve soup for breakfast. Soup is hydrating, nourishing, and healing, and warms you to the core. What better way to start your day? Soup for breakfast is especially restorative when you're feeling under the weather.

This miso soup is what we crave for "second breakfast" after a snowy winter run. The salty, umami broth is so simple to make and is really hydrating when you don't feel like guzzling a cold sports drink. The enzyme-rich miso, mineral-rich seaweed, and healing ginger will soothe your digestive system. We especially recommend including an egg with an oozy yolk to add richness to the broth. You could also add cooked rice or noodles to make it a meal.

---

2 tablespoons dried wakame*

2 tablespoons extra-virgin olive oil

2 carrots, cut into matchsticks

½ yellow onion, sliced into half-moons

½ teaspoon fine sea salt

2 heaping cups sliced mushrooms

4 garlic cloves, minced

1 tablespoon grated fresh ginger

6 cups filtered water

¼ cup barley miso or red miso paste

Soy sauce (shoyu or tamari)

4 soft-boiled eggs (see page 142), halved (optional)

Chopped scallions or fresh cilantro (optional)

1 Rinse the wakame in a fine-mesh sieve. Soak in cold water for 5 minutes, then drain and set aside.

2 Heat the oil in a large pot over medium heat. Add the carrots, onion, and salt and cook, stirring occasionally, until softened, about 5 minutes. Add the mushrooms and sauté for 5 minutes. Add the garlic and ginger and sauté, stirring often, for 1 minute.

3 Add the water and wakame. Bring to a boil, then reduce the heat to low, cover, and simmer for 10 minutes. Turn off the heat.

4 Transfer two ladlefuls of broth into a bowl. Add the miso and stir until fully dissolved (break up any clumps), then pour the mixture back into the pot. Add a dash of soy sauce to taste.

5 Ladle into bowls. Top with a soft-boiled egg and scallions or cilantro, if desired, and serve hot. This soup will keep in the fridge for up to 5 days. Warm leftovers over low heat on the stove. Be careful not to bring it to a full simmer to maintain the miso's probiotics.

Find wakame (a type of edible seaweed) and miso paste at most natural foods stores or online. Our favorite brands are Emerald Cove Pacific and Miso Master.

LONG RUN BAKED SWEET POTATO

for high-mileage adventures

SERVES 2

GLUTEN-FREE // **VEGAN:** Sub olive oil or coconut oil for the butter. //

We can't think of a single high-carb food that is easier to digest and more nourishing than the loyal sweet potato. That's why sweet potatoes are the fuel of choice for Shalane the night before a race. They are rich in essential electrolytes including potassium and magnesium, are high in vitamin A, vitamin C, and B vitamins, and provide complex carbohydrates for stamina.

You've probably never thought to try a baked yam for breakfast–neither did we, until we came up with this simple recipe that can be prepped the day before and topped with sweet or savory fillings. Any time you're meal prepping, toss a couple of sweet potatoes in the oven, and you'll have a nourishing meal at the ready.

---

2 small sweet potatoes or yams, scrubbed

2 tablespoons unsalted or salted butter

Fine sea salt

SWEET TOPPINGS: Chai Honey Nut Butter (page 275), Sprouted Almond Butter (page 269), or any nut butter; toasted coconut flakes; pecans or Chai-Spiced Pecans (page 126); Greek yogurt; honey or maple syrup

SAVORY TOPPINGS: fried egg (page 143), black beans (page 166), grated cheese, crumbled bacon (page 201), pesto (pages 262 and 264)

Nutrition Tip:
There is delicious nutrition in the skin of potatoes. Shalane remembers being told to eat her potato skin as a kid, and says, "We are an Irish family and we love our potatoes!"

1 **The day before:** Preheat the oven to 425°F.

2 Prick the potatoes with a fork and place on a baking sheet. Bake for 30 minutes, then flip the potatoes and bake for 30 minutes more, or until they feel super soft when pierced with a knife and begin to ooze (some charring on the skin is fine). Cooking times will vary based on the size. Cool, then store, covered, in the fridge for up to 4 days.

3 **In the morning:** For each potato, melt 1 tablespoon butter in a skillet over medium heat. Cut the potatoes in half lengthwise and place flesh-side down in the butter (if your potatoes are large, use more butter). Cook for 5 to 7 minutes, until the edges of the potato begin to brown and caramelize. Flip and cook on the skin side for 2 minutes. Remove from the heat.

4 Mash the flesh of the potatoes slightly with a fork, add a sprinkle of sea salt and your sweet or savory toppings of choice, and serve.

ALEXI PAPPAS, *an Olympian, the filmmaker behind* Tracktown *and* Olympic Dreams, *and the author of* Bravey, *says she's eaten sweet potatoes for breakfast before all her big races ever since her memorable first marathon experience in Chicago.*

"I was surprised that I liked this for breakfast. Frying it in butter really took it up a notch. I topped mine with Sprouted Almond Butter (page 269), yogurt, and chopped Chai-Spiced Pecans (page 126). The crispy skin was yummy!"

–pro recipe tester **NATALIE BICKFORD**

Love the combo of warm apples with crunchy pecans and cool yogurt. I stuck to the 8-minute cook time to ensure the apples stayed crisp, and that was key!

—COLLEEN QUIGLEY,
Olympian and recipe tester

APPLE-QUINOA PARFAIT
WITH CHAI-SPICED PECANS

for powering through your morning routine

SERVES 4

GLUTEN-FREE // **VEGETARIAN** // **VEGAN:** Substitute coconut oil for the butter and use nondairy yogurt. //

This fancy fall-inspired breakfast takes yogurt parfaits to a whole new level by adding protein-packed quinoa. We love the grab 'n' go convenience of prepping the jars in advance, but if you're eating this at home, store the apple-quinoa mixture and the nuts separate from the yogurt. Then you can warm it up before topping with the yogurt and pecans.

2 tablespoons unsalted butter

2 Granny Smith apples,* peeled, cored, and chopped into bite-size pieces

1½ teaspoons ground cinnamon

2 cups cooked quinoa (see page 85)

¼ cup maple syru5

¼ teaspoon fine sea salt

1 cup plain Greek yogurt

1 cup Chai-Spiced Pecans (page 126) or other toasted nut

The size of Granny Smith apples varies a lot. Most are fairly large. If your apples are small, increase the quantity to 3 apples.

1   Melt the butter in a large skillet over medium-high heat. Add the apples and cinnamon and sauté, stirring occasionally, until softened but still crisp, about 8 minutes. Stir in the quinoa, maple syrup, and salt. Cook briefly, stirring frequently, just until warm and thoroughly mixed. Remove from the heat. If you're meal prepping or serving this breakfast cold, set the apple-quinoa mixture aside to cool before adding the yogurt. If you prefer to eat it warm (like us), serve it right away or wait to add the yogurt until after you've warmed up your portion.

2   Line up four 1-pint widemouthed glass jars on the counter. Place about 1 cup of the apple-quinoa mixture in the bottom of each jar. Top each jar with ¼ cup of the yogurt. Cover the jars with lids and store in the fridge for up to 5 days. (Store the spiced pecans separately to keep them crunchy.)

3   Just before serving, sprinkle about ¼ cup of the spiced pecans on top of the yogurt in each jar and enjoy.

NOTE: This recipe is also delicious layered with our Pumpkin-Pear Butter (page 268) instead of the sautéed apples. For this substitution, simply layer plain cooked quinoa with the Pumpkin-Pear Butter, yogurt, and nuts.

PANCAKE AND WAFFLE MIX

for pancakes and waffles always at the ready

MAKES 12 CUPS MIX, ENOUGH FOR 12 BATCHES OF FLUFFY PANCAKES OR 6 BATCHES OF BELGIAN WAFFLES

GLUTEN-FREE: Use certified GF oats and replace the all-purpose flour with a cup-for-cup GF flour blend. // **VEGAN** //

We make pancakes or waffles every weekend, and we always double the recipe since the leftovers reheat perfectly in the toaster. If your family enjoys pancakes and waffles as frequently as we do, save time and money by making your own mix. This may seem like it uses a lot of flour, but you'll be surprised by how fast you go through it (the recipe can easily be halved for a smaller batch, if you prefer). Adding a small amount of all-purpose flour results in crispier waffles and less dense pancakes, but whole-wheat pastry flour or a cup-for-cup gluten-free flour blend can be substituted for the white flour. If you're grinding your own oat flour, buy about $2\frac{1}{2}$ pounds old-fashioned rolled oats. You'll have a little extra, which is great to have on hand to use in any of our Superhero Muffin recipes (see chapters 5 and 6).

9 cups oat flour
(see note, page 75)

3 cups all-purpose flour

¼ cup baking powder

2 tablespoons
ground cinnamon

1 tablespoon fine sea salt

In a large (4- or 5-quart) flour canister,* combine the oat flour, all-purpose flour, baking powder, cinnamon, and salt. Cover and store in the pantry for up to 3 months.

You'll want enough room in the canister to be able to thoroughly stir the mix. If you don't have a large canister, you can store the mix in a 1-gallon zipper bag.

Time Saver Tip: *Write the liquid ingredients and their quantities on your canister of Pancake and Waffle Mix so you always have the recipe handy.*

Next-Level Pancake Tips

▸ Wait until the skillet is hot before you add the batter. You want to achieve that immediate sizzle.

▸ Don't overcrowd the skillet with too many pancakes, or they'll be too close together to flip precisely.

▸ Peek underneath for doneness, but don't disturb the pancakes or flip them too soon.

▸ Adjust the temperature as you work. If the heat is too high, the pancakes will burn on the outside and not cook in the middle.

▸ Add more butter or coconut oil to the skillet between every batch. The fat is essential for pancakes with crispy edges.

(recipe continues)

I love the peacefulness of mornings. The day is about to get going and the streets are going to fill with busy people, but there is a quiet minute before the rush.

—MOLLY HUDDLE,
Olympian

FLUFFY PANCAKES

GLUTEN-FREE: see suggestions above. // **VEGETARIAN** //

This recipe can be made with one egg, but we like to sneak extra protein into breakfast, so we doubled the amount of eggs and Elyse's discerning kids didn't notice the change. The whole-milk yogurt helps the batter bubble for a fluffier stack, but if you're avoiding dairy, you can sub in mashed ripe banana or canned pure pumpkin puree.

⅓ cup whole milk, canned coconut milk, or rich nut milk (pages 250 and 253), plus more if needed

⅓ cup plain whole-milk yogurt

2 eggs

1 cup Pancake and Waffle Mix (page 158)

⅓ cup blueberries, or ¼ cup chocolate chips (optional)

2 to 3 tablespoons butter or virgin coconut oil, plus more butter for serving

Maple syrup, for serving

1 In a large bowl, whisk together the milk, yogurt, and eggs. Stir in the pancake mix. Stir in the blueberries (if using). If the batter seems too thick, add another splash of milk. Allow the batter to rest for 15 minutes (or while you run).

2 Heat a large cast-iron skillet or griddle over medium heat. Melt about 1 tablespoon of butter in the pan and swirl to coat. Spoon the batter into the skillet, using about 3 tablespoons per pancake. Cook until bubbles begin to form in the center of the pancakes, about 3 minutes. Flip and cook until lightly browned on the bottom, about 2 minutes. Transfer to a plate. Wipe out the pan with a cloth and add more butter before your next batch of pancakes. (If you'd like to make fewer pancakes, the leftover batter can be covered and stored in the fridge for up to 3 days.)

3 Serve warm, topped with maple syrup and more butter, if desired. Store leftover pancakes between layers of parchment paper in an airtight container in the freezer. Thaw, then pop in the toaster to reheat.

Nutrition Tip: Want to take these pancakes to the next level? Pulse ⅔ cup milk and ⅔ cup yogurt in a blender with 2 cups spinach, then add the mixture to the batter. This is enough liquid for a double batch of pancakes, so be sure to double the rest of the ingredients. Now you've got "green monster" pancakes, loaded with iron.

BELGIAN WAFFLES

MAKES 8 LARGE WAFFLES

DAIRY-FREE: Use nut milk and coconut oil. //
VEGETARIAN //

½ cup whole milk or nut milk

½ cup plain whole-milk yogurt

4 eggs

4 tablespoons (½ stick) butter or virgin coconut oil, melted

2 cups Pancake and Waffle Mix (page 158)

Peanut butter, Cacao-Hazelnut Spread (page 271), or Blueberry Chia Seed Jam (page 267), for serving (optional)

Maple syrup, for serving

Nothing beats homemade waffles hot off the press. We love Belgian-style waffles because the large nooks beg to be filled with nut butter and a generous drizzle of maple syrup. These waffles are high in protein and heart-healthy oats, so you can feel good about serving them on repeat. We make a large batch on Sundays so we can freeze them to have on hand for weekday toaster waffles. They're actually even better toasted straight from the fridge or freezer, as they get really crispy. If you plan to do this, you'll want to slightly undercook them in the waffle iron.

1 In a medium bowl (preferably with a pour spout), whisk together the milk, yogurt, eggs, and melted butter. Stir in the waffle mix. Allow the batter to rest for 15 minutes while you heat the waffle iron.

2 Pour batter into the waffle maker, being careful not to overfill, and cook according to the manufacturer's instructions. Transfer the waffle to a plate and repeat to cook the remaining batter.

3 Serve warm, with nut butter and maple syrup for drizzling on top, if desired. Store cooled leftover waffles in a 1-gallon freezer bag (reuse the bag!) in the freezer or refrigerate for up to 5 days. Toast until crispy on the outside and warm in the middle.

"My favorite post-long-run brunch food would be your classic eggs, bacon or sausage, and pancakes. I really love the sweet potato waffles/pancakes from Run Fast. Cook Fast. Eat Slow. *They're a good way to sneak in sweet potato and they taste just as good as, if not better than, traditional pancakes."*

–SHELBY HOULIHAN, *Olympian and American record holder*

ULTIMATE SAVORY WAFFLES

SERVES 1 OR 2

VEGETARIAN: Skip the bacon and top the waffles with grated cheese instead. //

Elyse's husband, Andy, gets the shout-out for this recipe. One summer Sunday, he surprised Elyse with this savory waffle combo when she walked in the door after a long sweaty run. Elyse craves salt after running, so this really hit the spot. If you don't eat bacon, you can fry the eggs and crisp the waffles in butter or olive oil.

4 slices bacon

2 Belgian Waffles (page 162)

2 eggs

Fine sea salt and ground black pepper

1 Heat a large skillet over medium-high heat. Place the bacon in the skillet and cook, flipping occasionally, until crispy, about 3 minutes per side. Transfer the bacon to a paper towel–lined plate to drain.

2 Carefully pour the bacon fat into a glass container, leaving about 2 teaspoons in the skillet. Return the skillet to medium heat. Place the waffles in the skillet and cook until crispy on both sides. Transfer each waffle to a plate.

3 If the skillet is dry, add more of the bacon fat to coat the bottom. Crack an egg into each side of the pan. Sprinkle with salt and pepper. Cook until the whites set, about 1 minute 30 seconds, then flip the eggs and cook on the second side for 30 seconds.

4 Top each waffle with 2 slices of bacon and a fried egg.

SAVORY RED LENTIL OATMEAL

for a sustaining breakfast

SERVES 5

GLUTEN-FREE: Use certified GF oats. //
DAIRY-FREE // VEGAN: Top with sliced
avocado instead of eggs. //

Do you ever find yourself hungry for lunch by ten a.m.? It happens to us all the time, especially if we don't eat a substantial breakfast after a morning run. As much as we love pancakes and waffles, sweet breakfasts don't always sustain. If you find yourself snacking throughout the morning, try switching to savory breakfasts.

We are completely hooked on this savory oatmeal bowl. It's packed with protein, fiber, and healthy fats to keep you full longer. The al dente texture of the steel-cut oats combined with the lentils is creamy and soul-satisfying. Elyse eats this on days when she is writing, as it helps her focus until lunch. Shalane savors this bowl for dinner, topped with sliced avacado.

---

2 tablespoons butter
or virgin coconut oil

1 small yellow
onion, chopped

1½ teaspoons fine sea salt

1 cup dried red lentils

1 cup steel-cut oats

2 teaspoons curry powder

4 cups water

2 bay leaves

4 cups loosely packed
chopped stemmed
kale leaves

1 cup canned unsweetened
full-fat coconut milk

Fine sea salt and
ground black pepper

5 fried eggs (see
page 143), for serving

Chopped fresh cilantro
or scallions (optional)

Sriracha or hot
sauce (optional)

1 Set your Instant Pot (or other multicooker) to the Sauté setting. Place the butter, onion, and salt in the pot and sauté, stirring occasionally, until the onion softens, 3 minutes.

2 Add the lentils, oats, and curry powder and sauté, stirring frequently, for 1 minute. Immediately add the water and bay leaves and stir to combine. Press the Keep Warm/Cancel button.

3 Secure the lid on the pot and close the pressure-release valve. Cook on high pressure for 10 minutes. Once the cook time is complete, allow the pressure to release naturally for 10 minutes, then quick-release the remaining pressure (or leave in Warming mode until ready to serve).

4 Remove the lid and discard the bay leaves. Stir in the kale and coconut milk. Put the lid back on for a couple of minutes to steam the kale (this is a good time to fry the eggs). If too thick, stir in a little more coconut milk or water. Taste and add salt, if needed.

5 Spoon the lentil oatmeal into individual bowls and top each with a fried egg. Sprinkle with cilantro or scallions and drizzle with hot sauce, if desired. Store leftovers in an airtight container in the fridge for up to 5 days. To reheat, stir in a tablespoon of water and warm in the microwave or on the stovetop over low heat.

STOVETOP INSTRUCTIONS: In a large pot, melt the butter or coconut oil over medium heat. Add the onion and salt. Sauté, stirring occasionally, until the onion softens, 5 minutes. Add the lentils, oats, and curry powder and sauté, stirring frequently, for 1 minute. Immediately add the water and bay leaves and stir to combine. Bring to a boil, then reduce the heat to low, cover, and simmer, stirring occasionally, for 20 minutes, or until the oats are soft and the lentils are falling apart. Remove from the heat and continue with the recipe as directed.

BASIC BLACK BEANS (INSTANT POT)

for a meal prep staple

MAKES 6 CUPS

GLUTEN-FREE // VEGAN //

Beans for breakfast?! Yes, please. If you find yourself hungry an hour after eating breakfast, beans might be your new bestie. They're high in protein and fiber, which will help keep you full longer. Black beans are great for keeping blood sugar levels in check, and they're a detox workhorse.

Try cooking your own beans instead of using canned. They're easier to digest, better for the environment (no aluminum!), and super inexpensive. Sold yet? Read on for our easy-peasy foolproof recipe. Enjoy these black beans in egg scrambles, breakfast burritos, quesadillas, bowls, and Black Bean Quinoa Pilaf (page 188).

If you're new to eating legumes, it's best to introduce them into your diet slowly, in small portions. This recipe makes a lot, so freeze the leftovers. See page 25 for information about the Instant Pot, the special equipment needed for this recipe.

---

1 pound (2¼ cups) black beans, soaked overnight

2 carrots, unpeeled, halved

1 yellow onion, halved and peeled (keep the halves intact by leaving root end on)

4 bay leaves

1 strip dried kombu (optional; helps with digestion)

1½ teaspoons fine sea salt

6 cups water

1 Drain and rinse the beans. Place the beans, carrots, onion, bay leaves, kombu, and salt in your Instant Pot. Add the water.

2 Secure the lid on the pot and close the pressure-release valve. Cook on high pressure for 20 minutes. Once the cook time is complete, allow the pressure to release naturally for 10 minutes, then quick-release the remaining pressure.

3 Remove the lid. Remove and discard the carrots, onion, bay leaves, and kombu. Remove the pot and set aside to cool.

4 Pour off some of the excess liquid, leaving just enough to cover the beans. Transfer the beans to glass storage containers. For easy freezing, we like to use 1-pint widemouthed freezer-safe glass jars. If freezing, include enough of the cooking liquid to cover the beans in each jar. When ready to use, thaw and drain the beans.

Time Saver Tip: To thaw the beans for last-minute meals, submerge the bottom of the jar in a pot with a couple inches of warm (not boiling) water. Thaw the beans enough that you can transfer them to a colander, then rinse them under cool running water until fully thawed.

WHIPPED WHITE BEAN AND AVOCADO TOAST

for the love of avocados

MAKES 1½ CUPS SPREAD

GLUTEN-FREE: Use gluten-free bread. // **VEGAN** //

We have yet to meet a runner who doesn't love avocado toast. Take your toast to the next level by whipping beans into your avocado. Besides adding protein, complex carbs, and fiber to transform your toast into a complete meal, a daily dose of beans provides energizing vitamins and minerals. Beans, beans, good for your heart . . . and they help us clear toxins from our hardworking bodies.

It's worth making an extra stop to buy your bread fresh from a local bakery (better yet, bake your own bread–see page 170 for our Whole-Wheat Bread recipe). Grocery store sandwich bread has an unsatisfying flavor and texture, plus unnecessary sugar, preservatives, and added gluten. Once you start toasting thick slices of fresh-baked bread, you'll never go back.

---

1 cup cooked or canned white beans, drained and rinsed

1 large or 2 small ripe avocados, halved, pitted, and peeled

1 garlic clove, minced

2 tablespoons fresh lemon juice

½ teaspoon fine sea salt

⅛ teaspoon ground black pepper

4 to 8 slices fresh bread

2 or 3 radishes, thinly sliced (optional)

Everything Bagel Seasoning Mix (page 265)

1 In a small food processor or high-speed blender, combine the beans, avocado, garlic, lemon juice, salt, and pepper. Process until smooth.

2 Toast your bread and allow to cool for a couple of minutes. Top with the bean-avocado spread. Garnish with a few slices of radish, if desired. Sprinkle generously with Everything Bagel Seasoning Mix.

3 Leftover spread will keep in an airtight container in the fridge for up to 2 days.

Time Saver Tip: This spread can be made the night before. After processing the ingredients, immediately transfer the spread to an airtight container and cover to prevent discoloration, then refrigerate overnight. Remove from the fridge 30 minutes prior to serving, as it tastes best at room temp.

Try my best, time will take care of the rest.
—ALEXI PAPPAS,
Olympian, filmmaker, and author

TEFF PORRIDGE
WITH PEAR AND PECANS
for breaking barriers

SERVES 4

GLUTEN-FREE //
VEGAN //

We asked Eliud Kipchoge, the first human to break the 2-hour marathon barrier, and his incredible training partner, Geoffrey Kamworor, what they eat for breakfast. This power duo shared with Shalane that their go-to long-run breakfast is teff porridge, fruit, bread, and tea.

Teff is a powerhouse for runners because it's packed with fiber, protein, B vitamins, iron, calcium, magnesium, potassium, and zinc. Teff is actually a seed, not a grain, making it an easy-to-digest alternative for those sensitive to grains. In Ethiopia and Kenya, elite runners rely on teff as an important protein source.

---

1 cup whole-grain teff (not teff flour)

1 tablespoon butter

½ teaspoon ground cinnamon

¼ teaspoon ground cardamom

3 cups filtered water

¼ teaspoon fine sea salt

½ cup whole milk, coconut milk, or nut milk

⅓ cup chopped dates

2 tablespoons blackstrap molasses

1 large ripe pear, cored and chopped, or 1 heaping cup seasonal fruit (chopped peach, mango, berries)

½ cup Chai-Spiced Pecans (page 126; optional)

Whole-milk yogurt, for topping (optional)

1 Heat a large saucepan over medium heat. Add the teff and toast, stirring frequently, until fragrant, 3 to 5 minutes. Add the butter, cinnamon, and cardamom and stir until the butter has melted.

2 Slowly add the water. Add the salt and stir to combine. Bring to a gentle boil, then reduce the heat to maintain a simmer, cover, and cook, stirring occasionally, for 15 minutes.

3 Remove the lid. Stir in the milk, dates, and molasses. Cook, uncovered, stirring occasionally, for 5 to 10 minutes, until the porridge thickens. Be sure to stir from the bottom of the pot to prevent sticking. If the porridge is too thick, add another splash of milk.

4 Ladle the porridge into bowls. Top with the fruit, then garnish with the pecans and a spoonful of yogurt, if desired.

5 Store leftovers, covered, in the fridge for up to 4 days. Add a splash of milk or water and reheat in the microwave on low power.

WHERE TO BUY: *Whole-grain teff (not teff flour) can be difficult to find, but it's worth seeking out, as this recipe will definitely convert you into a teff fan. Check with your natural foods store or buy it online at bobsredmill.com.*

WHOLE-WHEAT BREAD

for everything under the sun

MAKES ONE 9 X 5-INCH LOAF

VEGETARIAN // VEGAN:
Use brown rice syrup
or maple syrup instead
of honey. // **DAIRY-FREE** //

You can't write a breakfast cookbook without including a bread recipe. Once you start baking your own bread, you'll never go back to store-bought sandwich bread, which has the consistency of cardboard and a paragraph-long ingredient list.

We tested a lot of variations of bread recipes and came back to this most dependable one. You don't need a fancy bread machine or stand mixer but you do need time. Save this recipe for a day when you're home, as there is resting time between each step. This bread is so versatile. You'll love it for sandwiches, French toast (page 209), Whipped White Bean and Avocado Toast (page 167), eggs (see page 141), or with any of our go-to toast toppers (photo inspiration page 268).

Try this basic loaf first and then check out the variations on pages 171 and 175. New to baking bread? Check out Elyse's tips on page 173.

1½ cups warm water (not hot or boiling, 110° to 115°F)

2 tablespoons honey

1 tablespoon instant yeast (two ¼-ounce packets)

2 tablespoons extra-virgin olive oil, plus more for greasing

1¾ cups whole-wheat pastry flour

1 cup whole-wheat flour

1 cup white bread flour

1½ teaspoons fine sea salt

1 In a small bowl, stir together the water, honey, and yeast until dissolved. Set aside for 10 minutes, then stir in the oil. The mixture should bubble and smell yeasty.

2 In a separate large bowl, combine 1 cup of the whole-wheat pastry flour with the whole-wheat flour, white bread flour, and salt. Add the wet ingredients to the flour and use a rubber spatula to combine until the flour is fully incorporated. You should have a sticky dough that pulls away from the sides of the bowl.

3 Use ¼ cup of the remaining pastry flour to generously flour a clean work surface. Dump out the dough and begin kneading it by continuously folding, rolling, and rotating the dough onto itself. Any time it starts to stick, sprinkle a small amount of the remaining pastry flour onto the dough as you knead (you will likely have some flour remaining). Continue kneading for 8 minutes, or until you have a smooth dough that does not stick. You will likely have about ¼ cup of flour remaining.

4 Place the dough in a large, clean, lightly oiled bowl. Cover with a lid or damp towel and set in a warm place to rise for 45 to 60 minutes. The dough should double in size.

5 Position a rack in the center of the oven. Preheat the oven to 375°F. Lightly oil a 9 x 5-inch loaf pan.

6 Lightly flour your work surface. Dump out the dough and punch it down. Roll the dough into a ball and then form into a loaf shape. Place in the loaf pan. Cover with a damp towel and set in a warm place to rise for 30 to 60 minutes. The dough should again double in size.

7 Bake for 50 to 60 minutes, until the top is dark brown (might look burnt, don't worry) and very firm to the touch and the internal temperature is between 195° and 205°F.

8 Remove the bread from the pan by running a knife around the edges and flipping the loaf out onto a cooling rack. Freshly baked-bread is best stored unsliced in a clean brown-paper bag (lunch bag size) on the counter for up to 3 days. Or cool, slice, and store it in a 1-gallon bag in the freezer and reheat in the toaster.

OLIVE GARLIC WHOLE-WHEAT BREAD

MAKES ONE 9 X 5-INCH LOAF

3 tablespoons extra-virgin olive oil, plus more for greasing

3 or 4 garlic cloves, minced

1½ cups warm water (not hot or boiling, 110° to 115°F)

1 tablespoon honey

1 tablespoon instant yeast

⅓ cup chopped pitted kalamata olives

2 tablespoons minced fresh oregano, or 2 teaspoons dried

1¾ cups whole-wheat pastry flour

1 cup whole-wheat flour

1 cup white bread flour

1 tablespoon fine sea salt

1 Heat 1 tablespoon of the oil in a small skillet over medium heat. Add the garlic and sauté, stirring frequently, for 1 minute, or until lightly golden but not crispy. Set aside to cool.

2 In a small bowl, stir together the water, honey, and yeast until dissolved. Set aside for 10 minutes. The mixture should bubble and smell yeasty. Stir in the garlic, remaining 2 tablespoons oil, olives, and oregano.

3 In a separate large bowl, combine 1 cup of the whole-wheat pastry flour with the whole-wheat flour, bread flour, and salt. Add the wet ingredients to the flour and use a rubber spatula to combine until the flour is fully incorporated. You should have a sticky dough that pulls away from the sides of the bowl.

4 Use ¼ cup of the remaining pastry flour to generously flour a clean work surface. Dump out the dough and begin kneading it by continuously folding, rolling, and rotating the dough onto itself. Any time it starts to stick, sprinkle a small amount of the remaining pastry flour onto the dough as you knead (you will likely have some flour remaining). Continue kneading for 8 minutes, or until you have a smooth dough that does not stick.

(recipe continues)

5 Place the dough in a large, clean, lightly oiled bowl. Cover with a lid or damp towel and set in a warm place to rise for 45 to 60 minutes. The dough should double in size.

6 Position a rack in the center of the oven. Preheat the oven to 375°F. Lightly oil a 9 x 5-inch loaf pan.

7 Lightly flour your work surface. Dump out the dough and punch it down. Roll the dough into a ball and then form into a loaf shape. Place in the loaf pan. Cover with a damp towel and set in a warm place to rise for 30 minutes. The dough should again double in size.

8 Bake for 50 to 60 minutes, until the top is dark brown (might look burnt, but don't worry) and the internal temperature is between 195° and 205°F.

9 Remove the bread from the pan by running a knife around the edges and flipping the loaf out onto a cooling rack. Freshly baked-bread is best stored unsliced in a clean brown-paper bag (lunch bag size) on the counter for up to 3 days. Or cool, slice, and store it in a 1-gallon bag in the freezer and reheat in the toaster.

Elyse's 10 Bread-Baking Tips

1 Read the entire recipe before you begin. Baking bread takes time, so save it for a day when you're mostly at home.

2 Make sure your water is at the right temperature before adding it to the yeast. Use a liquid measuring cup for accuracy.

3 The loaf will look done before it is cooked through in the middle, so it's worth investing in an instant-read probe thermometer so you'll know when the bread is done baking (you can also use it to check your water temp).

4 Preheat the oven for at least 30 minutes. Your oven might indicate it is preheated sooner, but it takes time for the temperature to fully stabilize.

5 Don't shortchange the time needed for the dough to rise. The first and second rises are both essential; trust us, we tried to shorten this and it was not pretty.

6 A ceramic or cast-iron loaf pan works better than ones made from aluminum or glass, which don't retain heat well. My favorite is the Emile Henry basic loaf pan.

7 A small amount of honey is necessary to activate the yeast, but you can use a different sweetener if preferred.

8 We use the "scoop and level" method for measuring flour, which means lightly scooping the flour out of the bag with the measuring cup and leveling it off with the edge of a knife; it's the simplest method.

9 Put some stamina into your kneading. If you're unsure of the correct kneading technique, watch a quick YouTube video.

10 Have fun! Similar to running, the more you bake, the easier it will get. Your first loaf might not turn out perfect, but your bread will get better with every try.

Shalane's Fave Toast Toppings

1 Butter—you can't go wrong with the perfect simplicity of bread and butter. Kerrygold pure Irish butter (salted) is well worth seeking out.

2 To turn your bread into a balanced and satisfying meal, toast it and top it with smashed avocado, smoked salmon, and thinly sliced radishes.

3 For a sweet pick-me-up before a run, try fresh bread topped with Cacao-Hazelnut Spread (page 271) and sliced banana. Pure magic.

4 Take your avocado toast up a notch by topping it with a generous sprinkle of Everything Bagel Seasoning Mix (page 265).

5 In the summer, bread smeared with butter and Blueberry Chia Seed Jam (page 267) will make the whole family happy.

CINNAMON RAISIN SEED BREAD

MAKES ONE 9 X 5-INCH LOAF

1½ cups warm water (not hot or boiling, 110 to 115°F)

2 tablespoons honey

1 tablespoon instant yeast

1 cup mixed seeds (sunflower, pumpkin, sesame, and whole flaxseeds work best)

1 cup black or golden raisins

2 tablespoons extra-virgin olive oil, plus more for greasing

1 tablespoon ground cinnamon

1¾ cups whole-wheat pastry flour

1 cup whole-wheat flour

1 cup white bread flour

1½ teaspoons fine sea salt

NOTE: *This loaf makes a mean French toast. Check out our foolproof recipe on page 209.*

1 In a small bowl, stir together the water, honey, and yeast until dissolved. Set aside for 10 minutes. The mixture should bubble and smell yeasty. Stir in the seeds, raisins, oil, and cinnamon.

2 In a separate large bowl, combine 1 cup of the whole-wheat pastry flour with the whole-wheat flour, white bread flour, and salt. Add the wet ingredients to the flour and use a rubber spatula to combine until the flour is fully incorporated. You should have a sticky dough that pulls away from the sides of the bowl.

3 Use ¼ cup of the remaining pastry flour to generously flour a clean work surface. Dump out the dough and begin kneading it by continuously folding, rolling, and rotating the dough onto itself. Any time it starts to stick, sprinkle a small amount of the remaining pastry flour onto the dough as you knead (you will likely have some flour remaining). Continue kneading for 8 minutes, or until you have a smooth dough that does not stick.

4 Place the dough in a large, clean, lightly oiled bowl. Cover with a lid or damp towel and set in a warm place to rise for 45 to 60 minutes. The dough should double in size.

5 Position a rack in the center of the oven. Preheat the oven to 375°F. Lightly oil a 9 x 5-inch loaf pan.

6 Lightly flour your work surface. Dump out the dough and punch it down. Roll the dough into a ball and form it into a loaf shape. Place in the loaf pan. Cover with a damp towel and set in a warm place to rise for 30 to 60 minutes. The dough should again double in size.

7 Bake for 50 to 60 minutes, until the top is dark brown (it might look burnt, but don't worry) and the internal temperature is between 195° and 205°F.

8 Remove the bread from the pan by running a knife around the edges and flipping the loaf out onto a cooling rack. Freshly baked-bread is best stored unsliced in a clean brown-paper bag (lunch bag size) on the counter for up to 3 days. Or cool, slice, and store it in a 1-gallon bag in the freezer and reheat in the toaster.

9 | CELEBRATE WITH BRUNCH

(SAVORY TO SWEET)

CHORIZO BREAKFAST TACOS
WITH GUASACACA
for a post-run brunch

SERVES 2; MAKES 3 CUPS SAUCE

GLUTEN-FREE // VEGETARIAN:
Substitute Tempeh Breakfast Sausage
(page 183) instead of sausage. //

Natalie Bickford, our loyal assistant who has been a force behind the scenes on all three of our cookbooks, developed this recipe for us. Natalie's Venezuelan sister-in-law, Adriana, taught her how to make guasacaca (pronounced *WAH-sa-KAH-kah*), a Venezuelan avocado sauce that packs in the nutrients. This just might be our new favorite sauce for bowls and tacos.

You'll likely have leftover guasacaca, but lucky for you, it's good on everything. Natalie loves it spooned generously on scrambled eggs (page 141), potatoes (page 155), Breakfast Power Bowls (page 135), and grilled steak or chicken. The combo of antioxidants from the cilantro and healthy fats from the avocado and olive oil will help you recover better from Shalane's intense workouts (see chapter 3).

GUASACACA SAUCE
1 bunch cilantro

1 large or 2 small
avocados, pitted

1 small green bell
pepper, quartered

¼ yellow onion

1 small jalapeño, quartered

1 garlic clove, peeled

½ cup olive oil

¼ cup apple cider vinegar

¾ teaspoon fine sea salt,
plus more if needed

TACOS
1 tablespoon olive oil

5 ounces raw chorizo,
casings removed, or
3 Breakfast Sausage patties
(page 184), chopped

4 eggs, whisked

¼ teaspoon fine sea salt

4 small corn tortillas*

½ cup grated
cheddar cheese

¼ cup finely chopped
red onion (optional)

1 To make the guasacaca, separate the cilantro leaves and stems; finely chop the stems and set aside for garnish. Transfer the leaves to a high-speed blender and add the avocado, bell pepper, onion, jalapeño, garlic, oil, vinegar, and salt. Blend until smooth. Taste and add more salt, if needed. Transfer to a bowl and set aside.

2 To make the tacos, heat the oil in a large skillet over medium-high heat until hot and shimmering. Add the sausage and cook, breaking it up into smaller pieces with a spatula, until deeply browned and cooked through, about 5 minutes. Transfer to a bowl lined with a paper towel to drain. Pour excess fat from the skillet, leaving about 2 teaspoons in the pan.

3 Return the skillet to medium-high heat, add the eggs and salt, and cook, stirring gently to form large curds, until almost cooked through, about 1 minute. Return the sausage to the pan and stir everything together. Transfer the filling to a bowl and cover with foil or a clean dishcloth to keep warm. Carefully wipe out the skillet.

4 Place one or two tortillas in the skillet at a time and sprinkle 2 tablespoons of the cheese evenly onto each one. Warm over medium-low heat until the cheese has melted, about 1 minute.

5 Transfer the tortillas to plates and top evenly with the sausage-egg mixture, plenty of guasacaca, chopped cilantro stems, and red onion, if desired. Store leftover Guasacaca Sauce in an airtight container in the fridge for up to 5 days.

SECOND-BREAKFAST FRIED RICE

for repairing your circuits

SERVES 2

Do you ever feel like you're hungry all morning long when you run in the a.m.? Happens to us, too, when we're putting in the miles! The best thing you can do is eat a heartier post-run breakfast, so that you don't end up snacking all morning (speaking from experience!).

This is the ideal meal to replenish glycogen stores, repair muscles, and sustain you after a morning sweat session. This soul-satisfying fried rice is easy enough to pull off midweek or can be saved for "second breakfast" after your Sunday Long Run (see Shalane's Long Run pro tips in chapter 3).

We love the color combination of the purple cabbage and the kale, but feel free to toss in any other seasonal veggies. For those on a grain-free diet, this recipe is delicious made with riced cauliflower, quinoa, or lentils instead of rice.

---

2 tablespoons plus 1½ teaspoons virgin coconut oil

3 eggs, whisked

¼ teaspoon fine sea salt

2 cups cooked short-grain brown rice

½ small red or yellow onion, chopped

2 tablespoons soy sauce (tamari or shoyu)

2 cups thinly sliced red (purple) cabbage

2 cups chopped stemmed kale

1 garlic clove, minced

1 avocado, sliced (optional)

Spicy condiment like sriracha, kimchi, or chili oil (optional)

½ lime (optional)

Sesame seeds (optional)

1 Heat about 1½ teaspoons of the oil in a large nonstick sauté pan over medium heat. Add the eggs and salt and scramble until cooked through. Transfer to a small bowl.

2 In the same pan, heat the remaining 2 tablespoons oil over medium heat. Add the rice, onion, and soy sauce and cook, stirring frequently, until the onion softens, 5 minutes. Add the cabbage, kale, and garlic and cook, stirring frequently, until the veggies are cooked but still crisp, 2 to 3 minutes.

3 Turn down the heat to low. Return the eggs to the pan and stir to combine with the veggies and rice.

4 Divide the fried rice between two bowls. Top with the avocado, a spicy condiment or a squeeze of lime, and a sprinkle of sesame seeds, if desired.

Time Saver Tip: Leftover rice straight from the fridge works best in fried rice dishes, so plan ahead and cook extra rice. Cooked rice will keep for up to 5 days, but should be stored in the fridge within an hour of cooking.

TEMPEH BREAKFAST SAUSAGE

for a vegan protein boost

SERVES 2

GLUTEN-FREE // **VEGAN** //

This breakfast sausage is high in protein and essential micronutrients, and it doesn't skimp on flavor. Tempeh should be included regularly in any athlete's diet, as it's packed with protein, bone-building minerals, and digestion-enhancing fiber. We like tempeh more than tofu because it's naturally fermented and easier to digest.

There are so many uses for this satisfying breakfast "sausage" that we bet it will become a regular in your weekly repertoire. We like it best on top of sourdough toast with smashed avocado. Also try it with eggs or sautéed greens, wrapped into a burrito, served with Simply Roasted Potatoes (page 211) or flaky biscuits (page 197), or used as a substitute for the sausage in our Quinoa Veggie Superhero Muffins (page 84).

1 tablespoon white miso paste

½ cup water

1 (8-ounce) package tempeh

1 or 2 garlic cloves, minced

1 tablespoon maple syrup

1 teaspoon dried oregano

½ teaspoon ground cumin

½ teaspoon fennel seeds

¼ teaspoon fine sea salt

¼ teaspoon ground black pepper

2 tablespoons avocado oil or extra-virgin olive oil

1   In a medium bowl, whisk the miso into the water until dissolved. Use your hands to crumble the tempeh into small pieces into the bowl. Add the garlic, maple syrup, oregano, cumin, fennel, salt, and pepper and stir to combine. Cover and marinate at room temperature for 1 hour or overnight in the fridge.

2   Heat the oil in a large skillet over medium-high heat. Carefully add the tempeh and marinade (stand back in case there's any splattering) and sauté, stirring occasionally, until nicely browned and crispy, about 10 minutes. Serve immediately.

Nutrition Tip: Serve it like we do in the photo: Sauté kale in a little olive oil, set aside, then cook some tomatoes in the same skillet with another glug of olive oil just until they burst, about 8 minutes.

Don't write off tempeh until you try it! Our pro recipe tester, **NATALIE BICKFORD**, had her doubts, but this was her response: "Definitely exceeded my expectations! Super simple and flavorful. I ate it with the Basic Flaky Biscuits (page 197). So good! I loved how the fennel seeds and tempeh crumbles got a little fried and crispy in the oil."

MAKE-AHEAD BREAKFAST SAUSAGE

for protein lovers on a time crunch

MAKES 18 PATTIES

GLUTEN-FREE // DAIRY-FREE //

Getting Elyse's kids to eat anything other than pancakes and muffins for breakfast is a serious challenge. Both her six-year-old and her three-year-old have sworn off most egg dishes (hopefully just a phase!). In desperation to find a quick school-day breakfast that's high in protein and healthy fat, Elyse started buying frozen breakfast sausage. The store-bought sausage had an artificial maple taste and was overly sweet and salty.

Elyse knew she could probably make her own breakfast sausage using higher-quality meat sourced from her local butcher. This recipe was born out of that need, and it became an immediate hit with the fam. The flavor and ingredients are light-years better than anything store-bought.

Try this sausage chopped into our Quinoa Veggie Superhero Muffins (page 84), pair it with flaky biscuits (page 197) for a memorable brunch, add to Breakfast Power Bowls (page 135), or use it to level up your Sheet Pan Brunch (page 187).

1 pound ground turkey

1 pound ground pork

1 egg, whisked

¼ cup almond flour, almond meal, or oat flour (see note, page 75)

2 tablespoons maple syrup

2¼ teaspoons fine sea salt

2 teaspoons poultry seasoning blend*

½ teaspoon garlic powder

½ teaspoon ground black pepper

¼ teaspoon ground coriander

¼ teaspoon ground ginger

1 tablespoon high-heat neutral oil, like avocado oil, for browning

If you don't have a poultry seasoning blend, sub any combination of dried oregano, thyme, basil, and sage to equal 2 teaspoons.

1 Position racks in the middle and lower positions of the oven. Preheat the oven to 400°F. Line two baking sheets with parchment paper.

2 Place the turkey, pork, and egg in a large bowl. Sprinkle with the almond flour and drizzle with the maple syrup.

3 In a small bowl, combine the salt, poultry seasoning, and spices. Sprinkle the spice mixture evenly over the meat mixture. Use your hands to combine everything until evenly mixed.

4 Shape the mixture into small patties and place them on the prepared baking sheets, leaving some space between them.

5 Bake for 10 to 12 minutes, until the patties reach an internal temperature of 165°F. This step is just prebaking; the sausages will need to be browned in a skillet before serving.

6 If not serving the sausage immediately, cool completely before storing. Stack the patties between layers of parchment in a glass storage container or a reusable silicone bag. Store in the fridge for up to 3 days or in the freezer for up to 3 months. If frozen, thaw the patties quickly by microwaving for 30 seconds before browning.

7 To brown the patties (either directly from the oven or after storage), heat the oil in a skillet over medium-high heat. Transfer the patties to the skillet and cook until nicely browned on each side, 1 to 2 minutes per side. Serve hot.

SUBSTITUTIONS: You can leave out the egg and/or the flour if you have allergies. The sausage will be slightly denser, so we prefer to include them, but they aren't vital ingredients.

If you want to skip the ground pork, you can make this recipe with 2 pounds ground turkey instead. Just be sure to use higher-fat ground turkey (85% to 93% lean), not 99% lean. Higher-fat ground turkey includes the dark meat.

If your turkey has too much moisture and it's difficult to form the meat mixture into patties, add a couple more tablespoons of flour.

After a morning workout, I relish a hearty brunch! My spirits are high, so I feel inspired to cook. This meal powers me with positive energy through the rest of my day!

—SHALANE

SHEET PAN BRUNCH

for upping your veg lifestyle

SERVES 4

GLUTEN-FREE // VEGAN: Substitute a vegan breakfast sausage or skip the sausage and serve with a side of Basic Black Beans (page 166). //

In the fall and winter, we love to roast trays of colorful mixed veggies. Sheet pan creations are a staple for quick dinners, so why not try a brunch-inspired variation? This dish is hearty, balanced, and loaded with seasonal vegetables, and can stand alone as breakfast, brunch, or dinner. Sheet pan meals are a great way to use up any assortment of odd vegetables. The possibilities are endless.

For a next-level meal, top with Pico de Gallo (page 266) or leftover Guasacaca Sauce (page 178). For a vegetarian variation, skip the breakfast sausage and serve topped with a fried egg or scrambled eggs.

---

1 pound small potatoes, cut into bite-size pieces*

4 tablespoons olive oil

1 teaspoon fine sea salt

½ teaspoon garlic powder

8 ounces Brussels sprouts, trimmed and halved*

1 small head cauliflower, cut into bite-size florets

½ red onion, chopped into bite-size pieces

½ teaspoon ground cumin

½ teaspoon smoked paprika

¼ teaspoon ground black pepper

4 Breakfast Sausage patties (page 184), or 1 (7-ounce) package frozen breakfast sausages, thawed

Pico de Gallo (page 266), Guasacaca Sauce (see page 178), sliced avocado and/or spicy condiment for serving (optional)

The best potatoes for roasting are smaller varieties like red, fingerling, purple, or new potatoes. Keep it seasonal—great substitutes for the Brussels sprouts are broccoli, zucchini, and red bell pepper.

1   Position racks in the middle and lower positions of the oven. Preheat the oven to 425°F. Line two baking sheets with parchment paper.

2   Pat the chopped vegetables dry with a clean kitchen towel (removing the extra moisture helps them brown).

3   In a large bowl, toss the potatoes with 1 tablespoon of the oil, ½ teaspoon of the salt, and the garlic powder. Spread them out on one of the prepared baking sheets so they aren't touching.

4   In the same bowl, toss the Brussels sprouts, cauliflower, and onion with the remaining 3 tablespoons oil, ½ teaspoon salt, and the cumin, paprika, and pepper. Spread them out on the second prepared baking sheet.

5   Place the potatoes in the oven on the bottom rack and the mixed veggies on the center rack. Roast for 15 minutes, then remove both pans from the oven and stir. Add the sausage to the pan with the potatoes. Return the baking sheets to the oven, placing the potatoes on the center rack and the mixed veggies on the bottom rack. Roast for 15 minutes, or until the potatoes are golden and the vegetables are lightly charred. If you want crispy edges on the potatoes and sausage, roast them for an extra 5 minutes.

6   Combine all the veggies onto one sheet pan, arrange the sausage patties on top, and serve hot. If desired, top with Pico de Gallo, Guasacaca, sliced avocado, and/or a spicy condiment.

BLACK BEAN QUINOA PILAF

*for celebrating veggies
any time of day*

SERVES 5

GLUTEN-FREE // **VEGETARIAN** //
VEGAN: Skip the eggs. //
DAIRY-FREE //

Yes, veggies can be the star of the show at our favorite meal of the day! This easy vegetarian breakfast dish is a protein-packed alternative to your typical bacon and eggs. Quinoa is a complete protein, meaning it offers all nine essential amino acids that our muscles need for recovery.

We love any savory dish that beckons our favorite bowl toppings: think salsa (like Pico de Gallo, page 266), avocado, and cheese!

2 tablespoons extra-virgin olive oil

2 small carrots, diced

1 red bell pepper, diced

½ red or yellow onion, diced

¾ teaspoon fine sea salt, plus more if needed

1 tablespoon chili powder

1¼ cups water

1 cup quinoa, rinsed and drained

1 (15-ounce) can black beans, or 1½ cups Basic Black Beans (page 166), drained and rinsed

2 cups loosely packed chopped stemmed kale leaves (optional)

Ground black pepper (optional)

4 fried eggs (see page 143; optional)

OPTIONAL TOPPINGS: Pico de Gallo (page 266), sliced avocado, grated cheese, guacamole, a spicy condiment, and/or fresh cilantro

1 Heat the oil in a large heavy-bottomed saucepan over medium-high heat. Add the carrots, bell pepper, onion, and ½ teaspoon of the salt and sauté, stirring occasionally, for 5 minutes. Add the chili powder and sauté, stirring continuously, for 30 seconds. Immediately add the water to prevent the spices from burning.

2 Stir in the quinoa, beans, and remaining ¼ teaspoon salt. Bring to a boil. Reduce the heat to low, cover, and simmer until the quinoa is fully cooked (the individual grains will burst open, revealing the germ), 15 to 20 minutes. If there is any remaining water in the pot, stir and simmer, uncovered, for a couple of minutes more. Stir in the kale (if using), and cook just until wilted. Taste and add salt and black pepper if needed.

3 Divide the quinoa pilaf among four bowls. Top each bowl with a fried egg, if desired, and your toppings of choice.

Time Saver Tip: This is a great dish to meal prep on the weekends. Portion individual servings of the pilaf into glass containers and store in the fridge. Then reheat in the microwave and add your toppings. We love storing leftovers in glass because you don't have to transfer them to a different dish to warm them up.

Time Saver Tip: The night before you plan to make the frittata, grate the cheese and stash it in the fridge. Chop and sauté all the veggies, then store them, covered, in the fridge.

SUMMER VEGGIE FRITTATA

for a brunch celebration

SERVES 8 (AT A PARTY WITH SIDES) OR 4 HUNGRY RUNNERS

GLUTEN-FREE // VEGETARIAN //

The Mediterranean-inspired flavors and vegetables in this champion frittata appeal to all. Serve it at a brunch party, baby shower, or post-race party. Or cook it on a Sunday for dinner, and you'll have easy leftovers for a protein-packed breakfast or lunch.

For parties, we like to cook this frittata in a 9 x 11-inch baking dish so it can be easily sliced into 8 squares, but if you have a large 12-inch oven-safe skillet, that works great, too (slice it into 8 wedges). In the summer months, frittatas are a great way to use up an odd assortment of veggies from your farm share or garden. Get creative and swap in your seasonal favorites.

12 eggs

1 cup grated Gruyère or aged cheddar cheese

⅓ cup plain Greek yogurt or sour cream

⅓ cup chopped pitted kalamata olives

1 teaspoon fine sea salt

½ teaspoon ground black pepper

2 tablespoons extra-virgin olive oil

½ large red onion, chopped

2 cups broccoli florets or chopped zucchini

1 cup halved cherry tomatoes (small variety)

2 cups loosely packed chopped stemmed kale

2 teaspoons dried oregano

*If you plan to bake the frittata in the same skillet that you use to sauté the veggies, the skillet should be 12 inches in diameter, nonstick, and oven-safe. We love using our Le Creuset cast-iron braiser for this.

1 Position a rack in the center of the oven. Preheat the oven to 400°F. Lightly oil the bottom of a 9 x 11-inch ceramic baking dish (if using).*

2 In a large bowl, whisk together the eggs, ½ cup of the cheese, the yogurt, olives, ½ teaspoon of the salt, and the pepper. Set aside.

3 Heat the oil in a large oven-safe nonstick skillet over medium-high heat. Add the onion, broccoli, and remaining ½ teaspoon salt and sauté, stirring occasionally, until the veggies soften, 5 minutes. Add the tomatoes and cook, stirring occasionally, until the tomatoes soften and any excess moisture evaporates, 5 minutes. Add the kale and oregano and cook until the greens wilt, 1 minute. Remove from the heat.

4 Spread the veggie mixture evenly in the skillet or transfer it to the prepared baking dish in an even layer. Pour the egg mixture over the top and lightly stir to combine. Sprinkle the remaining ½ cup cheese on top.

5 Bake for 30 minutes, or until the eggs have set and the top is golden. Slice into 8 wedges or squares and serve hot. Store leftovers in an airtight container in the fridge for up to 5 days.

NEXT LEVEL: *Add 8 ounces uncooked breakfast sausage to the frittata. Remove the casings and sauté the raw sausage with the onions and broccoli, breaking it up into bite-size pieces with the spatula. You can skip the olives and oregano because the sausage adds tons of flavor.*

GLUTEN-FREE BREAKFAST PIZZA

for satisfying a pizza craving any time of day

MAKES TWO 8-INCH
PERSONAL PIZZAS

GLUTEN-FREE: Use certified GF oats. //
VEGETARIAN: Hold the meat. //

There are two things every runner loves for breakfast: oatmeal and leftover pizza. So why not combine them into a breakfast pizza with a gluten-free oat flour crust? With no kneading and no rising time, this crust is so easy to make. It has a crave-worthy crispy, cracker-y texture and can hold up to a lot of toppings (but don't expect it to have the chewy bite of a typical pizza crust, which is usually made with high-gluten bread flour).

This recipe is great for an interactive family brunch (or dinner!). Just double the recipe, arrange a spread of fun pizza toppings on the counter, and let everyone gather around to customize their own personal pizza.

CRUSTS
1½ cups oat flour
(see note, page 75)

1½ teaspoons dried oregano

1 teaspoon garlic powder

½ teaspoon fine sea salt

½ teaspoon baking powder

2 eggs, whisked

2 tablespoons extra-virgin
olive oil, plus more
for greasing

1 tablespoon water plus
more as needed

TOPPINGS
1½ cups diced veggies
(broccoli, zucchini, red bell
pepper, mushrooms)

1 tablespoon extra-virgin
olive oil

⅛ teaspoon fine sea salt

½ cup marinara sauce or
Presto Pesto (page 262)

1 cup grated firm mozzarella
or other cheese

3 or 4 slices cooked bacon,
chopped, or 6 to 8 slices
pepperoni or salami (optional)

1 Position a rack in the center of the oven. Preheat the oven to 450°F. Line a baking sheet with parchment paper (trim overhanging edges), drizzle with oil, and spread the oil over the parchment to coat.

2 To make the crusts, in a large bowl, combine the oat flour, oregano, garlic powder, salt, and baking powder. Add the eggs, oil, and water and stir until the mixture has a sticky, doughlike consistency. If it seems too dry, add another tablespoon of water. Set aside for 15 minutes to absorb moisture.

3 Use a rubber spatula to divide the dough in half in the bowl. Place the halves on opposite ends of the prepared baking sheet. Lightly oil your hands, then use your palms and fingers to press and shape the dough into two thin rounds about ¼ inch thick and 8 inches in diameter.

4 Bake for 10 minutes.

5 Meanwhile, prep the toppings. Toss the veggies with the olive oil and salt.

6 Remove the crusts from the oven and use a spatula to carefully flip them. Spread the sauce evenly over the top of each. Top evenly with the cheese and then the veggies and meat (if using). Return the pizzas to the oven and bake for 10 to 12 minutes, until the cheese has melted and the edges of the crusts are golden and crispy. Cut each pizza into quarters and serve hot.

PARSNIP "FRIES"

for salty french fry cravings

SERVES 4

GLUTEN-FREE // VEGAN //

The humble parsnip is often passed over in the grocery store, yet it deserves a place on every runner's table. Elyse came to love parsnips in 2020, when she saw they were one of the last veggies standing on wiped-out grocery store shelves during the pandemic. They store incredibly well and roast into sweet and earthy perfection with the texture of french fries. Like other root vegetables, parsnips are high in fiber, vitamin C, and minerals because of their contact with mineral-rich soil.

Even the most indulgent brunch menus should include a veggie. Filling up on fiber-rich vegetables in the morning helps minimize snack cravings later. These salty "fries" are especially satisfying after a sweaty run.

---

1 pound parsnips (2 to 4, depending on size), peeled

1 tablespoon tapioca flour (tapioca starch)

¾ teaspoon fine sea salt

½ teaspoon ground cumin

½ teaspoon garlic powder

½ teaspoon smoked paprika

2 tablespoons virgin coconut oil, melted

1. Preheat the oven to 425°F. Line a baking sheet with parchment paper.

2. Cut the parsnips in half crosswise, then cut them lengthwise into ¼-inch-thick slabs. Stack the slabs, cut them lengthwise into ¼-inch-wide french fries, and place in a large bowl.

3. In a small bowl, combine the tapioca flour, salt, cumin, garlic powder, and paprika.

4. Toss the fries with the melted coconut oil and then immediately toss with the spice mixture (before the coconut oil hardens). Spread them out on the prepared baking sheet, making sure not to crowd them to ensure crispiness. Bake for 15 minutes, stir, and bake for 10 to 15 minutes more, until browned and crispy. Serve immediately.

Time Saver Tip: Get your knives professionally sharpened every few months. A sharp knife is safer and makes chopping much more enjoyable. Between sharpenings, you can use a honing steel to maintain the blade's edge; while the steel itself won't sharpen the blade, it'll stretch how long the blade stays sharp by keeping the microscopic serrated teeth on the blade aligned.

BRUNCH POWER SALAD

for the love of kale

SERVES 5

GLUTEN-FREE // **VEGAN:** Substitute maple syrup for the honey and skip the bacon. //

Merge breakfast with lunch in style by serving this power salad that combines some of our favorite breakfast ingredients (chia seeds, blueberries, avocado, nuts, and bacon!) with hearty greens and a refreshing dressing.

Make this salad for Sunday brunch–it's rejuvenating after a long run. And as a bonus, you'll have awesome leftovers for work lunches during the week.

To make it vegetarian-friendly, skip the bacon. For a complete meal, top this salad with soft-boiled or hard-boiled eggs (see page 142). Stay seasonal–in the fall, swap in chopped pear or apple for the blueberries; in the winter, grapefruit is a delicious choice.

---

1 large bunch kale, stemmed and chopped (about 5 cups loosely packed)

1 small or ½ large head radicchio, chopped (about 3 cups)

1 recipe Lemon Chia Seed Vinaigrette (recipe follows)

1 cup fresh blueberries

1 avocado, chopped

1 cup chopped cooked bacon (optional)*

½ cup nuts (pecans, walnuts, almonds), toasted and chopped

*Cook the bacon a couple of minutes longer than you normally would to get it extra crispy (see our recipe for Easy Oven Bacon on page 201). Cool completely on a paper towel prior to chopping it and adding to the salad. The bacon can also be cooked the day before.

1 In a large salad bowl, toss the kale with three-quarters of the dressing. Use a spoon to really work the dressing into the kale (this helps soften it). Stir in the radicchio. Taste and add more dressing, if needed.

2 Just before serving, top the salad with the blueberries, avocado, bacon (if using), and nuts. Store leftovers, covered, in the fridge for up to 3 days.

LEMON CHIA SEED VINAIGRETTE
Makes 1¼ cups

½ cup extra-virgin olive oil

⅓ cup fresh lemon juice

2 tablespoons chia seeds

2 tablespoons honey

1 tablespoon Dijon mustard

½ teaspoon fine sea salt

¼ teaspoon ground black pepper

Combine the olive oil, lemon juice, chia seeds, honey, Dijon, salt, and pepper in a glass jar with a lid. Cover and shake vigorously to emulsify. Use immediately or store in the fridge for up to 1 week. If the oil solidifies, remove the lid and briefly microwave on low until it liquefies.

I run really early in the morning, around six a.m., for a couple reasons. Growing up in Kenya, early-morning running was the norm; every one of the pros did it! I like feeling like I have the rest of the day to myself to recover for the next big run.

—ALIPHINE TULIAMUK,
2020 US Olympic Marathon Trials champion

BASIC FLAKY BISCUITS

for a festive family meal

MAKES 12 SMALL BISCUITS

VEGETARIAN //

You can't write a breakfast cookbook without including a biscuit recipe, especially when the authors' twenty years of friendship started in the South.

These biscuits are delicious sliced open and topped with a fried egg and avocado or served with scrambled eggs, Tempeh Breakfast Sausage (page 183), bacon (page 201) and/or baked beans (page 200) for a classic Southern breakfast.

½ cup (1 stick) cold
unsalted butter

1 cup whole-wheat
pastry flour*

1 cup all-purpose flour

1 tablespoon
baking powder

1 teaspoon fine sea salt

¾ cup whole milk
or cold water

We use pastry flour because it's lower in gluten and results in a flakier finish. If you don't have whole-wheat pastry flour, you can sub all-purpose flour.

Time Saver Tip:
You can make the biscuit dough in advance and freeze it. Roll out the dough and cut the biscuits, then freeze them between sheets of parchment paper in an airtight container for up to 1 month. Thaw overnight in the fridge before baking.

1 Position a rack in the center of the oven. Preheat the oven to 375°F. Line a baking sheet with parchment paper.

2 Use a cheese grater to coarsely grate the butter. Place in a small bowl and chill in the freezer for 15 minutes (set a timer).

3 In a large bowl, combine the pastry flour, all-purpose flour, baking powder, and salt. Add the chilled butter and use your fingers to work it into the flour until you have crumbles. Add the milk and stir just until the dough begins to come together. If the dough seems dry, add another tablespoon of milk or water. Use your hands to shape it into a ball. Be careful not to overwork the dough.

4 Generously flour a large cutting board and set the dough on the cutting board. Flour your rolling pin and roll the dough into an oval about ½ inch thick. Fold the dough in half, then in half again (this creates layers). If the dough is sticking, add another dusting of flour. Lightly roll out the dough to 1 inch thick.

5 Cut out biscuits with a small round cookie cutter, or simply slice the dough into small (2-inch) squares with a sharp knife. Place the biscuits on the prepared baking sheet, spacing them 2-inches apart. If you have leftover scraps of dough, gather them together, lightly roll out, and cut out additional biscuits. Place the baking sheet with biscuits in the freezer for 10 minutes.

6 Bake the biscuits for 25 to 30 minutes, rotating the pan after 15 minutes, until golden brown on top and firm to the touch.

7 Store leftover cooled biscuits in an airtight container in the fridge for up to 1 week or in the freezer for up to 3 months. Reheat in the oven at 300°F for 6 minutes.

SWEET POTATO SAGE BISCUITS

for a celebratory post-run brunch

MAKES 15 SMALL BISCUITS

This interpretation of our flaky biscuits (page 197) includes sweet potatoes to raise the nutrient profile. The result is flaky-sweet-savory-buttery perfection. Serve with a side of scrambled eggs (see page 141), or Tempeh Breakfast Sausage (page 183), and sautéed kale for a nourishing start to your day. Pray for leftovers, because they're equally good with soup or chili for dinner. Plan ahead and bake your sweet potato up to three days in advance.

½ cup (1 stick) cold unsalted butter

1 cup whole-wheat pastry flour,* plus more for dusting

1 cup all-purpose flour

1 tablespoon baking powder

1 teaspoon fine sea salt

1 cup pureed sweet potato or yam (see note)

½ cup grated cheddar or Parmesan cheese

½ cup whole milk or cold water

2 tablespoons minced fresh sage

*We use pastry flour because it's lower in gluten and results in a flakier finish. If you don't have whole-wheat pastry flour, you can sub all-purpose flour.

NOTE: *To make sweet potato puree, prick 1 large (1- to 1½-pound) sweet potato or yam with a fork and wrap in foil. Bake at 400°F until super tender, about 1 hour. Cool completely, then unwrap, remove the skin, and mash the flesh with a fork until smooth.*

1 Position a rack in the center of the oven. Preheat the oven to 375°F. Line a baking sheet with parchment paper.

2 Use a cheese grater to coarsely grate the butter. Place in a small bowl and chill in the freezer for 15 minutes (set a timer).

3 In a large bowl, combine the flours, baking powder, and salt. Add the chilled butter and use your fingers to work it into the flour until you have crumbles. Add the sweet potato puree, cheese, milk, and sage and stir just until the dough begins to come together. Use your hands to shape it into a ball. Be careful not to overwork the dough.

4 Generously flour a large cutting board and set the dough on the cutting board (it will be sticky). Flour your rolling pin and roll the dough into an oval about ½ inch thick. Fold the dough in half, then in half again (this creates layers, for a flakier result). If the dough is sticking, add another dusting of flour. Lightly roll out the dough to 1 inch thick.

5 Cut out biscuits with a small round cookie cutter, or simply slice the dough into small (2-inch) squares with a sharp knife. Place the biscuits on the prepared baking sheet, spacing them 2 inches apart. If you have leftover scraps of dough, gather them together, lightly roll out, and cut out additional biscuits. Place the baking sheet and biscuits in the freezer for 10 minutes.

6 Bake the biscuits for 25 to 30 minutes, rotating the pan after 15 minutes to ensure even baking, until golden brown on top and firm to the touch. Transfer the biscuits to a cooling rack.

CLASSIC BAKED BEANS

for protein and fiber for days

MAKES 3 CUPS

GLUTEN-FREE // VEGAN: Substitute maple syrup for the honey. //

Time Saver Tip: *You can simmer the beans and stash them in the fridge a day ahead. Reserve the bean cooking liquid in a separate jar.*

Beans, beans, beans, oh how runners love thee. Beans for breakfast. Beans and toast. Beans and rice. Beans and fried eggs. They're an easy protein source that keeps us full longer. Beans are high in protein and fiber (helps remove toxins from the body), energizing B vitamins, magnesium, and folate.

We like to use a Dutch oven so the beans can go straight from the stovetop to oven, but if you don't have this style of pot, you can simmer the beans in a large saucepan and then transfer them to an oven-safe large casserole dish with a lid (or cover with foil) to bake.

These beans are baked full of sweet and salty flavor. They taste just like the canned varieties of our childhood, but without all the sugar and additives. Our version also happens to be vegan; you won't miss the bacon flavor thanks to the addition of miso, our favorite umami ingredient. Try serving them with toast, rice, or Simply Roasted Potatoes (page 211) and/or a fried egg (see page 143).

Don't forget to soak your beans the night before.

1½ cups dried navy beans or other white beans, soaked overnight

1 strip dried kombu (optional)*

1 tablespoon white miso paste

1 (15-ounce) can tomato sauce

¼ cup honey

2 tablespoons coconut aminos**

1 tablespoon Dijon mustard

½ teaspoon fine sea salt

*Kombu is a type of seaweed that aids digestion of the gas-causing carbohydrates in beans. You can find it at most health food stores.

**Coconut aminos is a salty-sweet condiment made from the fermented sap of the coconut palm tree. It is soy-free, gluten-free, and naturally sweet.

1   Drain and rinse the beans. In a Dutch oven, combine the beans, kombu (if using), and just enough water to cover by a couple of inches (6 to 8 cups). Bring to a boil, then reduce the heat to low, cover, and simmer over low heat for 1 hour to 1 hour 15 minutes, until the beans are very soft, creamy, and easily mashed between two fingers. (Alternatively, you can cook the beans in a pressure cooker, following the cook times in the manual.)

2   Position a rack in the center of the oven. Preheat the oven to 325°F.

3   Drain the beans, reserving ½ cup of the cooking liquid, and discard the kombu (if you used it). Return the beans to the Dutch oven.

4   In a small bowl, stir the miso into ¼ cup of the bean cooking liquid until fully dissolved. Add the miso mixture, tomato sauce, honey, coconut aminos, Dijon, and salt to the pot with the beans and stir to combine. Cover the Dutch oven.

5   Bake for 45 minutes, then stir the beans; if they seem dry, add a splash of the reserved bean cooking liquid. Cover again and bake for 15 minutes more, or until the sauce thickens. Remove from the oven and add salt and pepper to taste. Serve hot. Store leftovers in an airtight container in the fridge for up to 5 days or in the freezer for up to 3 months; reheat in a small saucepan.

EASY OVEN BACON

for special occasions

SERVES 4

GLUTEN-FREE // DAIRY-FREE //

Nothing cheers up the entire family more than bacon. While bacon isn't exactly a health food, we believe it's okay to indulge in it for special occasions. We've gotten hooked on the uncured, heritage-breed bacon from our friends at ButcherBox. Elyse's family especially loves bacon when they have "breakfast for dinner." Pancakes become a complete meal with a side of bacon and a fruit salad. And don't forget to wear your pj's to the party.

If the thought of splattering bacon fat makes you run the other way, try this no-mess oven technique.

1 pound thick-sliced uncured bacon*

*Check out ButcherBox.com for nitrate- and sugar-free bacon.

1 Position a rack in the center of the oven. Preheat the oven to 400°F. Line a large rimmed baking sheet with foil and place an oven-safe cooling rack** on top.

2 Lay the bacon slices in a row on the cooling rack, arranging them so they aren't overlapping. Bake for 8 minutes. Remove from the oven and use tongs to flip each slice of bacon. Return the bacon to the oven and bake, checking frequently to prevent burning, until crispy and golden brown, 8 to 12 minutes more. The exact cooking time will vary based on thickness; if any slices need more time, remove the crispy pieces and return the rest to the oven for 5 minutes more.

3 Line a platter or large plate with paper towels. Use tongs to transfer the bacon to the paper towels. Blot excess grease. Cool briefly, then serve. Store leftover bacon in an airtight container in the fridge for up to 4 days. Reheat on low power in the microwave.

4 Carefully pour the leftover bacon grease into a jar and store in the fridge (you can use it to sauté vegetables) or discard it. Never pour bacon grease down the drain, as it solidifies once cooled.

**If you don't have a cooling rack, you can simply line your baking sheet with foil or parchment paper. This may increase the cooking time by 5 minutes.

GOT LEFTOVER BACON? *Try our creative and oh-so-good Bacon Black Bean Superhero Muffins (page 74).*

MÉMÉ'S CREPES

for slow Sundays

SERVES 5 (MAKES 10 TO 12 CREPES)

VEGETARIAN // **VEGAN:** Use nut milk and sub coconut oil for the butter. //

Lily and Rylan's French grandma, Laurence, aka Mémé, introduced us to crepes, and they've now become a delicious weekend tradition. We usually make them for dinner, but they're also fun for a festive family brunch. We put out a whole spread of toppings, and the kids get to build their own creations. Then we roll them up and reheat them in the skillet. Mémé says, "I used to make them on weekends for all the kids. I had to double or triple the recipe and use two pans, as I could not make them fast enough. Bon appétit!"

Elyse has tweaked the family recipe, as she couldn't resist sneaking in a little whole-wheat flour, which her mother-in-law will probably protest. ☺

1 cup whole-wheat flour

1 cup all-purpose flour

½ teaspoon fine sea salt

4 eggs

2 cups cold whole milk or unsweetened nut milk

3 tablespoons unsalted butter, melted and cooled

High-heat oil, for frying (virgin coconut oil works great)

Sweet or savory fillings (ideas follow)

1 In a large bowl (preferably with a pour spout), combine the whole-wheat flour, all-purpose flour, and salt.

2 In a medium bowl, whisk together the eggs, milk, and butter. Slowly pour the wet ingredients into the dry while stirring with a rubber spatula, then switch to using a whisk to fully combine. The batter should be runny, without any lumps.

3 Heat ½ teaspoon to 1 teaspoon of oil in a 10- to 12-inch nonstick frying pan (or a crepe pan) over medium heat and swirl to coat the pan. Pour about ¼ cup of the batter into the center of the pan and immediately tilt the pan slowly to spread the batter as thin as possible. Cook the crepe, undisturbed, until the bottom is golden, about 1 minute, then flip it with a spatula and cook on the second side for 1 minute. If the crepe is cooking too quickly or too slowly, adjust the heat. Transfer the crepe to a platter, wipe out the pan, and repeat with the remaining batter. If this is your first time making crepes, it may take a couple of trials before you get the temperature and technique mastered.

4 Top each crepe with your fillings of choice and roll up. Once you add the fillings, you can reheat the crepe in the skillet or melt the cheese (if using) before serving. Store leftover crepes in an airtight container in the fridge for up to 1 week. Reheat in a skillet with your favorite toppings.

Time Saver Tip: To keep the crepes warm and ready to serve without needing to reheat them in the skillet, place them on a baking sheet lined with paper towels as you finish them and keep them in the oven at the lowest setting (just don't forget they're in there!).

FAVORITE CREPE FILLINGS

SAVORY: Grated cheese (Gruyère, cheddar, Swiss), sautéed spinach, sautéed mushrooms, shredded chicken, salami, Basic Black Beans (page 166), Make-Ahead Breakfast Sausage (page 184), Easy Oven Bacon (page 201), pesto (pages 262 and 264)

SWEET: Cacao-Hazelnut Spread (page 271), Chai Honey Nut Butter (page 275), Blueberry Chia Seed Jam (page 267), Salted Caramel Sprouted Almond Butter (page 269), sliced bananas or sliced strawberries, butter, honey, jam, powdered sugar with a squeeze of lemon

ASPARAGUS AND POTATO
SKILLET FRITTATA

for revamping
your egg routine

SERVES 4

DAIRY-FREE: Sub olive oil for the butter and ½ cup dairy-free cheese for the chèvre. //

Frittatas are clutch meals any time you're craving veggies and protein for brunch or dinner. We make them all year round, and when the first asparagus of the season pops up at the farmers' market, we lean wholeheartedly into this creative and delicious combination.

You could easily substitute any cheese, but we highly recommend using chèvre. It adds depth, richness, and a tangy bite, which transforms this frittata.

8 eggs

4 ounces chèvre (soft goat cheese)

½ teaspoon fine sea salt

½ teaspoon ground black pepper

2 tablespoons butter

2 cups chopped asparagus (about ½ bunch)

1 leek, halved lengthwise, rinsed well to remove grit between the layers, and chopped (1 cup)

1 cup Simply Roasted Potatoes (page 211)

Nutrition Tip:
Sub in any of your favorite seasonal veggies. Use about 3 cups chopped vegetables total. For picky kids, use less veggies and add a little breakfast sausage.

1 Position an oven rack in the top slot closest to the broiler. Preheat the oven to broil.

2 In a large bowl, whisk the eggs until well blended, then use a fork to stir in the chèvre, ¼ teaspoon of the salt, and the pepper.

3 Melt the butter in a 10-inch oven-safe skillet over medium-high heat. Add the asparagus and remaining ¼ teaspoon salt and sauté, stirring occasionally, for 3 minutes, or until slightly softened. Add the leek and potatoes and sauté, stirring occasionally, for 2 minutes.

4 Reduce the heat to medium. Pour the egg mixture over the veggies and lightly stir to evenly spread out the veggies. Cook, undisturbed, for 1 minute, then use a rubber spatula to lift the edges of the frittata so the liquid eggs flow to the bottom of the pan. Cook, continuously lifting the edges of the frittata and gradually working around the pan, until the eggs are mostly set (still a little liquidy on top), about 6 minutes.

5 Place the skillet under the broiler and broil for 2 to 4 minutes, until the eggs have fully set and the top of the frittata is slightly browned. Be careful not to overcook (the residual heat will continue to cook the eggs after removing the frittata from the oven).

6 Cool for 10 minutes. Cut into 4 slices and serve.

TROPICAL FRUIT SALAD
WITH FARRO

for a next-level fruit salad

SERVES 6

VEGAN //

When was the last time you got excited–like, *seriously* excited–about a fruit salad? This isn't your typical fruit salad: it's unique, gorgeous, and can stand alone as a meal. You know those days when you come back from a sweaty workout and all you want to eat is a huge bowl of juicy fruit? Well, now you can. This salad gives your body protein and complex carbs from the farro, an ancient whole grain, and healthy fats from the olive oil and nuts.

Use ripe, seasonal fruit for best results. We love the tropical fruit combinations we suggest here (don't skimp on the raspberries!), but feel free to substitute other seasonal fruits. It's also top-notch with apples, pears, or strawberries.

2 cups cooked whole-grain farro (see tip)

¼ cup extra-virgin olive oil

3 tablespoons fresh lime juice (about 1½ limes)

1 tablespoon coconut sugar or cane sugar

½ teaspoon ground cinnamon

¼ teaspoon fine sea salt

3 cups chopped pineapple or melon

3 cups chopped peaches (unpeeled) or mango (peeled)

1 cup blueberries

1 cup raspberries

½ cup pecans, walnuts, cashews, and/or coconut flakes, toasted

10 to 12 fresh mint or basil leaves, stacked, rolled, and thinly sliced crosswise

In a large bowl, toss the farro with the olive oil, lime juice, sugar, cinnamon, and salt. Just before serving, add the pineapple, peaches, and blueberries and stir to combine. Top the salad with the raspberries, nuts and/or coconut, and fresh herbs, if you're feeling fancy.

Time Saver Tip: Cooked farro will stay fresh in the fridge for up to 5 days, but the fruit is best freshly chopped. If you're making this for yourself and not a crowd, you can stash the seasoned farro in your fridge, then stir together as much farro as you want with an individual serving of freshly chopped fruit.

HOW TO COOK FARRO: To make enough farro for this recipe (plus leftovers), heat a medium saucepan over medium heat. Add 1 cup whole-grain farro and toast, stirring continuously, until fragrant, about 1 minute. Add 3 cups water and bring to a boil over high heat. Reduce the heat to low, cover, and simmer until the farro is tender but still chewy, 20 to 30 minutes (cooking times vary based on the type of farro, so check the package instructions). Drain thoroughly and set aside to cool. Store in an airtight container in the fridge for up to 5 days.

TOFU SCRAMBLE
WITH MUSHROOMS AND KALE

for a vegan breakfast that sustains

SERVES 3

GLUTEN-FREE // VEGAN //

Wow, we were skeptical about tofu for breakfast, but this is surprisingly good. It satisfies and nourishes like a delicious plate of creamy scrambled eggs. Even though we love our eggs, we'll be making this again and again—it's nice to mix up the routine, and we love that this dish is loaded with plant-based superfoods.

If you're vegan, mushrooms are an important food to eat regularly, as they supply energizing B vitamins and vitamin D, two essential nutrients for athletes that are difficult to obtain from a plant-based diet.

3 tablespoons extra-virgin olive oil

8 ounces cremini mushrooms, stems trimmed, sliced

¾ teaspoon fine sea salt, plus more as needed

2 cups loosely packed chopped stemmed kale

3 garlic cloves, minced

1 (16-ounce) block firm or extra-firm tofu, drained

1 teaspoon ground turmeric

¼ teaspoon red pepper flakes (optional)

¼ teaspoon ground black pepper, plus more as needed

Chopped fresh chives, cilantro, or parsley, for garnish (optional)

1 Heat 1 tablespoon of the oil in a 10- to 12-inch nonstick or cast-iron skillet over medium-high heat. Add the mushrooms and ¼ teaspoon of the salt and sauté, stirring occasionally, for 5 minutes, or until soft. Add the kale and garlic and sauté, stirring frequently, for 1 minute, or until wilted. Transfer to a bowl and cover to keep warm.

2 In the same pan, heat the remaining 2 tablespoons oil over medium heat. Slowly crumble the tofu directly into the pan (watch out for splattering). Add the remaining ½ teaspoon salt, the turmeric, red pepper flakes (if using), and black pepper. Sauté, stirring occasionally, for 5 to 7 minutes, until all the excess moisture has evaporated and the mixture has the consistency of scrambled eggs.

3 Reduce the heat to low, return the mushrooms and kale to the pan, and stir just long enough to reheat them. Season with salt and black pepper to taste. Serve immediately, garnished with a sprinkle of fresh herbs, if desired.

Nutrition Tip: Did you know that the texture of food is just as important as flavor for satiation? If the food you're eating is soft, you'll likely crave chips or crackers. Since this dish doesn't have a lot of variety in terms of texture, we recommend topping it with chopped toasted almonds or serving it with a side of toast or tortilla chips.

CINNAMON RAISIN FRENCH TOAST

for celebrating

SERVES 4

GLUTEN-FREE: Substitute GF bread. //
VEGETARIAN //

Sneak the incredible egg into family breakfast by making French toast. This recipe is delicious made with homemade Cinnamon Raisin Seed Bread (page 176).

If you don't have time to bake your own bread use thick slices of bakery-fresh bread. Try it with sourdough or brioche for a fancier French toast. True sourdough bread is easier to digest thanks to the fermentation. Skip store-bought sandwich bread, as it has hard-to-digest additives, sugar, refined gluten, and not much depth of flavor.

3 eggs

3 tablespoons whole milk or nut milk

¼ teaspoon ground cinnamon

⅛ teaspoon fine sea salt

2 tablespoons butter

4 thick slices Cinnamon Raisin Seed Bread (page 175), sourdough, or brioche

Maple syrup or Blueberry Chia Seed Jam (page 267), for serving (optional)

1   In a shallow bowl, whisk together the eggs, milk, cinnamon, and salt.

2   Melt 1 tablespoon of the butter in a large cast-iron or nonstick skillet over medium-high heat. Soak each slice of bread in the egg mixture for up to 1 minute per side (heartier whole-wheat bread needs more time to soak up the eggs; if using a white bread, a quick dip is sufficient).

3   Once the butter is hot and bubbling, shake any excess egg off the bread and place two slices at a time in the skillet. Fry until golden brown, 1½ to 2 minutes, then flip and cook on the other side until crispy, about 1 minute. Transfer to a plate and wipe out the skillet. Add the remaining tablespoon of butter and repeat with the remaining bread. Serve immediately, with a side of warmed syrup or jam.

Time Saver Tip: This recipe actually freezes surprisingly well. Thaw slices overnight and simply pop them in the toaster to reheat. The French toast will crisp up and taste freshly cooked.

SIMPLY ROASTED POTATOES

for an easy brunch side

**SERVES 4 AS A SIDE DISH
(MAKES ABOUT 3 CUPS)**

GLUTEN-FREE // VEGAN //

We like potatoes for breakfast. They're a back-to-basics comfort food that shouldn't be forgotten. For those who are sensitive to grains, potatoes are an easy-to-digest complex carbohydrate fuel source.

The next time you're at the farmers' market, check out all the varieties of potatoes–red, fingerling, purple, new, and sweet potatoes are the best types for roasting. (Sweet potatoes will cook faster than the white varieties, so keep an eye on them while they're in the oven.) Leftover roasted potatoes of any variety are great for tossing into a Breakfast Power Bowl (page 135) or a skillet frittata (pages 191 and 205). They're always good topped with a fried egg (see page 143) or a mound of cheesy scrambled eggs.

1½ pounds potatoes, cut
into bite-size pieces

2 tablespoons extra-
virgin olive oil

1 teaspoon garlic powder

½ teaspoon smoked paprika

¾ teaspoon fine sea salt

¼ teaspoon ground
black pepper

1 Position a rack in the center of the oven. Preheat the oven to 425°F. Line a baking sheet with parchment paper.

2 Pat the potatoes dry with a clean kitchen towel or paper towel (removing the extra moisture helps them get crispy edges) and place them on the prepared baking sheet. Add the oil, garlic powder, paprika, salt, and pepper and toss to coat (you can do this in a bowl, if you prefer, but we like the minimize the number of dishes we use). Spread the potatoes evenly over the baking sheet so they aren't touching.

3 Roast for 20 minutes. Stir and return to the oven for 15 to 20 minutes, or until the potatoes are well browned and crispy on the edges.

 Time Saver Tip: Add this dish to your meal-prep rotation. If you're doubling the recipe to ensure leftovers, you'll want to divide the potatoes between two baking sheets to prevent crowding.

Nutrition Tip: We love the humble potato. Potatoes are a great food for athletes, as they're inexpensive, available year-round, easy to digest, and high in complex carbs, potassium, energizing B vitamins, and vitamin C. Did you know vitamin C enhances iron absorption? Eat your potatoes in combination with iron-rich greens like broccoli, Brussels sprouts, or kale to keep your iron stores in check.

SHAKSHUKA
WITH HERB YOGURT DRESSING

for a hearty family-style meal

SERVES 3

GLUTEN-FREE // VEGETARIAN //

This recipe was created by our cookbook assistant, Natalie Bickford, who fell in love with shakshuka at a tiny Israeli restaurant tucked into the mountains of Patagonia. It's a staple dish throughout the Middle East and in North Africa. Classic shakshuka is made by poaching eggs in a spiced tomato sauce. Natalie gave it her own spin by adding kale and a tangy, herby yogurt dressing.

This dish is traditionally served for breakfast for a spicy start to the day, but it's equally delicious, and hearty enough, for dinner. Be sure to serve it with crusty bread, couscous, quinoa, or rice to sop up that luscious sauce!

3 tablespoons extra-virgin olive oil

3 tablespoons tomato paste

1 teaspoon ground cumin

1 teaspoon smoked paprika

¼ teaspoon ground cinnamon

¼ teaspoon red pepper flakes

½ yellow onion, chopped

1 teaspoon fine sea salt

3 cups loosely packed chopped stemmed kale

3 garlic cloves, chopped

1 (28-ounce) can crushed tomatoes (preferably San Marzano)

5 eggs

DRESSING
½ cup plain whole-milk yogurt

3 tablespoons chopped fresh herbs (dill, cilantro, and/or parsley), plus more for garnish

1 tablespoon fresh lemon juice

½ teaspoon fine sea salt

¼ teaspoon ground black pepper

Crusty bread, quinoa, couscous, or rice, for serving

1 Preheat the oven to 350°F.

2 Heat the oil in a large ovenproof (preferably cast-iron) skillet over medium heat until hot and shimmering. Add the tomato paste, cumin, paprika, cinnamon, and red pepper flakes and cook, stirring continuously, for 30 seconds. Add the onion and ½ teaspoon of the salt and cook, stirring occasionally, until softened, about 6 minutes (the tomato paste will darken). Stir in the kale and garlic and cook for 1 minute.

3 Stir in the crushed tomatoes and remaining ½ teaspoon salt and simmer for 15 minutes, or until the sauce thickens. Make three evenly spaced divots in the tomato sauce with the back of a spoon and crack an egg into each divot. Use a fork to break the egg whites (be careful not to disturb the yolks) and swirl the whites into the sauce. Spoon some tomato sauce onto the egg whites (this will help them cook more evenly).

4 Bring the sauce back to a gentle simmer, then transfer the skillet to the oven and bake for 8 to 10 minutes, until the egg whites are mostly cooked but the yolks are still runny. The eggs will continue to cook once out of the oven.

5 Meanwhile, to make the yogurt dressing, in a medium bowl, combine the yogurt, herbs, lemon juice, salt, and black pepper.

6 Serve the shakshuka topped with the yogurt dressing and garnished with fresh herbs, with a side of crusty bread, quinoa, couscous, or rice. If you have extra sauce, store it in an airtight container in the fridge for up to 5 days and use it for a weeknight pasta dish or on Breakfast Pizza (page 192).

RASPBERRY CHIA JAM CRUMBLE BARS

for celebrating friendship

MAKES 9 "BARS"

GLUTEN-FREE: Use GF-certified oats. //
VEGETARIAN //

This recipe celebrates twenty years of friendship between Elyse and Shalane by incorporating our favorite ingredients into a sweet treat. After we graduated from UNC Chapel Hill, we both had the opportunity to move to Oregon (in different years), and we've never looked back. In Oregon, berries and hazelnuts grow in abundance. Raspberries are Shalane's absolute favorite fruit. Butter and oats are both a mainstay in our kitchens.

This dish is a much healthier take on the overly sweet raspberry jam bars from our childhood. It's a cross between a raspberry bar and a berry crumble–taken to the next level. This is the dessert to serve when a friend is coming over for coffee after a run. Frozen raspberries work best.

16 ounces frozen raspberries (about 5 cups)

1 cup raw hazelnuts, pecans, walnuts, or almonds

⅓ cup plus ¼ cup coconut sugar or cane sugar

¼ cup chia seeds

1 tablespoon tapioca flour (tapioca starch)

1 cup oat flour (see note, page 75)

1 cup rolled oats

½ teaspoon ground cinnamon

½ teaspoon fine sea salt

½ teaspoon baking soda

½ cup (1 stick) unsalted butter, at room temperature

2 eggs

1 teaspoon vanilla extract

Plain Greek yogurt, for serving (optional)

1 **The night before:** Place the raspberries in a medium bowl and thaw overnight in the fridge.

2 Preheat the oven at 300°F.

3 Spread the hazelnuts over a rimmed baking sheet and toast in the oven for 10 to 12 minutes, until the nuts are fragrant, stirring once after 5 minutes. Allow the nuts to cool completely. Transfer the hazelnuts to a clean kitchen towel and rub to remove excess skins (if you are using another nut, you can skip this step). Pulse in a high-speed blender or food processor until broken down to resemble a coarse meal (do not overgrind). Transfer to a mixing bowl and cover.*

4 **In the morning:** Preheat the oven to 350°F. Line an 8-inch square baking dish with parchment paper, or butter the bottom and sides of the dish.

(recipe continues)

If you want to skip this step, you can substitute 1⅓ cups almond meal or hazelnut flour for the whole hazelnuts, but the freshly ground toasted hazelnuts add amazing flavor to the crust.

5 Add ⅓ cup of the sugar, the chia seeds, and tapioca flour to the bowl with the raspberries. Stir to combine (the raspberries should break down). Set aside to thicken.

6 In a medium bowl, combine the ground hazelnuts, oat flour, oats, cinnamon, salt, and baking soda.

7 In a separate large bowl, using a handheld mixer, cream the butter and remaining ¼ cup sugar until combined. Add the eggs and vanilla and beat again until smooth.

8 Add the dry mixture to the wet mixture and stir to combine. Roughly divide the dough into thirds in the bowl.

9 Place two-thirds of the dough in the prepared baking dish, crumbling it over the bottom of the dish. With a dampened hand, use your palm to press the dough into an even layer.

10 Bake the crust for 15 minutes, or until lightly golden. Remove from the oven. Pour the raspberry filling over the crust and spread into an even layer. Crumble the remaining dough evenly over the top and press it lightly into the jam. Bake for 30 to 35 minutes more, until the top is golden brown. Remove from the oven and allow to cool for at least 10 minutes before slicing.

11 Slice into 9 bars and transfer to individual plates (these crumble bars are not meant to be eaten by hand). Serve warm, with a side of Greek yogurt. Store leftovers in the fridge for up to 5 days or in the freezer for up to 3 months.

CINNA-RUN-ROLLS

for a celebratory post-run brunch with teammates

MAKES 9 CINNAMON ROLLS

VEGETARIAN //

We received hundreds of delicious submissions for the *Rise & Run* Recipe Contest. It was hard to narrow it down to just one winner, but this makeover of a classic brunch dish from Jacie Legois–and the moving story she shared–stole our hearts (and bellies).

Jacie told us: "A week before finals, my roommate, Gwynne Wright, and I were both hit with a not-so-fun bug. We decided that cinnamon rolls were an absolute necessity to help us feel better. We settled on making a store-bought container of cinnamon rolls and we finished off the entire pan. Two hours later, Gwynne headed off to one of our first indoor track workouts of the season. To this day, we are still amazed that cinnamon rolls fueled an entire track workout and managed to make us both feel better. It inspired me to create a homemade version of my own. While I have no doubt that my Cinna-Run-Rolls could fuel even the hardest of workouts, I find that these are truly best enjoyed with friends and teammates after your run."

Butter, for greasing

DOUGH

1 cup whole-wheat flour

1 cup all-purpose flour, plus more for dusting

3 tablespoons coconut sugar

2½ teaspoons baking powder

2 teaspoons ground cinnamon

¾ teaspoon fine sea salt

3 tablespoons unsalted butter

¾ cup whole milk or nut milk

FILLING

½ cup coconut sugar

2 tablespoons unsalted butter, melted

1 teaspoon ground cinnamon

1 Preheat the oven to 350°F. Lightly grease an 8-inch square baking dish with butter.

2 To make the dough, in a large bowl, combine the whole-wheat flour, all-purpose flour, sugar, baking powder, cinnamon, and salt.

3 In a small saucepan, melt the butter over low heat. Whisk in the milk, then pour the mixture over the dry ingredients and use a rubber spatula to combine until a shaggy, wet dough forms.

4 Generously flour a clean work surface. Transfer the dough to the work surface and knead until smooth and no longer sticky, 3 to 4 minutes. Add more all-purpose flour to the work surface as needed, up to an additional ¼ cup, to avoid sticking. Set the dough off to the side and lightly flour the work surface. place the dough back onto the work surface and use a floured rolling pin to roll it out into a 10 x 15-inch rectangle.

5 To make the filling, in a small bowl, combine the sugar, melted butter, and cinnamon and mix until no big clumps remain.

6 Sprinkle the filling evenly over the dough, making sure it reaches the corners and edges. Lightly press the filling down. Starting from one short side, roll up the dough, keeping it as tight as possible to avoid gaps, then pinch the seam to seal. Using a sharp knife,

FROSTING

4 ounces cream cheese, at room temperature

2 tablespoons maple syrup

¼ teaspoon vanilla extract

¼ teaspoon ground cinnamon

carefully slice crosswise into 9 rolls. Place them cut-side up in the prepared baking dish, leaving an even amount of space between each roll. Bake for 30 minutes, or until they have noticeably darkened in color and the filling is bubbling. Place the dish on a hot pad to cool for 15 minutes before frosting.

7 Meanwhile, to make the frosting, in a medium bowl using a handheld mixer, beat the cream cheese until smooth and fluffy, about 2 minutes. Add the maple syrup, vanilla, and cinnamon. Beat again until incorporated.

8 Spread the frosting over the cinnamon rolls while they are still warm. These are best enjoyed immediately, but leftovers can be stored, covered, in the fridge for up to 5 days. Reheat in the microwave until just warm, about 10 seconds.

RUSTIC APPLE GALETTE

for impressing your guests

SERVES 6

VEGETARIAN // VEGAN: Sub in virgin coconut oil for the butter. //

This stunning fruit-filled galette is made with whole-wheat flour, lots of buttah, and very little sugar. If you're stuck inside on a stormy weekend, this is the recipe to make to brighten the mood of your entire household. It's Instagram-worthy and ready for you to proudly photograph (tag us and use #riseandrun if you do post!).

We've wanted to include a pastry recipe in our previous cookbooks, but we always ended up cutting it because it seemed too complex. But by now, our fans are ready for an advanced recipe like this! We've cut unnecessary steps and provided very clear instructions. This recipe isn't super-labor-intensive, but it takes time because you need to allow the ingredients to chill and the dough to rest between steps.

Don't be intimidated by the thought of making your own flaky crust. You've got this!

CRUST
½ cup (1 stick) unsalted butter, cut into cubes

1½ cups whole-wheat pastry flour or all-purpose flour, plus more for dusting

¾ teaspoon fine sea salt

2 tablespoons maple syrup

¼ to ½ cup ice-cold water

FILLING
2 or 3 Granny Smith or Fuji apples (12 ounces total), peeled, cored, and sliced ¼ inch thick

2 tablespoons coconut sugar or cane sugar

1 tablespoon tapioca flour (tapioca starch) or cornstarch

1 tablespoon fresh lemon juice

½ teaspoon ground cinnamon

¼ teaspoon ground nutmeg

1 tablespoon maple syrup

Plain Greek yogurt, for serving (optional)

1. To make the crust, chill the butter in the freezer for 15 minutes (set a timer).

2. Whisk together the flour and salt in a large bowl. Use a pastry blender to cut the chilled butter into the flour until the mixture forms pea-size crumbles. (Alternatively, combine the ingredients in a food processor and pulse until crumbles form.)

3. Drizzle the maple syrup over the flour-butter mixture. While stirring, sprinkle ¼ cup of the water into the mixture, then add more water 1 tablespoon at a time until the dough begins to come together. (If using a food processor, pulse briefly between additions of water just until the dough begins to clump.) Use your hands to shape the dough into a ball, then flatten it slightly, return it to the bowl, cover, and chill in the fridge for 30 minutes.

4. Position a rack in the center of the oven. Preheat the oven to 375°F. Line a baking sheet with parchment paper.

5. To make the filling, in a large bowl, toss the apples with the sugar, tapioca flour, lemon juice, cinnamon, and nutmeg.

(recipe continues)

6 On a lightly floured work surface, roll out the chilled dough into a 12-inch round about ⅛ inch thick. Rotate the dough often while rolling it out and add more flour if needed to prevent sticking. Carefully transfer the dough to the prepared baking sheet.

7 Place the filling in the center of the dough round and spread it out, leaving a 2-inch border. Fold the exposed dough over the filling, forming evenly spaced pleats all the way around.

8 Bake for 20 minutes. Remove from the oven and brush the top of the crust and the exposed filling with the maple syrup. Rotate the baking sheet. Return to the oven and bake for 25 to 30 minutes, until the crust is a deep golden color and the apples are tender.

9 Use the parchment to carefully transfer the galette to a cooling rack. Cool completely before slicing. Serve with a side of Greek yogurt, if desired. This recipe is best the day it is made, but leftovers can be stored in the fridge for up to 5 days.

APPLE-BLUEBERRY
BREAKFAST CRUMBLE

for lazy, sweet mornings

SERVES 6

GLUTEN-FREE // VEGAN //

After years of relishing leftover apple crumble for breakfast, Elyse decided to give her favorite dessert a breakfast makeover. This version is less sweet, grain-free for those with sensitive digestion, and strengthened with protein-packed nuts and seeds. When served with a side of whole-milk yogurt (see page 149), this dish deserves a place on the breakfast podium.

The crumble topping can be made ahead and stays fresh in the fridge for up to a month. Elyse frequently doubles the topping so she'll have it on hand for a last-minute brunch treat (or healthy dessert). You can make individual servings of fruit crumble in ramekins (small white oven-safe bowls) any time the craving strikes.

Coconut oil, for greasing

TOPPING
¾ cup unsweetened coconut flakes

½ cup almond flour or almond meal

½ cup chopped raw walnuts or pecans

½ cup raw pumpkin seeds

¼ cup hemp hearts (hulled hemp seeds) or ground flax

½ teaspoon ground cinnamon

½ teaspoon ground ginger

¼ teaspoon fine sea salt

¼ cup maple syrup

3 tablespoons virgin coconut oil, melted

FILLING
3 crisp apples, peeled, cored, and chopped small (5 to 6 cups)*

2 cups frozen blueberries, thawed

2 tablespoons tapioca flour (tapioca starch) or cornstarch

1 tablespoon fresh lemon juice

Plain Greek yogurt or whole-milk yogurt, for serving

1   Preheat the oven to 400°F. Grease the bottom and sides of an 8-inch square ceramic baking dish with a small amount of coconut oil.

2   To make the topping, in a medium bowl, combine the coconut flakes, almond flour, walnuts, pumpkin seeds, hemp hearts, cinnamon, ginger, and salt. Add the maple syrup and melted coconut oil and stir until combined.

3   To make the filling, in a separate medium bowl, combine the apples, blueberries, tapioca, and lemon juice. Spread the filling over the bottom of the prepared baking dish. Distribute the topping evenly over the fruit and press down lightly.

4   Bake until the topping is golden brown and the apples are tender but still hold their shape, 25 to 30 minutes.

5   Serve warm, with a side of yogurt. Leftovers can be stored, covered, in the fridge for up to 1 week. Simply reheat in the microwave.

Our favorite apple varieties for baking are Granny Smith, Honeycrisp, and Braeburn. These varieties hold up well in the oven, so you don't end up with applesauce.

OAT BANANA BREAD
WITH CAULIFLOWER
for a wholesome makeover

MAKES ONE 9 X 5-INCH LOAF

GLUTEN-FREE: Use certified GF oats. //
VEGETARIAN // **DAIRY-FREE** //

We bet you can't find a healthier banana bread (that actually tastes good!) than this one. Most banana loaves are made with an entire cup of sugar. Our version uses a quarter of this amount, which allows the natural sweetness from the bananas to shine, and we up the ante by using gluten-free oat flour. And here's the secret–there's an entire cup of cauliflower hiding in there.

This quick bread is buttery and has that perfect balance of sweet and salty. You can smell the cauliflower when it first comes out of the oven. But we tested it on our pickiest eaters, and they asked for a second serving!

Typically, banana bread requires a handheld mixer to combine the butter and sugar and beat the eggs. In this recipe, we use a blender instead, which is essential for a smooth batter and helps save time. Just roughly mash the banana, enough to be able to measure it.

1½ cups oat flour
(see note, page 75)

1 cup rolled oats

1 cup almond flour
or almond meal

1 teaspoon baking powder

1 teaspoon baking soda

1 teaspoon ground
cinnamon

½ teaspoon fine sea salt

1 cup mashed banana
(2 to 3 very ripe bananas)

1 cup steamed
cauliflower florets (see
page 264), cooled

2 eggs

⅓ cup virgin coconut oil

¼ cup coconut sugar
or cane sugar

½ cup chopped
walnuts (optional)

1 Position a rack in the center of the oven. Preheat the oven to 350°F. Line a 9 x 5-inch loaf pan with parchment paper.

2 In a large bowl, combine the oat flour, oats, almond meal, baking powder, baking soda, cinnamon, and salt.

3 In a high-speed blender, combine the banana, cauliflower, eggs, coconut oil, and sugar. Blend on high speed for 1 minute. Check for any lumps and blend again until smooth.

4 Pour the wet ingredients over the dry ingredients and use a rubber spatula to scrape out the blender. Add the walnuts (if using) and stir to combine.

5 Pour the batter into the prepared loaf pan and shake the pan to spread the batter evenly. Bake until the top and edges are deep golden brown and the banana bread is firm to the touch, 60 to 65 minutes.

6 Use the parchment paper to carefully lift the loaf out of the pan and transfer it to a cooling rack. Cool completely before slicing, about 1 hour (yes, patience!). This is a tender loaf and will crumble if you slice it too soon.

7 Store the bread, covered, at room temperature for up to 3 days or in an airtight container in the fridge for up to 1 week.

Time Saver Tip: If you don't have the patience to wait for your bananas to ripen, here's a little trick: Put the bananas (with their peels on) in the oven at 300°F for about 20 minutes, until the peels turn completely black. Let cool. Now you have bananas that are perfect for banana bread.

10 | DRINKS AND SMOOTHIES

MATCHA GREEN TEA SMOOTHIE

for balanced energy

SERVES 2 (MAKES 24 OUNCES)

GLUTEN-FREE // VEGAN //

This decadent and energizing smoothie tastes like a cross between green tea ice cream and a matcha latte. The dairy-free crowd will celebrate its creamy flavor and smooth, earthy sweetness. This uplifting smoothie is packed with antioxidants, calcium, and potassium, to name just a few of its benefits—but most important, it just tastes damn good. Sip and savor, friends!

1 cup loosely packed chopped stemmed kale

1 frozen small banana (peel before freezing)

½ cup raw cashews, soaked overnight and drained

1 to 2 tablespoons honey, to taste

2 teaspoons matcha green tea powder

1 cup filtered water, plus more if needed

1 cup ice

2 tablespoons chocolate chips, dark chocolate chunks, or cacao nibs (optional)

1 In a high-speed blender, combine the kale, banana, cashews, honey, matcha, water, and ice. Blend on high for 1 minute, or until smooth. Check for any remaining pieces of ice or banana and blend again if needed. If too thick, add an additional ¼ cup water.

2 For a more decadent smoothie, add the chocolate chips and pulse briefly just to coarsely chop and blend into the smoothie. Serve immediately or store in 1-pint glass jars in the fridge for up to 2 days.

Nutrition Tip: If you have a good-quality blender, it's not completely necessary to soak your cashews for this recipe, but soaking makes nuts easier to digest. Simply place the cashews in a jar, cover with water, and store in the fridge overnight. In the morning, drain and rinse the nuts before adding to the smoothie.

RASPBERRY RIVAL SMOOTHIE

for a power smoothie to ready for competition

SERVES 2 (MAKES 24 OUNCES)

GLUTEN-FREE // VEGAN //

This energizing smoothie highlights Shalane's favorite fruit–raspberries. Raspberries are high in vitamin C for immune support and vitamin K and manganese for bone health. They're antioxidant powerhouses, which runners need for healing and recovery.

We paired raspberries with carrot, orange, and our rich Vanilla Almond Milk for a creamy, dreamy smoothie. This smoothie is high in omega-3s and healthy fats. To make it a meal, see our Protein Boost and Nutrition Tip below.

1 cup frozen raspberries or frozen mixed berries

1 large navel orange, peeled, halved, and seeded

1 carrot, halved

3 Deglet Noor dates, pitted

2 tablespoons hemp hearts (hulled hemp seeds)

1 cup Vanilla Almond Milk (page 253) or store-bought nut milk*

1 cup ice

*If using store-bought nut milk, which is lower in protein and fat than homemade, add 2 tablespoons raw cashews or 1 tablespoon almond butter to make it deliciously creamy.

In a high-speed blender, combine the raspberries, orange, carrot, dates, hemp hearts, milk, and ice. Blend on high speed for several minutes, until smooth (use the tamper tool to keep the ingredients moving). Serve immediately or store in 1-pint glass jars in the fridge for up to 2 days.

PROTEIN BOOST: *Add ¼ cup plain Greek yogurt or 2 tablespoons collagen peptides or hemp protein powder. These are our preferred protein sources for smoothies. Skip pea protein, rice protein, and whey protein powders, which are difficult to digest and often high in additives and toxins. In general, we prefer to get our protein from whole-food sources or from reputable brands like Vital Proteins, Great Lakes Gelatin Company, and NOW Real Food (organic hemp protein).*

Nutrition Tip: *If you like to "chew" your smoothie so that it feels more like a meal, stir in a handful of granola (like the Molasses Tahini Granola on page 128).*

I'm definitely a morning person. My favorite part about mornings: It's a new day and a fresh start. I love watching the sun come up during morning practice, being productive, and enjoying a good cup of coffee.

—LINSEY CORBIN,
pro triathlete and Ironman champion

CAN'T BEET ME SMOOTHIE III

for a morning power boost

SERVES 2

GLUTEN-FREE //
VEGAN: Use nondairy yogurt. //

Every Sunday as part of Elyse's meal prep routine, she steams a few beets for smoothies. Beets are a nutritional powerhouse and are nearly undetectable when combined with the berries, yogurt, and seeds in this creamy and refreshing smoothie. Elyse likes to include yogurt in her smoothies for the probiotics and bone-building minerals it contains, but this recipe can easily be made vegan by substituting dairy-free yogurt, nut milk, or half an avocado.

This vibrant smoothie provides a balanced breakfast, which is perfect for rushed mornings. Prep it ahead, pack it in a mason jar, and store in the fridge, then grab it to sip on your way to work or school. Stir in shredded coconut or granola if you like to "chew" your smoothies, which is great for satiation and digestion.

1 beet, steamed and peeled (see note)

1 heaping cup frozen strawberries

½ cup frozen blueberries

½ cup plain whole-milk yogurt

¼ cup raw pumpkin seeds

2 tablespoons peanut butter

1 (1-inch) knob fresh ginger, peeled, or ¼ teaspoon ground ginger

1½ cups coconut water*

The coconut water provides electrolytes and sweetens up the smoothie. If you prefer, you can substitute filtered water and then add a few dates to sweeten to taste.

In a high-speed blender, combine the beet, strawberries, blueberries, yogurt, pumpkin seeds, peanut butter, ginger, and coconut water. Blend on high speed for several minutes, until smooth. Serve immediately in two tall glasses (smoothies made with blueberries are best served fresh, as the pectin in the blueberries will give the smoothie a gloppy texture if stored overnight in the fridge).

STEAMED BEETS: *Steaming is the best cooking technique to preserve the nutrients in beets: Fill a pot with 1 inch of water and set a steamer basket in the pot. Quarter the beet and place it in the steamer basket. Cover, bring the water to a simmer, and cook for 20 minutes, or until the beet is soft when pierced with a fork. Allow to cool, then peel the beet and use it as you like, or store in an airtight container in the fridge for up to 5 days. If you're using a high-speed blender like a Vitamix, you can also leave the beet raw (simply wash and peel it).*

PUMPKIN PIE SMOOTHIE

for a festive fall smoothie

SERVES 2

GLUTEN-FREE // VEGAN //

Training for a fall marathon or a PR in the Turkey Trot? Make this fruit-and-veggie-loaded smoothie weekly to replenish your body's vitamins and minerals. Use the leftover pumpkin to whip up a batch of our favorite grain-free muffins (page 92), and you'll be hot to trot.

1 cup frozen steamed cauliflower florets (see page 264)

½ cup canned pure pumpkin puree

¼ cup raw walnuts or cashews

½ apple, quartered and cored

1 carrot, halved

4 Deglet Noor dates, pitted

1 tablespoon fresh lime juice (optional)

1½ teaspoons Chai Spice Mix (page 274) or pumpkin pie spice

1½ cups filtered water

1   In a high-speed blender, combine the cauliflower, pumpkin, nuts, apple, carrot, dates, lime juice (if using), chai spice mix, and water. Blend on high speed for several minutes, until smooth (use the tamper tool to keep the ingredients moving).

2   Serve immediately or store in 1-pint jars in the fridge for up to 2 days.

SMOOTHIE BOWL: This recipe is also delicious as a fall-inspired smoothie bowl. Use just ½ cup water and top it with Goddess Grain-Free Granola (page 127) and chopped apple.

CHOCOLATE AVOCADO SMOOTHIE

for an indulgent recovery drink

SERVES 2

GLUTEN-FREE // VEGAN //

This decadent smoothie is a treat any time of day. It's creamy and refreshing, and surprisingly loaded with nourishing ingredients like heart-healthy avocado, vitamin-rich zucchini, and antioxidant-rich chocolate. It's Shalane's new favorite smoothie after a hot run, as it's also high in essential electrolytes to help you hydrate.

To take this recipe to the next level, don't skimp on the chocolate. We like to briefly pulse in chocolate chips at the end to add texture. This helps you sip the smoothie more slowly, which is great for digestion.

---

1 small or ½ large ripe avocado, pitted and peeled

1 cup steamed frozen zucchini rounds (see note)

3 Medjool or 5 Deglet Noor dates, pitted

2 tablespoons unsweetened cocoa powder

2 tablespoons almond butter or cashew butter

2 cups coconut water

1 cup ice

2 tablespoons dark chocolate chips, chopped dark chocolate (from a bar), or cacao nibs

1 In a high-speed blender, combine the avocado, zucchini, dates, cocoa powder, nut butter, coconut water, and ice. Blend on high speed for 1 minute, until smooth. Check for any remaining whole chunks of ice and blend again if needed.

2 Add the chocolate and pulse briefly, just to coarsely chop and blend it into the smoothie. This smoothie is best served immediately.

STEAMED ZUCCHINI: *Wash 3 zucchini, discard the ends, and slice into 1-inch-thick rounds. (You should have 3 to 4 cups, depending on the size of your zucchini.) Fill a large pot with 1 inch of water and fit a steamer basket in the pot. Put the zucchini in the basket, cover, and bring the water to a boil. Reduce the heat to maintain a simmer and steam the zucchini until fork-tender, about 8 minutes. Spread the steamed zucchini over a baking sheet and cool completely. Transfer 1-cup portions of the zucchini into individual silicone or plastic zipper bags and freeze to use in this recipe or other smoothies.*

GREEN VITALITY SMOOTHIE

for sipping the vitamin alphabet

SERVES 2

GLUTEN-FREE // VEGAN: Use dairy-free yogurt or sub in nut milk. //

This vitamin-loaded smoothie will wake you up better than coffee. It will remind you of your favorite $8 green juice, but with fat for staying power instead of sugar. It's high in essential electrolytes, including potassium, calcium, and magnesium, and rich in vitamins A, B, C, and K.

If you like apples dipped in peanut butter, you'll love the flavor combos in this creamy smoothie. Cheers to sipping the alphabet at sunrise.

---

1 large Granny Smith apple, quartered and cored

½ frozen banana (peel before freezing)

1 cup tightly packed chopped stemmed kale

1 cup frozen steamed cauliflower florets (see page 264)

½ cup plain whole-milk yogurt

3 tablespoons creamy peanut butter

½ teaspoon ground cinnamon

1½ cups coconut water*

*We use coconut water as a smooth way to sweeten this smoothie, but you can use filtered water instead. If using water, we recommend adding a few dates or a spoonful of honey to enhance the flavor.

In a high-speed blender, combine the apple, banana, kale, cauliflower, yogurt, peanut butter, cinnamon, and coconut water. Blend on high speed for several minutes, until smooth.

NOTE: *If you like your smoothie icy (especially satisfying on a hot day), add a handful of ice cubes before blending.*

Nutrition Tip: Steam your greens! If you drink a lot of green smoothies, we recommend lightly steaming the kale prior to adding it to this smoothie. Raw greens are high in oxalic acid, an antinutrient, which may interfere with your absorption of minerals—not good for athletes. To do this, fill a pot with about 1 inch of water and set a steamer basket inside. Place the kale in the steamer basket. Cover, bring the water to a simmer, and cook for 1 minute, or until just slightly wilted (vibrant green color). Transfer the kale to a bowl and stash in the fridge until ready to use.

Time Saver Tip: This smoothie holds its creamy texture well and can be blended the night before and stored in 1-pint jars in the fridge for up to 2 days.

ELECTROLYTE SMOOTHIE

for replenishing post-run

SERVES 2

GLUTEN-FREE // VEGAN //

Every ingredient in this smoothie was carefully selected for maximum electrolyte replacement. After a hard sweat session, drinking plain water can cause an electrolyte imbalance, which can lead to sudden-onset nausea or headaches. Been there–not fun!

The electrolytes that your body depletes while running, especially on a hot day, include sodium, chloride, calcium, magnesium, and potassium. Coach Shalane says this smoothie is so perfect after Long Runs on warm days. Check out the chart below to see which foods are highest in each of these vital minerals. Sip smarter!

1 cup frozen chopped pineapple

½ frozen banana (peel before freezing)

1 cup tightly packed baby spinach or stemmed kale (see Nutrition Tip, page 234)

2 celery stalks, halved

2 tablespoons almond butter or cashew butter

2 tablespoons hemp hearts (hulled help seeds)

⅛ teaspoon fine sea salt

1 cup coconut water

1 cup ice

1 lime (optional)

1 In a high-speed blender, combine the pineapple, banana, spinach, celery, nut butter, hemp seeds, salt, coconut water, and ice. Blend on high speed for several minutes, until smooth (use the tamper tool to keep the ingredients moving).

2 If desired, add a squeeze of fresh lime juice and garnish with a slice of lime. Best served immediately.

Eat Your Electrolytes

CALCIUM: milk, yogurt, cheese, nuts, seeds, beans, leafy greens

CHLORIDE: celery, tomatoes, olives, salt

MAGNESIUM: nuts, seeds, banana, avocado, whole grains, legumes, blackstrap molasses, dark chocolate, leafy greens

POTASSIUM: banana, orange, watermelon, potatoes, sweet potatoes, leafy greens

SODIUM: table salt, sea salt, olives, pickles

BLUEBERRY BLISS SMOOTHIE BOWL

for easing into your morning

SERVES 2

GLUTEN-FREE // **VEGETARIAN** //

Every summer we road trip to Hood River to pick local blueberries. We rinse, dry, and store them in bags in our freezer. They never last as long as we hope, since frozen blueberries are so good in muffins, smoothies, oatmeal, pies, and crumbles. Definitely the most perfect breakfast fruit.

The whole family will enjoy this decadent, thick, creamy smoothie bowl. It's a beauty, especially when decorated with your fave toppings. Put out a spread of nuts, dried fruit, and granola and let everyone come up with their own creation.

1 cup frozen blueberries

1 frozen small banana (peel before freezing)

½ cup plain whole-milk Greek yogurt

½ cup nut milk (such as Vanilla Almond Milk, page 253), plus more if needed

2 tablespoons chia seeds

2 tablespoons peanut butter or almond butter

¼ teaspoon ground cinnamon (optional)

TOPPINGS: fresh berries, sliced banana, Molasses Tahini Granola (page 128), Goddess Grain-Free Granola (page 127), nuts, coconut flakes, hemp seeds, chia seeds, pumpkin seeds, cacao nibs or chocolate chips, honey

1 In a high-speed blender, combine the blueberries, banana, yogurt, nut milk, chia seeds, nut butter, and cinnamon (if using). Blend on high speed for 1 minute, or until smooth (use the tamper tool to keep the ingredients moving). The texture should be thick, but if your blender sticks, add an extra tablespoon or two of milk. Use a rubber spatula to scrape down the sides and blend again.

2 Divide between two bowls. Top with fresh berries and your favorite toppings and enjoy.

Time Saver Tip: This smoothie can be prepped the night before. Divide between two 1-pint widemouthed glass jars and store in the fridge. Add the toppings just before serving.

Nutrition Tip: If you want to sneak a veggie into this smoothie, add a raw carrot or steamed beet (see page 231). Avoid using raw greens like spinach, kale, and Swiss chard in smoothies, as they're high in oxalic acid, an antinutrient, which may interfere with your absorption of minerals. Consume raw greens in moderation or gently steam them (see page 234) before adding to your smoothie.

PREP-AHEAD SMOOTHIE PACKETS

for rushed mornings

MAKES SIX 2-SERVING PACKETS

GLUTEN-FREE // **VEGAN** //

Ya'll know how much we love smoothies. Smoothies taste best when they're freshly blended, but adding all the individual ingredients to the blender every morning became tedious, so we started making smoothie packets in bulk—and it's been a game changer.

This might seem like a lot of effort up front, but it will save you significant time when you need it most (mornings!). After steaming your vegetable of choice, chop it into bite-size pieces so it blends up easily when frozen. We used seeds in this recipe because they're easy to blend. Alternatively, you could put a spoonful of peanut butter or almond butter in each packet or add your fat of choice later.

6 cups mixed frozen fruit (strawberries, blueberries, raspberries, mango, pineapple, or peaches)

3 cups chopped steamed vegetable of choice (zucchini, cauliflower, or beets)*

3 ripe bananas, peeled and halved

6 (1-inch) pieces fresh ginger, peeled (optional)

¾ cup raw pumpkin seeds

¾ cup hemp hearts (hulled hemp seeds)

1½ cups liquid of choice (coconut water; Vanilla Almond Milk, page 253; filtered water), for serving

How to steam veggies for smoothies:
Beets: see page 231
Zucchini: see page 233
Cauliflower: see page 264

1. Place 1 cup of fruit, ½ cup of veggies, ½ banana, and 1 piece of ginger (if using) in each of six 1-quart zipper bags (preferably silicone or other reusable bags). Add 2 tablespoons of pumpkin seeds and 2 tablespoons of hemp hearts to each bag. Seal the bags and lay them flat in the freezer. Freeze overnight or until ready to use.

2. To serve, transfer the contents of one packet to a high-speed blender and add your liquid of choice. Blend on high speed for several minutes, until smooth (use the tamper tool to keep the ingredients moving). Since the ingredients are frozen, you'll need more liquid than usual; if the smoothie is too thick to blend, add a splash of water.

ADDITIONS: To sweeten your smoothie, add a few pitted dates. For a creamier smoothie, add ⅓ cup whole milk or Greek yogurt (do not freeze). For a protein boost, add peanut butter, almond butter, collagen peptides powder, or hemp protein powder.

CREAMY CHAI CAULIFLOWER SMOOTHIE BOWL

for a healing jump-start

SERVES 2

GLUTEN-FREE // **VEGAN** //

We were a bit skeptical when we heard that putting cauliflower in smoothies is a thing. Super-duper healthy, but would it actually taste good?! Elyse decided to take the hit for the team and give it a try. She paired the cauliflower with cashews to up the creaminess factor and added dates and healing spices to satisfy morning cravings.

She was blown away by the end result. This smoothie bowl is so good, we could eat it for dessert with granola. (Ice cream for breakfast, anyone?!) It's also surprisingly filling, especially when you sprinkle on your favorite toppings. It's dreamy topped with Goddess Grain-Free Granola (page 127) or Molasses Tahini Granola (page 128).

You can whirl this breakfast together faster than Shalane can run a mile, but be sure to follow the instructions and get things started the night before.

---

2 cups filtered water

½ cup raw cashews

4 to 6 Deglet Noor dates, pitted

1 (1-inch) knob fresh ginger, peeled*

½ teaspoon ground cinnamon*

¼ teaspoon ground cardamom (optional)*

Pinch of sea salt

1 cup frozen steamed cauliflower florets

1 frozen small banana (peel before freezing)

TOPPINGS: granola, chopped nuts, coconut flakes, berries, chopped peaches or apples, honey or blackstrap molasses, hemp seeds or pumpkin seeds

*To save time, you can substitute ½ teaspoon Chai Spice Mix (page 274) for the ginger, cinnamon, and cardamom.

1 **The night before:** In a 1-quart mason jar, combine the water, cashews, dates, ginger, cinnamon, cardamom (if using), and salt. Cover and store in the fridge overnight. Prep the cauliflower (see page 264).

2 **In the morning:** In a high-speed blender, combine the contents of the mason jar, the cauliflower, and the banana. Blend on high speed for 1 minute, or until smooth (use the tamper tool to keep the ingredients moving). Check for any remaining whole pieces of cauliflower and blend again if needed.

3 Divide between two bowls. Decorate with your favorite toppings and serve. Leftovers (without toppings) can be stored in a jar in the fridge for up to 2 days.

🕐 *Time Saver Tip: To have your cauliflower at the ready, after steaming, spread it out on a sheet pan to cool completely. Transfer 1-cup portions of the cauliflower into individual silicone zipper bags and freeze to use in smoothies.*

SUNRISE JUICE

for an instant glow

MAKES 30 OUNCES (ABOUT 3½ CUPS)

GLUTEN-FREE // VEGAN //

We prefer smoothies over juice because there is less waste, and a lot of the great nutrition in fruits and vegetables is in the fiber, which you can't get when you make juice. But every so often a really good juice hits the spot, especially post-run. This recipe is inspired by Elyse's favorite juicer-y/eatery, Sunny Yoga Kitchen. Drink this any time you're feeling run down, for an instant glow. This concoction is spicy and heavy on the carrots, which we love, but feel free to tweak the amounts to suit your taste buds.

When you do break out your juicer, consider juicing more ginger than you need—like a whole pound—and freezing it for Lemon Electrolyte Water (page 244), tea, smoothies, and Digestion Tonic (page 246).

6 navel oranges, peeled (use a paring knife)

6 carrots, unpeeled (if the carrots are large, reduce to 4)

1 (4-inch) piece fresh ginger

1 (3-inch) piece fresh turmeric (optional)

Sparkling mineral water (optional)

1 Follow the instructions that came with your juicer to juice the oranges, carrots, ginger, and turmeric (if using) into the pitcher. Taste the juice; if it's too sweet or spicy, dilute it with sparkling mineral water.

2 Stir, then pour into tall glasses over ice and serve, or store in glass jars in the fridge. Since fresh juice is unpasteurized, it should be consumed within 3 days.

NOTE: *This recipe requires a high-powered juicer (with a hard vegetable setting to break down the ginger). We recommend using a cold-press juicer to preserve nutrients. Elyse likes the Breville brand, but there are other options available online.*

LEMON ELECTROLYTE WATER

for smart hydration

MAKES 34 OUNCES (ABOUT 4 CUPS)

GLUTEN-FREE // VEGAN //

This recipe is so simple but essential. It's become our go-to for hydration both before and after sweaty runs. Sports drinks are definitely beneficial, but they're often high in added sugar or artificial sweeteners, making them handy but not something to drink every day.

When it comes to smart hydration, chugging plain water doesn't always cut it. Without the right electrolyte balance, our bodies have difficulty absorbing water. Too much water can cause the sodium levels in your blood to drop to below normal, which leads to a very serious condition called hyponatremia. Symptoms include headaches, nausea, dizziness, and vomiting as the body tries to rid itself of the excess water. Learn more about essential electrolytes on page 236.

When Elyse shakes up this concoction, she always includes fresh ginger to soothe digestion and inflammation.

2 cups coconut water

2 cups filtered water

¼ cup fresh lemon juice

2 tablespoons fresh ginger juice (optional; see tip, page 246)

¼ teaspoon fine sea salt

In a pitcher, combine the coconut water, filtered water, lemon juice, ginger juice (if using), and salt. Stir to combine. Serve or store in a covered pitcher in the fridge for up to 1 week.

Nutrition Tip: Everyone's hydration needs vary greatly. This recipe can easily be customized to suit you. Sweaty run and craving salt? Add more. Sensitive digestion? Include the ginger. Sipping during a long run and need the calories? Add more coconut water, honey, or a scoop of your favorite sports drink powder. Too sweet? Use less coconut water.

DIGESTION TONIC

for awakening your digestion

MAKES ABOUT 4 CUPS

GLUTEN-FREE // VEGAN //

This tonic combines all our favorite ingredients for healing a stressed digestive system. Ginger, apple cider vinegar, and lemon juice have earned their respect as gut-healing foods. When we combined these powerhouse ingredients into one beverage, we were surprised at just how delicious and refreshing it turned out. Elyse now makes this drink weekly. She especially likes to drink it the day before her Sunday Long Run (see page 45).

Drink one cup first thing every morning or sip a little before every meal to awaken your digestive fire. The enzyme-rich apple cider vinegar, alkalizing lemon juice, and anti-inflammatory ginger will help you start your day right. Ginger has been used for centuries as a digestive aid to relieve gas and soothe the belly. If the flavor is too strong, add sparkling water.

3 cups filtered water

1 tablespoon raw or local honey

2 tablespoons unfiltered apple cider vinegar

2 tablespoons fresh lemon juice

2 teaspoons fresh ginger juice (see notes)

1 Heat 1 cup of the water on the stove or in the microwave and pour into a 1-quart mason jar. Add the honey and stir to dissolve. Add the remaining 2 cups cold water. Stir in the vinegar, lemon juice, and ginger juice. Put the lid on the jar and refrigerate until chilled before serving.

2 Since the ginger juice is not pasteurized, this should be stored in the fridge and consumed within 3 days.

GINGER JUICE: *You'll need a high-powered juicer to extract the juice from whole ginger root. Juicing ginger can be a pain due to the mess of cleaning the juicer. To make it worth the effort, Elyse juices a couple of pounds of ginger all in one fell swoop and then freezes the ginger juice in small freezer-safe glass jars to always have it at the ready. Freezing the juice in an ice cube tray would also give you the right size portions to make this tonic.*

GINGER TEA: No juicer? No problem. You can still make this recipe by first making a strong ginger tea: Bring all 3 cups of the water to a boil in a pot over high heat. Peel and grate a 3-inch piece of fresh ginger. Place the grated ginger in a tea ball and add it to the pot (or just add the ginger directly to the water). Reduce the heat to low, cover, and simmer for 20 minutes.

Remove the tea ball or pour through a tea strainer fitted inside a 1-quart widemouthed glass jar. Stir in the honey. Allow to cool. Stir in the apple cider vinegar and lemon juice. Put the lid on the jar and chill before serving. Store in the fridge for up to 3 days.

IMMUNE-BOOSTING TONIC

for firing up all your systems

MAKES 2½ CUPS

GLUTEN-FREE // **VEGAN** //

This concoction sounds like a witch's potion, and it kind of is. And it works. Pungent and invigorating, it will definitely wake you up, firing up your digestive and immune systems any time you're under the weather. It goes down easily, thanks to the addition of apple juice. Drinking just a little goes a long way. Keep it fresh by storing it in an ice cube tray in the freezer, so you'll always have small portions at the ready.

Immune-boosting foods seem to work when we're able to catch a virus in the early stages, before it has the chance to settle into our systems. Elyse has found that if she consumes raw garlic when she starts to feel a scratchy throat, a telltale sign of a cold coming on, she's often able to head it off.

Funny enough, this is the only recipe in this cookbook that we are still waiting on Shalane to test. Be brave, girl!

1 cup unfiltered apple juice (store-bought or freshly juiced)

1 cup filtered water

1 lemon, peeled, halved, and seeded

2 garlic cloves, peeled

1 (2-inch) piece fresh ginger, peeled

⅛ teaspoon cayenne pepper

1. In a high-speed blender, combine the apple juice, water, lemon, garlic, ginger, and cayenne. Blend on high speed for 1 minute, or until smooth. Pour into a jar, cover, and refrigerate.

2. Drink a shot-glass–size amount about 15 minutes before a meal and chase with water. Store in the fridge for up to 3 days if using fresh apple juice and up to 5 days if using pasteurized apple juice. Or freeze in ice cube trays, transfer the cubes to a zipper bag, and store in the freezer for up to 3 months.

DISCLAIMER: *Do not drink this tonic before running. Do not drink this before a date! You may want to brush your teeth immediately after consuming!*

What will get you to the finish line is nothing compared to what got you to the start.

–ADRIANNE HASLET,
Boston Strong survivor and para athlete

MATCHA COLLAGEN LATTE

for post-run protein bliss

MAKES 1 LATTE

GLUTEN-FREE //
VEGAN: Skip the honey. //

We aren't big on protein powders since they can inflict digestive troubles, but if there is one protein supplement that we do embrace, it's collagen peptides. The best collagen supplements have just one ingredient and the highest sourcing standards (grass-fed, free-range, contaminant-testing protocols).

Modern diets are lacking in collagen, which is found naturally in homemade bone broth (you can find our recipe on page 152). It's an essential nutrient for high-mileage runners looking to give their skin, nails, bones, and joints a much-needed boost.

When Shalane told Elyse that she drinks collagen daily in her morning tea, Elyse thought that sounded rather unappetizing. Together they came up with this healing recipe—the collagen is nearly undetectable. Sip and contemplate your day ahead.

1 tablespoon collagen peptides powder

1 teaspoon matcha green tea powder

8 ounces boiling water

1 teaspoon honey, or more to taste

Splash of whole milk or Vanilla Almond Milk (page 253)

Place the collagen and matcha in your favorite mug. Pour the boiling water into the mug, leaving room for milk. Stir thoroughly with a fork. Add the honey and milk to taste, stir, and enjoy.

PRACTICE "MINDFUL MORNINGS" *while you sip your a.m. beverage of choice. Check out page 19 for inspiration from our favorite yoga instructor.*

Nutrition Tip: Matcha is expensive, but a little goes a long way. It's high in antioxidants and phytonutrients. It's energizing and contains about a third of the caffeine of coffee. Matcha is Elyse's beverage of choice when she's writing and needs a brain boost. We also love it in our Matcha Green Tea Smoothie (page 227).

ANTI-INFLAMMATORY CASHEW MILK

for a golden start

MAKES 4 CUPS

GLUTEN-FREE // VEGAN //

Store-bought nut milk has a ton of additives that can be difficult to digest and is often low in nutrients since there are so few nuts actually hiding in that carton. Making your own nut milk saves you moola and cuts down on landfill waste. Win-win.

We're fans of homemade almond and hazelnut milks, but making them is a time commitment. Cashew milk is the easiest dairy-free milk to make because the nuts get really soft when soaked so you don't have to strain the milk.

This is our go-to nut milk for so many recipes. We use it in Chai Chia Seed Parfaits (page 140), Overnight Oats (page 137), our Apple Maple Butter Oatmeal Bake (page 132), Steel-Cut Oatmeal (page 150), smoothies, and coffee or tea. For best results, use a high-speed blender like a Vitamix.

¾ cup raw cashews

6 Deglet Noor or 3 Medjool dates, pitted

1 (1-inch) knob fresh ginger, peeled*

1 (1-inch) knob fresh turmeric,* peeled, or ½ teaspoon ground turmeric

About 3 cups filtered water

If you don't have fresh ginger and turmeric, you can use ½ teaspoon Chai Spice Mix (page 274) instead.

1 Place the cashews, dates, ginger, and turmeric in a 1-quart glass jar. Fill to the top with water. Seal with a lid and place in the fridge to soak overnight.

2 In the morning, pour the contents of the jar into a high-speed blender. Blend on high until smooth and creamy.

3 Store in the same jar in the fridge for up to 4 days.

NOTE: *This ratio of nuts to water results in a creamy "whole milk"-style cashew milk, but more water can be added for a lighter result.*

Time Saver Tip: *One-quart mason jars are our favorite containers for storing family-size smoothies, homemade tea, and sports drinks, but if you don't have this size jar, you can use a pitcher or bowl with a lid (just add 3 cups water; don't fill to the top).*

CHOCOLATE CASHEW MILK

for a post-run chocolate milk craving

MAKES 4 CUPS

GLUTEN-FREE // VEGAN //

Runners love chocolate milk as a post-workout hydrating drink. Store-bought chocolate milk is loaded with sugar and made with ultra-pasteurized and homogenized milk, which is difficult to digest. This simple nondairy chocolate milk promises to satisfy, and delivers glycogen, minerals, protein, and fat without slowing you down.

¾ cup raw cashews

6 Deglet Noor dates, pitted

1 tablespoon plus 1½ teaspoons unsweetened cocoa powder

¼ teaspoon vanilla extract

Pinch of fine sea salt

About 3 cups filtered water

1 Place the cashews, dates, cocoa powder, vanilla, and salt in a 1-quart glass jar. Fill to the top with water. Seal with a lid and place in the fridge to soak overnight.

2 In the morning, pour the contents of the jar into a high-speed blender. Blend on high until smooth and creamy.

3 Store in the same jar in the fridge for up to 4 days.

RECOVERY CASHEW MILKSHAKE

for a replenishing post-run snack

Makes 1 milkshake

GLUTEN-FREE // **VEGAN:** Leave out the collagen peptides. //

Transform your cashew milk into a refreshing and indulgent recovery "milkshake" by adding frozen bananas, easy-to-digest protein (peanut butter), and whole-food omega-3 fatty acids (seeds), which are good for fighting inflammation.

1 cup homemade cashew milk (page 250)

1 frozen small banana (peel before freezing)

1 cup baby spinach or stemmed kale leaves (see tip, page 234)

1 tablespoon ground flax or hemp hearts (hulled hemp seeds)

1 tablespoon peanut butter

1 tablespoon collagen peptides powder (optional)

1 cup ice

1 In a high-speed blender, combine the cashew milk, banana, spinach, ground flax, peanut butter, collagen peptides (if using), and ice. Blend on high speed for several minutes, until smooth.

2 Serve immediately or store in 1-pint glass jars in the fridge for up to 2 days.

IRON ALMOND MILK

for a creamy and delicious mineral boost

MAKES 40 OUNCES (ABOUT 5 CUPS)

GLUTEN-FREE // **VEGAN** //

This rich and creamy almond milk serves up a daily dose of iron. It's satisfying as a snack simply served over ice, or take it up a notch and serve it alongside our beloved Trail Mix Breakfast Cookies (page 115).

This functional beverage is a lifesaver for female distance runners who need the extra iron. We've combined calcium-rich nuts with iron-loaded blackstrap molasses and mineral-rich cocoa powder for an ideal recovery drink. Soaking the almonds overnight helps remove phytic acid and enzyme inhibitors, which increases digestibility and nutrient bioavailability.

1½ cups raw almonds, soaked overnight

4 cups cold filtered water

3 tablespoons blackstrap molasses

2 tablespoons unsweetened cocoa powder

⅛ teaspoon fine sea salt

1 Drain and rinse the almonds. Place the almonds and water in a high-speed blender. Begin blending on low speed, slowly increasing the speed to the blender's highest setting, and whir for 1 to 2 minutes, until smooth and creamy.

2 Pour into a nut-milk bag* set over a bowl with a pour spout. Twist the top of the bag to seal it and then knead and squeeze the bag over the bowl to collect the milk, extracting as much liquid as possible.

3 Give the blender a quick rinse and pour the almond milk back into it. Add the molasses, cocoa powder, and salt. Blend briefly to combine.

4 Pour the milk into a 1-quart glass jar, seal, and store in the fridge for up to 4 days. Separation is normal; shake before serving.

5 Save the fiber-and-protein-rich pulp. You can use it in smoothies or sneak it into oatmeal, granola, or muffins. Store in an airtight container in the fridge for up to 5 days or in the freezer for up to 3 months.

If you don't have a nut-milk bag, you can use cheesecloth. Rinse a 12-inch piece of cheesecloth in cold water and wring it out. Fold it in half and use it to line a mesh sieve. Set the sieve over a bowl, pour a small amount of the nut mixture into the sieve, gather up the edges of the cheesecloth, and twist and squeeze to extract as much liquid as possible. Set aside the pulp and repeat with the remaining nut mixture. Do not use a sieve without the cheesecloth to strain the nut milk.

VANILLA ALMOND MILK

for a basic rich nut milk

MAKES 40 OUNCES (ABOUT 5 CUPS)

GLUTEN-FREE // **VEGAN** //

We can't get enough of our Iron Almond Milk (page 252), so we also came up with this rich, rewarding all-purpose vanilla-flavored nut milk, which can be used in many of our recipes as a substitute for whole milk.

It's delicious in Sunrise Overnight Oats (page 139), pancakes and waffles (pages 162 and 163), and smoothies (pages 228, 237, and 249), or just sipped straight up. We love it as a base for iced coffee, chai tea, and Matcha Collagen Lattes (page 249). Once you start making your own nut milk, it's hard to go back to the store-bought stuff, which has zero nourishment and subpar flavor.

Be sure to soak the almonds overnight, which increases their digestibility and nutrient bioavailability by removing phytic acid and enzyme inhibitors.

1½ cups raw almonds, soaked overnight

4 or 5 dates, pitted

4 cups cold filtered water

½ teaspoon vanilla extract

⅛ teaspoon fine sea salt

1 Drain and rinse the almonds. Place the almonds, dates, and cold water in a high-speed blender. Begin blending on low speed, slowly increasing the speed to the blender's highest setting, and whir for 1 to 2 minutes, until smooth and creamy.

2 Pour into a nut-milk bag (or use cheesecloth; see page 252) set over a bowl with a pour spout. Twist the top of the bag to seal it and then knead and squeeze the bag over the bowl to collect the milk, extracting as much liquid as possible.

3 Pour the almond milk into a large (1½-quart) glass jar or pitcher. Add the vanilla and salt and stir to combine. Cover with a lid. Store in the fridge for up to 5 days. Separation is normal; shake before serving.

Time Saver Tip: Freshly made almond milk freezes really well. Freeze any portion that you won't drink within 4 days in freezer-safe glass half-pint jars for up to 3 months. Thaw overnight in the fridge and shake before using.

MARATHON MOCHA

for long-lasting energy

MAKES 1 MOCHA

GLUTEN-FREE // VEGAN //

This drink is crazy good. Make it once, and you'll be craving it all summer long. Sip slowly and savor it as you stretch outside post-run, to recharge and seize the day ahead.

Handful of ice

½ cup brewed coffee, cooled (or cold-brew coffee)

½ cup Iron Almond Milk (page 252)

Place the ice in a tall glass. Pour the coffee and almond milk over the top. Stir and serve with a straw.

"My morning ritual is all about the coffee! I either go to my favorite coffee shop or I make a fancy coffee at home. I'm pretty picky about it, so it's a process: I use a hand grinder, my favorite beans, and either an AeroPress or pour-over with steamed rice milk. It's the best 15 minutes to sit there with a cup and mentally prepare for my workout!"

—MOLLY HUDDLE, *Olympian*

SIP ME HOT COCOA

for winter comfort

SERVES 1

GLUTEN-FREE // VEGETARIAN //

When life gives you snow, drink hot cocoa. Blustery winter days call for warming up from the inside out. Get inspired to get outside for an icy run by promising yourself a mug of hot chocolate, a good book, and maybe even lounging fireside upon your return (okay, dreaming!).

Store-bought hot cocoa mixes are loaded with mysterious ingredients. Make your own decadent mug with a few simple ingredients that you probably already have on hand. Bonus: A cup of this cocoa provides antioxidants, iron, calcium, and other minerals.

1½ cups whole milk*

1 tablespoon plus 1 teaspoon coconut sugar

1 tablespoon plus 1 teaspoon unsweetened cocoa powder

¼ teaspoon vanilla extract (optional)

1 (½-ounce) square dark chocolate (70% cacao or higher; optional)

1 Heat the milk in a small saucepan over low heat until hot but not boiling, about 3 minutes. Remove from the heat. Add the sugar, cocoa powder, and vanilla (if using) and whisk to combine.

2 Pour into your favorite mug. Add a square of chocolate for a melty treat at the end, if desired.

Whole milk works best for hot chocolate, but if you're sensitive to dairy, this cocoa is also good with store-bought unsweetened hemp milk or homemade Vanilla Almond Milk (page 253). We found that store-bought almond milk didn't have a great result.

TURMERIC TEA

for self-care mornings

MAKES 32 OUNCES (4 CUPS)

GLUTEN-FREE //
VEGAN: Skip the honey. //

Turmeric is a proven healing spice. Rich in the anti-inflammatory and immune-boosting compound curcumin, it is used medicinally across cultures to help treat a variety of ailments, from arthritis to IBS. This caffeine-free herbal tea can be sipped throughout the day. The addition of black pepper and milk (or any fat) helps with absorption for maximum benefits.

4 cups water

¼ cup grated fresh turmeric* (about two 4-inch pieces)

¼ teaspoon ground black pepper

Coconut milk, whole milk, or rich nut milk (such as Vanilla Almond Milk, page 253), for serving

Honey, for serving

*If using fresh turmeric, there is no need to peel it—just wash it well. If you can't find fresh turmeric root, you can substitute 1 tablespoon ground turmeric (find it in the spice aisle).

Bring the water to a boil. Remove from the heat and stir in the turmeric and pepper. Cover and steep for 10 minutes. Strain into a 1-quart glass jar to store in the fridge for up to 5 days or pour individual servings into mugs. Add milk and honey to taste.

FOR A TURMERIC LATTE: Combine 1 cup hot turmeric tea, ¼ cup warm milk, and 1 teaspoon honey.

NOTE: *Turmeric's vibrant yellow color is not easy to wash off cutting boards and counters. Handle the turmeric carefully when grating and pour into mugs over the sink.*

DREAMER'S TEA

for restorative sleep

MAKES ENOUGH TO BREW
25 CUPS OF TEA

To find the best pre-bedtime, mineral-rich tonic for athletes, we consulted with Katelyn Dexter, owner of the Peoples Apothecary, our favorite medicinal tea shop in Oregon. Katelyn sent us endless varieties of medicinal-strength loose-leaf teas. While in Bend for the photo shoots for this book, Shalane and Elyse taste- and sleep-tested each blend. The Dreamer's Tea was the clear winner.

The Run Fast Eat Slow + Peoples Apothecary Dreamer's Tea includes organic botanicals to encourage relaxation, restful sleep, and dream connection. It tastes of familiar flowers, woven with the aromatics of peppermint, lemon balm, and holy basil. We know you'll want to sip it every evening, especially when you need to unwind.

To learn more about the benefits of each of these herbs, read the descriptions on page 259. These dried herbs can be found at herbal tea specialty shops to create your own blend, or you can buy the blend on our website at runfasteatslow.com.

0.5 ounce organic food-grade dried rose petals

0.4 ounce organic holy basil

0.4 ounce organic dried rosemary

0.4 ounce organic dried peppermint

0.4 ounce organic chamomile

0.4 ounce organic damiana

0.3 ounce organic mugwort

0.25 ounce organic dried lemon balm

0.1 ounce organic calendula

Boiling water, for brewing

Honey, for serving

1 Combine the rose petals, holy basil, rosemary, peppermint, chamomile, damiana, mugwort, lemon balm, and calendula in a 1-pint glass jar or tea tin and shake until evenly combined. Store in the pantry for up to 3 months.

2 To brew the tea, place 2 to 3 teaspoons of the herb blend in a tea infuser and pour 1 cup boiling water over the top. Cover and steep for 10 minutes. Remove the tea infuser and, if desired, stir in honey to taste.

FOR A MEDICINAL-STRENGTH TEA: Place ¼ cup of the herb blend in a 1-quart mason jar. Fill the jar with 4 cups almost-boiling water. Cover and steep for 1 to 2 hours (or longer) for a strong brew. Strain the brewed tea into a jar, cover, and store in the fridge for up to 1 week. Reheat the amount you want to drink in a microwave-safe mug.

NOTE: *While this formula is generally regarded as very safe, we are all individuals and can react differently to herbal teas. If you are pregnant, nursing, taking a medication, or have medical concerns, consult with your doctor prior to consuming this tea.*

HOLY BASIL: This herb is rich in antioxidants and anti-inflammatory properties that protect the body against stress, and support repair and recovery. As an adaptogen, its nature is to restore balance to the body, mind, and spirit. It feeds a tired, overworked nervous system and helps you handle stress with greater ease.

LEMON BALM: This common plant has a wide range of medicinal uses. It's antispasmodic and sedative, helping to reduce muscle cramps, soothe nerves, release tension, and support healthy digestion and nutrient absorption.

MUGWORT: This herb encourages healthy circulation and blood flow. It has a long tradition of being used as a dream-enhancing ally when added to teas and herbal baths.

ROSEMARY: This prolific herb is rich in minerals, vitamins, and anti-inflammatory compounds to support circulation. Rosemary also eases muscle pain and recovery. Known as "the herb of remembrance," it has been revered for centuries as a cognitive ally to increase focus and memory.

PEPPERMINT: This aromatic herb has relaxant and antispasmodic properties, helping to relieve pain, reduce tension, and calm digestive distress.

DAMIANA: Damiana is an herb with so much medicine to offer. Best known for its mood-elevating and aphrodisiac properties, it also increases circulation, boosts physical and mental stamina, and supports healthy blood flow and libido.

ROSE PETALS: A favorite for all issues of the heart, rose is often overlooked for its ability to reduce heat and inflammation in the body, tone tissue, ease muscle tension, and encourage restful sleep.

CHAMOMILE: The gentle, calming nature of chamomile helps soothe stomach and nervous-system stress and is particularly useful for those with anxious/nervous tummies.

CALENDULA: One of the most revered medicinal plants, these flowers are anti-inflammatory and rich in antioxidants, and provide nutrients essential for tissue repair.

11 | SPREADS AND TOPPERS

(SAVORY TO SWEET)

PRESTO PESTO

for a meal prep staple

MAKES 2 CUPS

GLUTEN-FREE //
VEGETARIAN //

We've brought back the coveted pesto recipe from *Run Fast. Cook Fast. Eat Slow.* because it's still a staple in our kitchens. You'll want this recipe when making our Pesto-Zucchini Superhero Muffins (page 75). Also try it on top of toasted Whole-Wheat Bread (page 170), scrambled eggs, or whisked into a simple frittata.

---

2 cups tightly packed fresh basil leaves or arugula

1 (6-ounce) wedge Parmesan cheese, rind removed, quartered

½ cup roasted unsalted almonds

1 garlic clove, peeled

½ cup extra-virgin olive oil

¼ cup fresh lemon juice

½ teaspoon fine sea salt

MIX UP YOUR NUTZ:
This pesto is amazing made with almonds, walnuts, cashews, or hazelnuts.

1 In a food processor or high-speed blender, combine the basil, Parmesan, almonds, and garlic. Pulse until finely ground. Add the oil, lemon juice, and salt. Process until completely smooth, stopping to scrape down the sides as needed.

2 Transfer to a widemouthed glass jar and store in the fridge for up to 5 days or freeze in small containers for up to 3 months for the convenience of easy-to-thaw proportions.

SUBSTITUTIONS

TO AVOID NUTS, *substitute ½ cup toasted pumpkin seeds for the almonds.*

TO AVOID DAIRY, *substitute ½ cup canned or cooked white beans (drained and rinsed) and 1 tablespoon plus 1 teaspoon white miso paste for the Parmesan.*

VEGAN SPINACH-WALNUT PESTO

for an eat-more-veggies life hack

MAKES ABOUT 2 CUPS

GLUTEN-FREE // VEGAN //

You already know how much we love pesto. Pesto recipes appear in our first two cookbooks, so naturally, this book wouldn't be complete without another unique pesto creation. Pesto is a podium-worthy spread because it's packed with iron-rich greens, immune-boosting garlic, mineral-rich nuts, and inflammation-busting olive oil.

This vegan pesto sneaks in a second nourishing veggie that we bet you won't detect. Cauliflower steps in for Parmesan, making this the ideal condiment for the dairy-free crowd. The addition of probiotic-rich miso means you won't miss out on that cheesy flavor.

We especially love it as a topper for toast (try our Whole-Wheat Bread, page 170), Breakfast Power Bowls (page 135), or scrambled eggs, as a dip with crudités, or tossed with pasta (okay, it's not just for breakfast!).

---

1 heaping cup steamed cauliflower florets (see below), cooled

4 cups loosely packed baby spinach or stemmed kale leaves

1 cup walnuts, toasted

1 tablespoon plus 1 teaspoon white miso paste

1 garlic clove, peeled

⅓ cup extra-virgin olive oil

¼ cup fresh lemon juice

½ teaspoon fine sea salt

¼ teaspoon ground black pepper

1 Pat the cauliflower dry, removing any excess moisture. In a food processor or high-speed blender, combine the spinach, cauliflower, walnuts, miso, garlic, oil, lemon juice, salt, and pepper. Process until completely smooth, stopping to scrape down the sides as needed.

2 Transfer to a widemouthed glass jar and store in the fridge for up to 5 days or freeze in small containers for up to 3 months for the convenience of easy-to-thaw proportions.

STEAMING CAULIFLOWER: *Wash 1 head of cauliflower and cut it into bite-size florets. (You should have 3 to 4 cups florets, depending on the size of your cauliflower.) Fill a large pot with 1 inch of water and fit a steamer basket in the pot. Put the cauliflower in the steamer, cover, and bring the water to a boil. Reduce the heat to maintain a simmer and steam the cauliflower until fork-tender, 10 to 15 minutes. Use freshly steamed in banana bread (page 222) and pesto (page 262).*

EVERYTHING BAGEL SEASONING MIX

for a power seed topping

MAKES ¾ CUP

GLUTEN-FREE // VEGAN //

We've upped the ante on traditional everything bagel seasoning by incorporating our favorite omega-3 rich seeds, including hemp, flax, and chia. This seasoning blend is good sprinkled on just about everything. We especially love it on avocado toast (page 167), Breakfast Power Bowls (page 135), and our Everything Bagel Superhero Muffins (page 77).

½ cup NOW Real Food Organic Triple Omega Seed Mix*

2 tablespoons dried onion flakes

2 teaspoons flaky or coarse sea salt (we like Jacobsen Salt Co. Pure Flake Sea Salt)

In a small glass jar, combine the seeds, onion flakes, and salt. Cover with a lid and shake to combine. Store in the pantry for up to 1 month or in the fridge for up to 6 months.

*NOW Real Food's Organic Triple Omega Seed Mix can be found online at nowfoods.com or in natural foods stores. To make your own power seed mix, combine any of your favorite raw tiny seeds to equal ½ cup. Seed suggestions include black sesame seeds, white sesame seeds, whole flaxseeds, hemp seeds, chia seeds, and poppy seeds.

"I keep a journal next to my bed, and before I get up, I write down a goal for the day and something I'm grateful for. This sets an intention and a vibe for my day. It's a practice that helps you focus on what's important to you and can help you through difficult times. When you write things down, you bring your thoughts and goals to life. At night when I go to bed, I can look at it and reflect on how those words influenced my day."

—TRACEY KATONA, *elite Pilates instructor*

PICO DE GALLO

for spicing up your morning routine

MAKES 4 CUPS

GLUTEN-FREE // VEGAN //

Pico de Gallo is a fresh Mexican-style chunky salsa. It pairs beautifully with so many of our favorite brunch dishes that we had to include it in this book. It's traditionally made with fresh lime juice, but our version is made with apple cider vinegar, which adds another flavor dimension (and is great for digestion).

Save this recipe for the summer months when your backyard garden or farmers' market is bursting with fresh tomatoes. Spoon it generously on top of scrambled eggs, breakfast burritos, quesadillas, Black Bean Quinoa Pilaf (page 188), Breakfast Power Bowls (page 135), or Second-Breakfast Fried Rice (page 181).

1½ pounds fresh tomatoes (preferably from the farmers' market)

1 cup finely chopped red onion (about 1)

2 jalapeños, finely diced (remove the seeds for less spice)

2 garlic cloves, minced

¼ cup finely chopped fresh cilantro

2 tablespoons apple cider vinegar

1 teaspoon fine sea salt

Use a small serrated knife to finely chop the tomatoes and place them in a medium bowl. Add the onion, jalapeños, garlic, cilantro, vinegar, and salt and stir to combine. Transfer to an airtight container and chill in the fridge for at least 2 hours before serving. Store leftovers in the fridge for up to 5 days.

BLUEBERRY CHIA SEED JAM

for a champion topper

MAKES ABOUT 2 CUPS

GLUTEN-FREE // VEGAN: Substitute maple syrup for the honey. //

This jam is our jam. Store-bought jams are high in sugar and low in real fruit and fresh flavor. This single 1-pint jar is loaded with a pound of blueberries and has zero preservatives. Chia seeds add staying power and help thicken the jam to achieve the ideal texture for spooning on top of toast, Fluffy Pancakes (page 161), Belgian Waffles (page 162), and French toast (page 209). We especially love it stirred into whole-milk yogurt with Goddess Grain-Free Granola (page 127) or Overnight Oats (page 137).

1 pound (3 cups) fresh or frozen blueberries, thawed

3 tablespoons honey

¾ teaspoon ground cinnamon

⅛ teaspoon ground nutmeg

3 tablespoons chia seeds

Zest of 1 lemon (optional)

2 tablespoons fresh lemon juice, plus more if needed

1 In a medium saucepan, combine the blueberries, honey, cinnamon, and nutmeg and cook over low heat, uncovered, stirring occasionally, until the blueberries break down, about 8 minutes.

2 Stir in the chia seeds. Simmer over very low heat, stirring every couple minutes, for 10 minutes, or until thickened. Remove from the heat. Stir in the lemon zest (if using) and lemon juice. Taste and add more lemon juice or sugar, if needed (see tip).

3 Let cool (the jam will thicken further as it cools). If you prefer a smooth jam, use an immersion blender to blend it to the desired consistency. Transfer to a 1-pint widemouthed glass jar. Cover with a lid and store in the fridge for up to 2 weeks.

Nutrition Tip: If you're serving this to someone with a sweet tooth (kids), you can stir in 1 tablespoon coconut sugar or cane sugar at the end. It will still have a lot less sugar than store-bought jam, but will satisfy that craving. You also might want to include the spoonful of sugar if you're using out-of-season blueberries, which tend to be less sweet.

PUMPKIN-PEAR BUTTER

for a quick warm-up

MAKES 5 CUPS

GLUTEN-FREE // VEGAN //

This spiced pumpkin topper warms our souls on cooler fall days. We like it best as a sweet layer in yogurt parfaits topped with Molasses Tahini Granola (page 128), or in an Apple-Quinoa Parfait (page 157). The thick and velvety texture means you can also use it as a topper on toast or waffles (page 162). It's delicious spread in a thick layer on homemade Whole-Wheat Bread (page 170).

Spice up your breakfast routine by keeping small jars of pumpkin butter stashed in your freezer. Elyse likes to warm a small bowl of it on low power in the microwave before adding it to yogurt, overnight oats (pages 137 and 139), or Steel-Cut Oatmeal (page 150).

---

2 (15-ounce) cans pure pumpkin puree

2 ripe pears, peeled, cored, and chopped

½ cup unfiltered apple juice

½ cup coconut sugar

1 tablespoon Chai Spice Mix (page 274) or pumpkin pie spice

3 tablespoons fresh lemon juice

1 In a medium saucepan, combine the pumpkin, pears, apple juice, sugar, and chai spice mix. Bring to a light simmer over medium heat. Reduce the heat to low and simmer, stirring occasionally, for 25 minutes, or until thickened. Remove from the heat and stir in the lemon juice.

2 We like the pumpkin-pear butter chunky, but if you prefer a smoother texture, use an immersion blender to blend it to the desired consistency. Transfer to glass jars and store in the fridge for up to 2 weeks or in the freezer for up to 3 months (be sure your jars are freezer-safe).

 Nutrition Tip: Stir in 2 to 3 tablespoons chia seeds to add staying power.

"Steel-cut oats, toast, and muesli are on my breakfast rotation. Before big workouts or races, my go-to meal is something easy to digest. Oatmeal and a sandwich of some kind do the trick."

–MOHAMMED AHMED, *IAAF World Championship medalist*

SPROUTED ALMOND BUTTER

for healthy digestion

MAKES 1½ CUPS

GLUTEN-FREE // VEGAN

This simple recipe can be made with toasted almonds, but sprouting your nuts, when you have the time, takes this nut butter to a whole new level of flavor and nutrition. Learn more about why we like to sprout almonds on page 121.

3 cups Sprouted Almonds (page 121)

2 tablespoons virgin coconut oil

¼ teaspoon fine sea salt

1 In a high-speed blender, combine the almonds, coconut oil, and salt. Begin blending on low speed, gradually increasing to high, and whir until smooth (use the tamper tool to keep the ingredients moving). It will take several minutes to get a smooth texture. Stop as needed to scrape down the sides and underneath the blade.

2 Transfer the almond butter to a jar and store in the fridge for up to 1 month. It's easier to spread at room temperature, so remove from the fridge 30 minutes prior to using.

SALTED CARAMEL SPROUTED ALMOND BUTTER

for a spoonful of delicious energy

MAKES 1½ CUPS

3 cups Sprouted Almonds (page 121)

2 tablespoons virgin coconut oil

2 tablespoons coconut sugar

1 teaspoon vanilla extract

¼ to ½ teaspoon fine sea salt, to taste (see tip)

A spoonful of this nut butter saves the day before an early run. It's deliciously satisfying and easy to digest, with a touch of sugar for quick energy and fat for stamina.

1 In a high-speed blender, combine the almonds, coconut oil, sugar, vanilla, and salt. Begin blending on low speed, gradually increasing to high, and whir until smooth (use the tamper tool to keep the ingredients moving). It will take several minutes to get a smooth texture. Stop as needed to scrape down the sides and underneath the blade.

2 Transfer the almond butter to a jar and store in the fridge for up to 1 month. It's easier to spread at room temperature, so remove from the fridge 30 minutes prior to using.

Nutrition Tip: Runners needs more salt in their diets than sedentary folks because we lose this essential electrolyte when we sweat. Consuming food with salt in it alongside your morning beverage will help you hydrate better.

My power breakfast usually takes place after my first workout of the day. I love a combo of eggs, veggies, avocado, and toast. You can't forget the coffee, of course! I feel like this meal sets me up for a great day.

—LINSEY CORBIN,
professional Ironman triathlete

CACAO-HAZELNUT SPREAD

for preventing hitting a wall

MAKES 1 CUP

GLUTEN-FREE // VEGAN //

Be warned–you'll want to eat this nut butter straight out of the jar. It tastes like Nutella, but with half the sugar and zero refined oils or additives, you can feel good about starting your day with a spoonful. Try it on Belgian Waffles (page 162) for a winning combo. It's also crazy good on our Cinnamon Raisin Seed Bread (page 175).

Here in Oregon, we have the perfect climate and rich soils for growing hazelnuts. We love this snackable nut because it's high in folate and trace minerals like manganese and copper, essential nutrients for strong bones and better iron absorption.

2 cups raw hazelnuts

3 tablespoons coconut sugar or cane sugar

2 tablespoons virgin coconut oil

2 tablespoons unsweetened cocoa powder or cacao powder

¼ teaspoon fine sea salt

1 Position a rack in the center of the oven. Preheat the oven to 275°F. Line a rimmed baking sheet with parchment paper.

2 Spread the hazelnuts in a single layer on the baking sheet. Toast in the oven for 10 minutes, then stir and toast for 10 to 15 minutes more, until the nuts are golden in color and fragrant. Transfer the warm hazelnuts to a clean kitchen towel and rub to remove their skins. (Don't worry about getting every last skin off, just the loose ones.) Let cool.

3 Transfer the hazelnuts to a high-speed blender or food processor and blend on high or process for several minutes, until finely ground, stopping as needed to scrape down the sides and underneath the blade with a rubber spatula. Add the sugar, coconut oil, cocoa powder, and salt. Process again until smooth.

4 Transfer to a glass jar with a lid. Store in the fridge for up to 2 weeks or in the freezer for up to 3 months (be sure your jar is freezer-safe). Leave out at room temperature for 15 minutes before serving.

MARATHON PEANUT BUTTER

for skipping across the finish line

MAKES 2½ CUPS

GLUTEN-FREE // VEGAN //

You know you're a runner if you eat peanut butter by the spoonful straight out of the jar. And you're definitely a distance runner if you top that spoonful of peanut butter with a few chocolate chips. Are we right?! We've taken the beloved peanut-butter-and-chocolate combination to the next level with this energizing nut-and-seed butter.

Our better butter features swirls of dark chocolate, dates, chia seeds, and hemp seeds. It's packed with omega-3 fatty acids for energy. We like it best straight outta the jar. Try a spoonful before an early run to motivate yourself to get out the door, or serve it on yogurt, oatmeal, or toast for a post-run treat.

3 cups unsalted roasted peanuts (just under 1 pound)

12 Deglet Noor or 6 Medjool dates, halved and pitted

¼ cup hemp hearts (hulled hemp seeds)

¼ cup chia seeds

2 tablespoons virgin coconut oil

1 teaspoon ground cinnamon

1 teaspoon fine sea salt (leave out if peanuts are salted)

3 ounces dark chocolate (from a bar), coarsely chopped

1 In a food processor or high-speed blender, combine the peanuts, dates, hemp hearts, chia seeds, coconut oil, cinnamon, and salt. Process until there are no visible chunks of nuts or dates and the mixture begins to look smooth (if using a blender, use the tamper tool to keep the ingredients moving). Stop as needed to scrape the sides and underneath the blade with a rubber spatula.

2 While the peanut butter is still warm from blending, use the rubber spatula (not the processor/blender) to stir in the chocolate. You want the chocolate to melt just enough to swirl it into the peanut butter, but you don't want to fully incorporate it.

3 Divide the peanut butter between two half-pint glass jars with lids. For longer shelf life and to prevent oil separation, store in the fridge for up to 3 months. To make it easier to spread, leave it out at room temperature for 30 minutes before using.

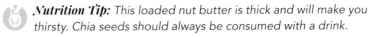 ***Nutrition Tip:*** *This loaded nut butter is thick and will make you thirsty. Chia seeds should always be consumed with a drink.*

CHAI SPICE MIX

for digestion and healing

MAKES ABOUT 5 TABLESPOONS

GLUTEN-FREE // **DAIRY-FREE** //
VEGAN: Substitute maple syrup for
the honey (store in the fridge). //

Warming spices are incredibly healing–soothing to digestion, inflammation-fighting, immune-boosting, and naturally stimulating. We always keep our favorite chai spice mix on hand. See a list of all our recipes that celebrate chai below.

3 tablespoons
ground cinnamon

1 tablespoon ground ginger

2 teaspoons ground
cardamom

½ teaspoon ground cloves

½ teaspoon ground nutmeg

½ teaspoon ground
turmeric

Combine the cinnamon, ginger, cardamom, cloves, nutmeg, and turmeric in a ½-pint mason jar. Store in the pantry for up to 6 months.

"So freakin' easy to make! I sprinkle this on buttery toast and I use it in coffee and tea. Brilliant."

—SHALANE

Recipes that Use Chai Spice Mix

Chai Honey and Chai Nut Butter // *page 275*

Chai Chia Seed Parfait // *page 140*

Long Run Baked Sweet Potato // *page 155*

Anti-Inflammatory Cashew Milk // *page 250*

Creamy Chai Cauliflower Smoothie Bowl // *page 240*

Pumpkin Pie Smoothie // *page 232*

Pumpkin Streusel Superhero Muffins // *page 96*

Nutty Chai Energy Bites // *page 117*

Chai-Spiced Pecans // *page 126*

Pumpkin-Pear Butter // *page 268*

CHAI HONEY
for next-level tea

MAKES ½ CUP

We can't go a day in the winter without our warming and digestion-soothing chai tea fix. This recipe makes it so simple to convert a mug of black tea, oolong tea, or green tea into a luscious chai latte. Simply stir in a small spoonful of this spiced honey and add a splash of milk to taste. You can also try it stirred into Chai Chia Seed Parfait (page 140), drizzled on yogurt with chopped apples, added to Overnight Oats (pages 137 and 139), or smeared on toast with butter. This honey makes a great holiday gift–simply double the recipe to fill a half-pint jar and tie a ribbon onto the lid.

> ½ cup raw honey*
> 2 teaspoons Chai Spice Mix (page 274)

In a half-pint mason jar, stir together the honey and spice mix until blended. Seal with the lid and store in the pantry for up to 6 months.

It's worth seeking out raw honey from a producer in your area. Local honey contains enzymes and pollen to help soothe digestion and relieve allergies.

CHAI HONEY NUT BUTTER
for a spoonful of energy

MAKES 6 TABLESPOONS

This chai-infused nut butter tastes like Christmas cookie dough–you'll want to eat it right off the spoon. Stir a spoonful into a bowl of oatmeal to convert it into a breakfast for champions. This spiced butter is also delicious smeared on toast or a banana, or try it on a baked sweet potato (see page 155) for a unique and energizing breakfast.

We love to make this recipe with cashew butter, but any nut butter works great. For early-morning runs, a spoonful of this before heading out the door provides lasting energy and calms a nervous tummy. We recommend doubling this simple recipe.

> 2 tablespoons Chai Honey (this page)
> ¼ cup creamy nut butter (peanut, almond, or cashew)

In a small jar with a lid, use a fork to stir together the honey and nut butter until blended. Store in the pantry for up to 2 months.

YOGURT BUTTERCREAM FROSTING

for transforming Superhero Muffins into cupcakes

MAKES 1¼ CUPS

GLUTEN-FREE // VEGETARIAN //

Instead of artificial food coloring, we used the drippings from steamed beets to dye this frosting a beautiful pink color. It doesn't take much beet juice to add a pop of color, so you don't need a fancy juicer to make this work. Another way to naturally add a pop of color is to squeeze a little juice from dark red cherries.

This recipe makes enough frosting to spread on 24 mini or 12 large Superhero Muffins. We especially love it on Lily's Chocolate Superhero Muffins (page 104), Dark Chocolate Banana Superhero Muffins (page 90), and Red Velvet Superhero Muffins (page 106). We recommend doubling* this recipe if you want to add a more elaborate cupcake-style swirl of frosting on each muffin. To achieve this pro look, you'll need a piping bag.

½ cup (1 stick) unsalted butter, at room temperature

2 cups powdered sugar

2 tablespoons plain whole-milk Greek yogurt

1 teaspoon vanilla extract

1 teaspoon beet juice (see note)

If you're doubling the recipe, you can use a stand mixer instead of a handheld mixer.

Nutrition Tip:
Want natural green or yellow frosting instead of pink? Recipe tester Michael Weisberg recommends stirring a small amount of matcha green tea powder or ground turmeric into the yogurt before beating it into the butter-sugar mixture. Or better yet, mix both powders for a baby blue (we haven't tested these color variations, but they sound fun!).

1 Place the butter in a medium bowl and beat with a handheld mixer on medium speed until creamy, about 1 minute. Add the sugar and beat until incorporated, stopping as need to scrape down the sides of the bowl with a rubber spatula (some clumps at this stage are okay).

2 Add the yogurt, vanilla, and beet juice and beat until fully incorporated and fluffy. If the frosting gets stuck on the beaters, lift them above the frosting (but still below the edge of the bowl) while they are rotating.

3 Use the frosting to decorate muffins, or cover and store in the fridge for up to 5 days. Leave out at room temperature for 1 hour prior to using. Decorate muffins just before serving.

BEET JUICE: *Fill a large pot with 1 inch of water and set a steamer basket in the pot. Quarter 2 beets, leaving the skins on, and place in the steamer basket. Cover, bring the water to a simmer, and cook for 20 to 25 minutes, until soft and easily pierced with a knife. Allow the beets to cool, then peel them and place in a glass storage container. Pierce multiple times with a fork. The beets will release a small amount of juice into the bottom of the glass container. Use these drippings to color your frosting. The leftover cooked beets are great in smoothies or salads (or slice and freeze for future smoothies).*

ACKNOWLEDGMENTS

We would like to thank the dream team behind *Rise & Run*. Many of you have been with us from the beginning, 2015, when we started writing this series. We never imagined it would evolve into three cookbooks (and two *New York Times* bestsellers). In particular, we have relied on the support of:

At Rodale/Penguin Random House: Our dedicated editor, Dervla Kelly, who has put up with our numerous requests. The very talented Rae Ann Spitzenberger, who designed and created the page-by-page layouts for both *Rise & Run* and *Run Fast. Cook Fast. Eat Slow.* Brianne Sperber,

marketing guru, who goes above and beyond. Thank you for your love and support over many years. And the rest of the talented crew–Diana Baroni, Stephanie Huntwork, Tammy Blake, Jessica Heim, Terry Deal, Merri Ann Morrell, and Ivy McFadden–who brought our vision to life.

At LGR Literary, our devoted and brilliant agent, Danielle Svetcov. Thank you for the mentorship, friendship, and priceless guidance for over six years.

Flexing between Portland and Bend, our kitchen angel, Natalie Bickford, who has been our loyal and talented assistant since day one and who brings delicious ideas to each book.

On shoots, our dazzling food photographer, Erin Scott, and the

Special thanks to Natalie Bickford, MS in nutrition, who has been a part of the *Run Fast. Eat Slow.* team from the very beginning, helping to test and develop recipes alongside Elyse.

incredible food stylist, Lillian Kang; and our adventurous sports and lifestyle photographers, Tiffany Renshaw (Bend) and Cortney White (Portland).

Everywhere: Our team of recipe testers who helped us perfect each recipe. Professional recipe tester Michael Weisberg deserves a special shout-out for testing every single recipe in both *Rise & Run* and our previous cookbooks. And gratitude to our team of volunteer testers: Colleen Quigley, Linsey Corbin, Julie Stackhouse, Brianne Sperber, Yvette Jacobs, Sarah Bousman, Holly Marquez, Bridget Foote, Jackie Kunnemann, Tina Capparell, Alma Aldrich, Naomi Ryan, Carol Feaga, Melissa Cummings, and Mark Posey.

Gracious shout-out to our recipe testing sponsors, ButcherBox and NOW Foods. They helped offset the huge cost of testing hundreds of recipes and provided us with essential ingredients when the grocery store shelves were wiped out during the pandemic.

Love to our footwear sponsors, Nike (Shalane) and Saucony (Elyse). Thanks for keeping us inspired for many miles on the roads and trails.

Our expert contributors, Colleen Little, Tracey Katona, Rosie Acosta, and Brad Stulberg. Thank you for sharing your valuable knowledge.

The Bowerman Babes and Bowerman Track Club for testing, tasting, and training with our recipes. Thank you for your dedication to the sport.

The grandparents, husbands, and kiddos for being our biggest fans and best eaters, and for putting up with a lot of dishes! Shalane: Steve Flanagan and Monica Flanagan, Steven Edwards, Jack Dean Edwards. Elyse: Caren Arlas, Andy Hughes, Lily Kopecky, Rylan Kopecky.

This third cookbook would not have been possible without the steadfast support from the running community. Thank you for sharing your inspirational stories with us. Your heartfelt letters, emails, reviews, and drool-worthy Instagram posts provide the fuel to keep us going.

RECIPE INDEX

INDEX

ABOUT THE AUTHORS

ELYSE KOPECKY

Driven to help others eat right and live healthy, Elyse Kopecky is a two-time *New York Times* bestselling cookbook author, culinary instructor, and inspirational speaker. She has coauthored *Run Fast. Eat Slow.* and *Run Fast. Cook Fast. Eat Slow.* with four-time Olympian and New York City Marathon champion Shalane Flanagan. Elyse is also a mom and an avid trail runner, which inspires her passion to fuel others and the future through enriching food.

Elyse's work has been featured in *Women's Health*, *Runner's World*, *Outside* magazine, *Sports Illustrated*, *People*, and ESPN.com and on *Good Morning America*, *Today*, CBS, and NBC News. She writes a monthly column for *Women's Running Magazine* and is a Saucony ambassador. Elyse lives in Bend, Oregon, with her husband and two adventurous kids. Follow her on Instagram @elysekopecky or at elysekopecky.com.

SHALANE FLANAGAN

Dedicated to giving back to the sport she loves, Shalane Flanagan is now an elite coach to the Bowerman Track Club, global spokesperson, and a mom, after retiring as one of America's most decorated distance runners. Shalane's accolades include four-time Olympian, Olympic silver medalist, 2017 TCS New York City Marathon champion, IAAF World Cross Country bronze medalist, and multiple American record holder. She is the third fastest American marathoner in history, with a time of 2:21.14. Shalane is the fastest American woman to run the Boston Marathon, with a time of 2:22.02.

Along with her coauthor, Elyse Kopecky, she is the two-time *New York Times* bestselling author of *Run Fast. Eat Slow.* and *Run Fast. Cook Fast. Eat Slow.* Shalane attributes her long career and incredible success to her nutrient-dense diet. Shalane has left the track behind, but you'll still find her logging high mileage on trail-run adventures with friends!